MW00982280

Modern Bride.®

Honeymoons
and Weddings Away

Also available from Wiley's *Modern Bride®* Library:

Modern Bride® Wedding Celebrations
The Complete Wedding Planner for Today's Bride
by Cele Goldsmith Lalli and Stephanie H. Dahl

Modern Bride® Guide to Etiquette
Answers to the Questions Today's Couples <u>Really</u> Ask
by Cele Goldsmith Lalli

Modern Bride® Just Married
Everything You Need to Know to Plan Your New Life Together
by Stephanie H. Dahl

Modern Bride®
Honeymoons and Weddings Away

The complete guide to planning
your most romantic trip ever

GERI BAIN
Travel Editor, *Modern Bride*

JOHN WILEY & SONS, INC.
NEW YORK • CHICHESTER • BRISBANE • TORONTO • SINGAPORE

This publication is designed to provide accurate and authoritative information in regard to the subject matter covered. It is sold with the understanding that the publisher is not engaged in rendering professional services. If legal, accounting, medical, psychological, or any other expert assistance is required, the services of a competent professional person should be sought.

Although the author has made every effort to provide the most up-to-date and accurate information possible, the author and the publisher accept no responsibility for any loss, injury, or inconvenience arising out of the use of the information in this book. Please call ahead before relying on any information. We also appreciate feedback from our readers. Please direct comments and suggestions to:

Geri Bain
c/o John Wiley & Sons, Inc.
605 Third Avenue
New York, NY 10158-0012

Library of Congress Cataloging-in-Publication Data:
Bain, Geri
    Modern bride honeymoons and weddings away: the complete guide
  to planning your most romantic trip ever / Geri Bain.
      p. cm. — (Wiley's Modern bride library)
    Includes index.
    ISBN 0-471-00722-6 (pbk. : acid-free)
    1. Travel. 2. Honeymoon. I. Modern bride. II. Title.
  III. Series.
  G151.B32 1995
  910'.2'02—dc20   95-1298

Printed in the United States of America
10 9 8 7 6 5 4 3 2 1

*To my parents, Sanford and Ruth Bain, who opened
the world to me and my brother;
and to my husband, Robert Keroack,
who continues to turn every trip into a honeymoon—
even with our newest companion,
our daughter Jenny Lucienne!*

CONTENTS

FOREWORD

With all of the time and effort involved in planning a wedding, engaged couples might not realize that selecting their honeymoon destination requires similar attention. As they get caught up in the wedding details, the tendency to postpone researching for and organizing this very special trip is quite common. Those who are frequent travelers tend to think it's just like any other trip, and those with little travel experience often don't know where to start, so they tend to procrastinate and then panic. To the former group, let me say that this is not like any other trip you might have taken together and you're mistaken to think of it as such. To the latter group, you have no reason to worry with this book in your hand.

Geri Bain has compiled *the* best resource of solid information, emotional support, and practical advice for honeymooners. Through her travels and her mail, Geri is constantly in touch with engaged and newlywed couples. That, combined with her extensive knowledge of the travel industry, provides you with all the help you need to make yours the honeymoon you have always dreamed about.

Whether you have received this book as a gift or purchased it yourself, you are indeed fortunate to have the most clearly organized, thoroughly personalized honeymoon travel guide available. Share the book with one another and enjoy the planning together so that when you reach your honeymoon haven, it will be everything you hoped for and a lot more!

Cele Goldsmith Lalli
Editor-in-Chief, *Modern Bride*

PREFACE

As travel editor of *Modern Bride* magazine, the most frequent questions I am asked are: "Where should I go on my honeymoon?" and "Can you suggest an exotic place where we can get married?" Most readers ask these questions without telling me anything about themselves or what they are looking for, as though there were one place that is right for everyone.

Similarly, the strangest letter I've received asked: Do you think we should go to Aruba or Hong Kong? *Aruba or Hong Kong!* I had to call and find out why the same couple would be considering such completely different types of honeymoons. Well, her parents loved Aruba; his friends had taken their honeymoon in Hong Kong. But what did *they* want? Your decision of where to go should begin with the two of you and your preferences. This book is designed to help you sort out your priorities and plan your dream honeymoon or wedding away.

Modern Marriages

Although the commitment to marriage and the importance of a romantic honeymoon have intensified in the past decade, couples today are far from traditional. Many have traveled and lived together before marriage. They may come from very different backgrounds, and their friends and family are likely to be scattered across the country or even around the world. Often older and more established than couples of previous decades, they may be paying for their own wedding and honeymoon. Many have been married before, and some have children from previous marriages.

These factors are motivating a growing number of couples to exchange their vows at their honeymoon destination—"destination weddings," as *Modern Bride* calls them. Unlike elopements, destination weddings are usually announced in advance and often include guests.

Some couples choose to have a destination wedding for its exotic appeal, but for many, getting married away is the solution to challenging situations. It removes from the wedding tensions over different religions and complex family situations and allows a couple to focus on what they want, not what family and friends think they should do. And if money or time is limited, a destination wedding can enable a couple to have a special ceremony for little more than the cost of their honeymoon and with very little effort.

None of this diminishes the importance of the marriage ceremony. On the contrary, couples are creating new and more personal ways of celebrating. So although perhaps less conventional, today's weddings are extremely meaningful.

The traditional idea of a honeymoon has changed as well. Today's honeymooners are more sophisticated and find romance in sharing new experiences. Overall, they are an outgoing and going-out lot. They still are looking for beautiful hideaways, but most aren't looking to cut themselves off from the world.

They are as likely to be hang gliding as hanging out in their rooms. You'll find newlyweds taking jeep safaris across the desert; sightseeing by helicopter, horseback, and submarine; scuba diving and cycling; or exploring exotic new locales together.

The word *honeymoon* brings up a special set of expectations, so honeymoons and getaway weddings elicit excitement and special treatment from almost everyone. The boss who frowns on employees taking more than one-week vacations may suggest that you take more time. The high-pressured executive who can never be away from a phone may opt for a resort with no telephones. And everyone has ideas of where you should go.

With so much importance placed on this trip, no wonder even experienced travelers get nervous about making the arrangements. Yet planning is part of the fun. It's a time to share dreams and perhaps discover new facets of each other. Hopefully, this book can take the tension out of planning by providing you with a step-by-step approach to guide you through the maze of choices you face when selecting a honeymoon or wedding destination.

USING THIS BOOK

First, answer the questions in "Your Honeymoon Profile" in chapter 1. This will help both of you crystallize your preferences and keep you focused on *your* needs and desires. "Honeymoon and Wedding Planning Checklists" will help organize your planning. Throughout the book, highlighted "Honeymoon Facts" and "Wedding Facts" tell you about what other couples are doing. "Honeymoon Tips" and "Wedding Tips" boxes offer suggestions on special touches to weave romance into your trip and help you get the most for your money. "Stress Control" boxes offer suggestions to head off problems before they occur. And "Questions to Ask" and "Learning the Lingo" will give you an insider's look at the travel and wedding industries.

The book is divided into three parts: Part One, Honeymoon Planning; Part Two, Planning a Destination Wedding; and Part Three, Destination Snapshots.

Part One is designed to work on two levels: as a travel primer to help inexperienced travelers plan like pros and as a tip sheet for experienced travelers. This section will show you how to focus on what you want for your honeymoon, where to turn for free expert advice, how to shop for the best travel deals, how to make the best decisions *for your needs,* and how to avoid scams and common honeymoon pitfalls.

If you are thinking about combining your wedding and honeymoon, flip to Part Two before reading the honeymoon-planning section. This section provides all the information you'll need to plan a hassle-free destination wedding. You'll find that legal weddings can't be arranged everywhere, so some terrific honeymoon destinations make impossible wedding destinations. And you'll learn about free and almost-free options, professional planners who handle all the details, and how to personalize your ceremony and celebration. If you have children from former marriages, you'll find suggestions on how to include them in your wedding and still have an intimate honeymoon. And if you're getting married without guests, you'll find suggestions on how to make the people who are important to you feel included, even if they don't come with you.

Part Three provides an overview of some of the most popular honeymoon destinations, and the Appendixes provide sources for more information.

I hope this book makes planning your wedding trip almost as much fun as the voyage itself! Congratulations and bon voyage!

PART ONE
Honeymoon Planning

CHAPTER 1

Picking a Destination

I met Carolyn walking along the beach on Grand Cayman Island and looking quite melancholy. She was on her honeymoon, but it was not what she had hoped for. She turned to me and began to explain: "Bill is an avid scuba diver; I had never tried it, but we figured I could take a short course here and then we could do some diving together. I guess with all the wedding stuff going on, I really didn't think that much about it. As it turns out, I have something wrong with my ears and can't dive at all. But even if I could, I really would have had to go through much more training to keep up with Bill. I just don't know what he was thinking when he planned this. Now we both feel guilty. He's cut back on his diving, and I can see he's not happy about that; and he says when he's diving, he feels guilty about not being with me."

Find Shared Interests

A honeymoon is not the time to go to a golf resort if only one of you loves golf. Nor should you plan to spend a week in Europe visiting museums if you don't share a passion for art and history. Although some compromise is inevitable and you don't need to spend every minute of your trip together, your honeymoon destination should be a place you can both get excited about. It doesn't matter if you and your fiancé have been traveling together for years; your wedding trip will be a chance to discover new things about each other and the world—and planning a honeymoon that satisfies your needs is a very important part of that process.

A Different Kind of Trip

Joan and Paul had both been married before. "We wanted to just flop on a beach after the wedding, but we felt it was important to go someplace neither of us had been with our previous spouses," Paul said. "Between us, we'd gone to almost all the traditional places people go on their honeymoons. And since we only had a week, we didn't want to go too far. We were really at a loss for what to do. Then

---

✿ HONEYMOON TIPS ✿
Plan Together

Your ideal honeymoon may be a relaxing week spent basking in the sun, while your partner may want seven action-packed days of adventure. No matter how well you think you know one another, there is always something new to learn. Unless you plan your honeymoon together, one of you isn't going to be very happy. And by working together, neither one of you will be at fault when something doesn't go exactly as planned—which seems to happen at some point in every trip—and you can laugh it off together.

---

a travel agent suggested we go to the island of Anguilla, in the Caribbean. It was the perfect choice. Not much to do. Great beaches. And if you get bored, you can take a ferry to St. Martin. We never did get around to that."

Like Joan and Paul, most couples want their honeymoon to feel different from other vacations. For some, it's a time to splurge on luxury or on doing something exotic and perhaps a bit adventurous. But don't be surprised if it takes a bit of introspection to distinguish appealing images from your true preferences.

Take Sam and Barbara. They had been together for ten years when they decided to get married. "You'd think it would be no big deal," said Barbara. "We'd always had a very easygoing, take-it-as-it-comes relationship. But suddenly, every decision about our wedding and honeymoon became a source of tension, and everything he did got on my nerves. I even remember going into the bathroom and seeing the tops off the toothpaste and shampoo—he's never put them on—and thinking, 'Oh no, do I have to live with this for the rest of my life?' It had never bothered me before and hasn't since. Anyway, we had traveled quite a bit together, but we couldn't seem to agree on what we wanted to do for our honeymoon."

Sam explained: "I felt this was our chance to do something really stimulating and adventurous. Barbara's idea of a honeymoon was just lazing on a beach for two weeks, even though we'd agreed a long time ago that beach vacations bored us."

✿ HONEYMOON FACTS ✿
The Top Ten

Curious about where most honeymooners go? Here are the ten most popular honeymoon destinations: Florida, Hawaii, Mexico, Jamaica, U.S. Virgin Islands, Bahamas, California, Pennsylvania, Antigua, and Puerto Rico/Barbados (tied).

Source: Modern Bride Honeymoon Market Report

❧ HONEYMOON FACTS ❧
Honeymoon Wish List

What do most honeymooners look for in a destination? Beautiful natural scenery, warm weather, lots of sightseeing and outdoor sports, and something that fits their budget. Also important to many: diving/snorkeling; seclusion and privacy; luxury; an exotic, well-known honeymoon locale; and good shopping.

Source: Modern Bride Honeymoon Report

Barbara added: "Somehow, when I thought of a honeymoon, I pictured a sunny, romantic hideaway where we could just relax. But finally, we talked it out, and I realized getting married didn't mean we had to fit into preordained roles, which was what I was trying to do. I began to relax, and everything got easy again. I realized that I did want to go someplace where there was a lot of exploring to do."

Sam also realized that he would want his honeymoon to start out with some quiet, private time. "When we read about Australia, it sounded perfect. We started out with five days at a resort near the Great Barrier Reef and did some diving; then we hiked around the Outback," Sam said. "I only wish we'd planned a longer trip. There was so much more we wanted to do."

Like Sam and Barbara, many couples have a hard time sorting out what they want for their honeymoons. Often, couples try to second-guess each other and find compromise solutions before even conceptualizing their own individual preferences.

Although it's important to be able to compromise and try to please each other, the first step should be to find out what you each want.

Your Honeymoon Style

Here are some things to consider when selecting a destination. Before you begin discussing these questions together, each of you should write answers on your own. When you compare notes, you may be surprised at your fiancé's answers—and even some of your own.

1. *Are there places where you have always dreamed of spending your honeymoon?* Are you drawn to explore your roots? Which places do you think would be perfect for a honeymoon? What makes those places so appealing?
2. *How do you want to spend your days?* Are there sports you want to learn or facilities you'd like to have available? Do you enjoy visiting historic places? Shopping? Exploring cities? Or is doing nothing everything?

3. *How do you want to spend your evenings?* Do you want to dance under pulsating lights, under the stars, or not at all? Do you want to try your luck at a casino, catch Las Vegas–style floor shows, or be in a setting where a quiet dinner is the only evening activity?

4. *How much seclusion do you want?* Would you really like to play Robinson Crusoe, or do you want a telephone, television, and air-conditioning? Is a beach enough, or do you want volleyball games, party boats, and foursomes for golf?

5. *Would you enjoy adapting to a foreign culture?* Would it be fun to experiment with another language, or would it be a hassle? Do you enjoy tasting exotic foods? Are you intrigued by customs very different from your own?

6. *What does your ideal honeymoon setting look like?* Is it lush and flowerful? Mountainous? An endless stretch of white-sand beach? The narrow streets of a medieval city? Or a bustling urban center? Is there snow? Autumn foliage? Or is "hot, hot, hot" what you want?

7. *What kind of accommodations do you want?* Would you prefer the tranquillity of an inn or guest house or the services of a hotel? Do you want a choice of restaurants and activities on-site? A fancy, impressive lobby? Round-the-clock room service? A condo or villa with lots of space and a full kitchen?

8. *When will you be going? What type of climate do you want?* Some areas, such as the Rocky Mountains or New England, have climates that vary greatly by season. In much of the Caribbean and Mexico, however, the biggest seasonal change is the prices; rates drop as much as 50 percent in summer, which is considered the "off" season.

9. *How much time can you take?* If you want to go someplace far away, see if you can get a longer vacation. You probably won't want to spend twelve hours or more getting to your honeymoon locale if you have only a week.

10. *What kind of splurges do you think are important?* Are gourmet dining, shopping, or elegant accommodations a priority for you?

Once you've answered these questions individually, sit down together and compare notes. Don't worry if your answers are quite different; there are ways for you both to have what you want. For example, if one of you wants a beach and the other wants to do a lot of sightseeing, choose a place where both are available (such as Greece, Puerto Rico, California, or Florida). You can even combine snow skiing and tropical beaches (on the Big Island of Hawaii). Part III of this book can help you find places that offer the features you're both looking for.

Be sure to agree on a budget and (equally important) discuss how you want to allocate your money. That way you won't find yourselves arguing en route about whether or not you can afford to buy an expensive sculpture or take a dinner cruise.

Your next step will be to begin checking out different destinations.

৯৬৯৯ৡ HONEYMOON FACTS ৯৬৯৯ৡ
The Average Honeymoon

Almost every newlywed couple takes a honeymoon; most leave within a day or two of their wedding. The average *Modern Bride* reader takes a honeymoon that lasts nine days and costs about $3,500.

Source: Modern Bride Honeymoon Market Report

Gather Information

Now that you have some idea of what you're looking for, it's time to start doing some research. Most couples start the process of picking a honeymoon destination by asking their friends and family for suggestions, and even if you don't ask them, you can be sure that they'll tell you! When they do, be sure to find out more than just where they went. Ask why they chose that destination, what they did there, and what they enjoyed most. Then ask yourselves if your tastes are similar.

Magazines are another good source of ideas. The honeymoon sections of bridal magazines, which provide information about the most popular and romantic honeymoon spots, can be especially helpful. At first, every place may sound equally appealing. But as you read, stop to think about how much each destination appeals to you and why.

You'll also want to visit a travel agent. A good, well-traveled agent who knows your priorities can help guide you to the honeymoon of your dreams and make your money go much further than you might think. He or she can also make all the arrangements.

The Honeymoon Checklist on the following pages can help you keep everything organized and remind you of what to do each step of the way. Use it and refer back to it as you plan.

Honeymoon Checklist

Soon after You Get Engaged
- Discuss the type of honeymoon you want.
- Set a tentative budget.
- Begin reading bridal publication honeymoon sections and travel magazines for ideas.

- Talk to friends and family members with tastes similar to your own about their favorite places.
- Start sending for information about places that interest you.
- Select a travel agent and visit together to discuss your honeymoon.

Four to Six Months before You Go

- Arrange for vacation time from your jobs.
- Make your reservations.
- Arrange for any necessary passports, visas, and inoculations. (Allow plenty of time to recover from any side effects from inoculations.)
- Set up a file for confirmations, brochures, guidebooks, and other information that you want to bring on your trip. Be sure all arrangements are confirmed *in writing*.
- Set up another file for copies of passports, visas, a complete itinerary, and other documents. When you go, give this file to a trusted friend or family member (in case you run into problems or lose your documents on the way).
- Make a tentative packing list and shop for major items you want to bring, such as new cameras.
- Check with your bank to be sure your ATM card will work if you plan to use it to withdraw cash while you're traveling. Ask if there are any fees and request a list of ATMs in your destination.

Three to Four Weeks before You Go

- Reconfirm all arrangements, including complete flight information (airports, departure times, and flight numbers). If you're cruising, be sure that you're confirmed for a room with a double bed.
- Make a packing list and begin preparing your clothes. Shop for new clothes, film, toiletries, and other items you want to bring. Buy a surprise honeymoon gift for your fiancé.
- Arrange for someone to care for pets, plants, lawns, and other responsibilities while you are away.

The Week before You Go

- Be sure you have all the documents, tickets, and confirmations you need.
- Lay out your clothing, suitcases and carry-ons, and all other items you're planning to bring. (Consider bringing your address book, notepaper, and a record of gifts not acknowledged. You might want to get a leg up on your thank-you notes while you're relaxed and can share the writing.)
- Get traveler's checks and exchange currency.
- Store valuables and documents.
- Arrange to stop deliveries and put mail on hold, effective *the day before* your departure.

The Day before You Go

- Reconfirm your flights.
- Reconfirm arrangements for care of pets, plants, and other responsibilities.
- Give the appointed friend a copy of your itinerary with phone numbers of the places you'll be staying, along with your document file that includes the identification pages of your passports (with your passport number), confirmations, traveler's check numbers, credit card numbers (and emergency contact numbers), and other important documents as well as house, car, and office keys (in case there's an emergency while you're away).

Day of Departure

- Pack your suitcase and check against your list.
- Check thermostat and unplug TV, lamps, and air conditioners.
- Lock windows, doors, basement, and garage. Connect security lights to timer.
- Dispose of perishable foods.
- Be sure you have all tickets and travel documents in carry-on luggage.

CHAPTER 2

Free Expert Advice

Your engagement period will probably be the busiest and most decision-filled time of your life. Sometimes you'll wish someone would just step in and handle all the details. Well, when it comes to planning your honeymoon, there is an expert who will do just that. And it probably won't cost you a penny!

Using a Travel Agent

A good travel agent should be your most valuable ally in travel planning. He or she will do far more than simply make reservations. After asking questions about what you want your honeymoon to be, your agent should be able to suggest destinations that will fulfill your dreams. Then, once you've picked a destination, a good agent will help you sift through the confusing array of hotels, airfares, packages, and other options to help you find the best accommodations and deals. Your agent also should be able to answer questions on packing, climate, local transportation, attractions, and more.

Through their computer reservation services, travel agents have up-to-the-minute information on fares and availability for most airlines and, in some cases, for hotels, cruises, and tours. Many also have extensive libraries of videos and guidebooks as well as brochures that you can browse through. And best of all, in most cases, travel agents will charge you nothing or a small fee for their services.

How do they make money? In general, travel agents are paid commissions by the airlines, hotels, and tour operators. This implies, for the most part correctly, that travel agents are most familiar with services that pay commission. In fact, one of the exceptions to the "no charge" rule would apply if you decided to stay in a small guest house or hotel that did not pay a commission. Then you might be asked to pay for phone calls and/or fax charges to make the reservations. Some agents also charge a processing fee for low-fare air tickets, especially if they are not making other arrangements for you.

Can you get better rates on your own? The answer is rarely for airfares or packages—if you have a knowledgeable travel agent. (See the following section for tips on finding a good agent.) And because rates change so often, your best bet is to have a travel agent who will keep on top of things. Some even have

---

✿ HONEYMOON FACTS ✿
Honeymooners Use Agents

More than 70 percent of all couples use a travel agent to help arrange their honeymoon trip.

Source: Modern Bride Honeymoon Market Report

---

computer programs to scan for sales on tickets they've already booked. Most travelers find that a good travel agent is invaluable for guiding them to the right place for the best price. (However, if you're looking for information on home-stay programs, small bed-and-breakfast inns, or camping, guidebooks will usually be a better source of information.)

How to Find a Good Agent

Think of a travel agent as a professional, such as a doctor or a financial consultant. If you haven't used one before, here are some sources of referrals:

Word of mouth. Your best bet is to ask friends and family for recommendations. Try to ask people with interests that are similar to your own, and be sure to get the name of the agent as well as the agency.

Call the tourist office. Many governments, regions, and states maintain travel information offices. Some offices can give you a list of agents in your area who specialize in their country or region. (See Appendix B for listings.)

Look for specialists. Agents with CTC (Certified Travel Counselor) after their names have completed a 200-hour program of travel industry studies, whereas those with DS (Destination Specialist) credentials have completed training in a particular region. You can contact the Institute of Certified Travel Agents for CTC and DS Agents in your area. (See Appendix A.)

Respond to ads. You'll find travel agency ads in the travel pages of your local newspaper and Yellow Pages. Agencies that are members of ASTA, the American Society of Travel Agents, agree to adhere to a code of ethics and often post the ASTA logo in their ads and on their windows.

Evaluating Your Agent

You should feel completely comfortable with your travel agent's expertise and understanding of your needs and wishes. A good agent will take the time to know exactly what you are looking for. You can make the process easier by sharing the information from the "Honeymoon Style" questions you answered in chapter 1. It's especially important to tell an agent about your budget as well as any activities you'd like to have available.

As in any profession, some agents are more competent than others; some have good overall knowledge, whereas others have an area of specialty. And as you'll see from some examples in the following chapters, some can be fairly characterized as inept. If you feel your travel agent is not knowledgeable, isn't taking the time to ask questions about what you want, or doesn't pay attention to what you are saying, then it's time to change agents. Understanding how the travel industry works—which you'll also learn in following chapters—will help you appraise how well your travel agent is serving you.

Questions to Ask a Travel Agent

1. **Can you provide us with client references who have interests that are similar to our own?** Most agents will provide you with names but may want to call their clients first, so as not to intrude on their privacy.
2. **Have you been to the destinations we're considering?** Although agents can advise you about destinations without having been there, you'll get more complete information from someone who has.
3. **Can you advise us about passports, visas, travel and health insurance, no-fee traveler's checks, and so on?** Many agencies can handle all these arrangements for you.
4. **Do you have guidebooks and/or videos we can look at?** Some agencies keep libraries for their clients' use.
5. **Do you work with consolidators to obtain discounted airline tickets?** If you're going overseas and want to get the lowest fare (see chapter 4), this can be important.
6. **Because you receive higher commissions or incentives from certain airlines, hotel chains, cruise lines, and the like, will there be any advantages for us? Will you also check into other suppliers?** Most travel agencies earn higher commissions from certain suppliers, but because agents are trying to build a lifelong relationship with you, most will put your needs first.
7. **Do you have a twenty-four-hour help line in case we encounter problems during our trip?** This is very important. Most agencies either maintain their own help line or contract with a service that will help you in case of emergencies, such as canceled flights or hotel problems.

More Free Information

Other excellent sources of free information are the official tourist offices or chambers of commerce of the countries and regions you plan to visit. You'll find a listing for the most popular destinations in Appendix B. Most tourist offices will provide you with free brochures on activities, accommodations, and restaurants and will answer any specific questions you may have. And because their offices are often staffed with people from the country they represent, they can be a wonderful source of ideas for romantic things to do.

❧ CHAPTER 3

Checking into Accommodations

A terrace overlooking the ocean. A fireplace. A private pool. Plush robes. Baroque decor with overstuffed furniture. For better or for worse, your honeymoon accommodations are something you'll never forget, so they're an important consideration in picking a destination.

Just ask Ginger, whose tropical honeymoon was, in her words, "not a great start for our marriage." What happened? She and Brett had purchased the lowest-priced package they could find. Their hotel was several blocks from the beach; their room was spartan and overlooked a parking lot. "It was our honeymoon, and I hated being in that room," she said.

Although most couples don't let a disappointing room cast a pall over their whole trip, the most common lament I hear from couples is that they wish they'd splurged a bit more on their honeymoon accommodations. In this chapter, you'll learn about the different types of lodgings popular with honeymooners, where the best values are, and most important, which will provide the best experiences—and happiest memories—for you.

Randy and Louise, who had an oceanfront suite in Cancún, said that the nicest part of their honeymoon was getting back to their room in time to sip wine and watch the sunset from their terrace every evening. "It was a wonderful time to relax together and review the day; it's a ritual we'd like to continue forever, although unfortunately, we don't have an oceanfront terrace at home!" said Louise.

You don't have to spend a fortune to have fine accommodations. Some couples opt to spend their whole honeymoons close to home so that they can stay at a special hotel or inn. Many take advantage of money-saving packages or off-season rates. And some stay at condominiums or villas, which often offer far more space than comparably priced hotel rooms, with the additional cost-saving potential of being able to have snacks, drinks, and meals—if you feel like cooking—at supermarket rather than restaurant prices. Bed-and-breakfast inns may also be fairly inexpensive alternatives.

In addition to your room or suite, your lodgings may have other features that would help to make your trip special. At an all-inclusive resort, you can enjoy dining, sports, and entertainment without ever opening your wallet. Or you

---

ᘓᔆᕋ HONEYMOON TIPS ᘓᔆᕋ
Revel in the Romance

Everyone loves lovers. Let people know you're honeymooners and watch them roll out the red carpet. Don't be bashful, especially with hotels, cruise lines, and restaurants—tell them you're honeymooners when you make your reservations, and you're likely to enjoy special treatment, such as a gift basket in your room or complimentary champagne. Some honeymoon packages even include photo albums, crystal or china, or a gift certificate to be used for an anniversary trip.

---

might opt for a private villa with a cook and a chauffeur on staff, a full-service resort, or a rental cottage.

You'll generally pay more for the best locations, luxurious service, spacious accommodations, in-room amenities, impressive lobbies, or swimming pools and other sports facilities. There are numerous rating systems, so you need to ask a lot of questions to understand what you're getting. For example, "first-class accommodations" may sound like the top of the line, but they're usually less luxurious than the deluxe variety, and the word *luxury* is often used indiscriminately. Similarly, the word *hotel* is used to refer to a wide range of prices and facilities. What best suits you? On the following pages, you'll find a rundown of the most popular types of accommodations for honeymooners and what you can expect from each.

Questions to Ask about Accommodations

Here are some basic questions to ask to be sure you're getting what you want; you'll find more specific questions to ask for each type of accommodation in the sections that follow.

Location: Is it in a special setting: on the beach, in the middle of the city, near sightseeing attractions, or in beautiful natural surroundings? What is the view from your room? (Get this confirmed in writing.)

Meals: What type of dining is available on-site? Is there a choice of casual and formal dining? Are other restaurants nearby?

Facilities: Which activities are available on the premises? Is there a full-service spa and health club? An indoor pool? Can you expect all the facilities and restaurants to be open during your visit? Are they free to guests? Will there be construction during your stay that will affect your use of the facilities or your comfort?

Amenities: Are rooms equipped with air-conditioning? Minibar? Combination safe? Telephone? Radio? Television? VCR (usually with a rental library available)? Oversized whirlpool baths? Hair dryers? Fancy soaps and lotions?

Additional charges: Are tips for bellhops and maids included? Is a fixed percentage added to all restaurant and room service bills? (Unless you ask, you'll probably end up tipping *and* paying the charges on your bill.) What taxes are applicable? (These can add more than 20 percent to your bill.) Are there energy or other surcharges? Will you receive a written confirmation of your arrangements from the hotel, including the rate and what it pays for? (You should receive this as soon as you make your reservations.)

All-Inclusive Resorts

The modern concept of all-inclusive honeymoon resorts started in the Poconos during and just after World War II, when hotels began catering to returning soldiers and their brides by charging a single price for accommodations, meals, and use of whatever facilities they provided. Club Med popularized the concept in the 1960s, creating all-inclusive resorts in exotic destinations around the world, where the only extras were drinks and some sports. SuperClubs brought the concept to Jamaica in 1975, soon followed by another well-known Jamaican resort company, Sandals.

These days, all-inclusive resorts are popping up all over the Caribbean and the rest of the world, too. And many traditional hotels are offering all-inclusive packages. The nice thing about all-inclusives is that you'll be able to budget very accurately for your honeymoon, and you may find yourselves trying new sports and activities because you won't have to think about the cost. But all all-inclusive resorts are not the same.

Here are some questions to ask when making your selection:

Ambience: Does the resort cater to a particular group—couples only, singles, families—or everyone? Will there be many newlyweds? (If so, you'll have lots of couples with whom to share wedding stories and, maybe, begin lifetime friendships.)

Meals: Does the rate include three meals a day? Are snacks available around the clock? Is there a choice of restaurants? Are meals served sit-down or buffet-

---

❧ HONEYMOON FACTS ❧
Honeymoon Wish List

What do most honeymooners want in a hotel? Here are the top five considerations: cost within budgetary goals, beachfront/oceanview, outdoor sports facilities, a choice of restaurants, and luxurious rooms.

Source: Modern Bride Honeymoon Market Report

Ȥ *HONEYMOON TIPS* Ȥ
Ways to Save

1. Ask your travel agent about honeymoon and similar packages as well as other special discounts. City hotels often offer weekend discounts and packages, whereas resorts generally offer low- and shoulder-season rates.
2. Compare package rates—and what they include—to what you would pay à la carte for the features that you are looking for.
3. Examine a discount or travel club; many offer 50 percent off hotel rates and other benefits, although you should check out the restrictions on using the discount before joining. (See Appendix A.)

---

style? Is there room service? During what hours? Are alcoholic beverages and wine included?

Tipping: Are tips included? (Many couples view this as a real advantage. Said one newlywed, "It's relaxing not to worry about tipping each time someone brings you a drink or opens a door for you." Other couples feel uncomfortable not tipping for good service.)

Value: Are the sports, drinks, and activities you want included? If you're not drinkers and all you plan to do is lie on the beach, are you still getting good value?

Grand Resorts

Often boasting more than a thousand rooms, these resorts are like miniature cities. Like all-inclusives, grand resorts usually offer a wide array of activities. Although you'll probably pay as you go for meals and activities, most resorts offer packages that include specific options such as scuba diving, golf, tennis, or meals. The advantage: you can enjoy a wide array of dining, shopping, and sports options without leaving the resort and pay only for the facilities you use. You will probably also enjoy twenty-four-hour room service as well as nice touches such as twice-a-day maid service, chocolate mints on your pillow at night, and concierges ready to help with just about anything. Here are some questions to ask:

Ambience: How big is the property? Is it formal or informal? Grand or intimate? High-rise or low-rise? What percentage of the resort's guests come with business or civic groups at the time of the year you're planning to visit? (You probably won't want to be one of the few people not wearing a name tag.) Does the resort have a children's program? If so, are there separate pools and play areas for children? (If not, children may break the romantic mood wherever you go.)

Views: What will you see from your room? If you are at a beach hotel, will you have an oceanfront room? (This doesn't mean you'll walk out your door to the ocean, but you should have an unobstructed view of the sea.) An oceanview room? (This might mean you have to crane your neck a bit to see the sea.) Or a garden or mountain view? (This is usually what it sounds like, but there may be a parking lot in between you and the view.)

Condominiums and Villas

If you want space, privacy, and the convenience of your own kitchen, this could be for you. The prices are often comparable to those of hotels, and some condo and villa complexes offer comparable facilities. Room service meals are generally not available, and daily maid service may cost extra. However, some villas come complete with maid, chef, and chauffeur services for roughly the price of a hotel room. Here are some questions to ask:

Services: Is maid service included? Is it available? At what cost? What other services are included?

Meals and supplies: Is there a restaurant on the premises or nearby? Is room service available? Is there a grocery store?

✣ *Honeymoon Tips* ✣
About Meal Plans

Some resorts include meals in their rates or for a surcharge. If you plan to eat most of your meals at the resort, these can be a good deal. However, it's wise to find out which restaurants are included and whether you'll be able to order from the full menu or pay surcharges for premium dishes. Here are the most common hotel meal plans:

1. Modified American Plan (MAP): Full breakfast and lunch or dinner daily are included.
2. American Plan (AP) or Full Pension/Full Board: Price includes three meals a day.
3. European Plan (EP): No meals are included.
4. Continental Plan (CP): Continental breakfasts provided daily. In the Western Hemisphere, this usually means breakfast rolls and coffee or tea. In Europe, it can also include cheeses and sliced meats.
5. Bermuda Plan (BP): Full breakfast daily, usually including juice, eggs, toast, and coffee or tea.

Note: Alcoholic beverages, including wine, are usually not included in these prices.

Tipping: What kind of tips should we expect to give the staff? (This is especially important in villas where you may have a large staff at your service.)

Inns and Bed-and-Breakfasts

These terms cover a wide range of accommodation styles. You might be renting a room in a farmhouse, a suburban home, a city apartment, or a historic landmark.

Generally, bed-and-breakfasts are private homes that rent a few rooms to visitors. Breakfast, included in the price of your room, will probably be the only meal available, and your hosts will probably make you feel like personal guests. These are generally the least expensive but also the least private. Hosts may share their living room with their guests, and you may not have your own bathroom.

Inns often offer more services and amenities (perhaps a tennis court or swimming pool). Many are known for their gourmet food as well as their per-

---

༘ HONEYMOON TIPS ༘
Learning the Lingo

Hotels have a language all their own, and as is the case with all idioms, learning the jargon gives you an insider's view. The following are some of the most common hotel terms.

Rack rates: The full (retail) price of the room before discounts are applied. Hopefully, you won't have to pay this rate.

Guaranteed late arrival: To hold your reservation, no matter how late you arrive, you'll have to pay for your first night in advance. That money won't be refunded, even if you don't arrive until the next day. However, without this guarantee, most hotels will not hold your room past 6 P.M.

Standard rooms: At some resorts, all guest rooms are quite special; "spartan" best describes the rooms at others. Look at recent brochures and ask if the room pictured is standard or a special suite that may cost more.

Suites: Suites can be quite elaborate, perhaps with an in-room Jacuzzi and large sitting room, while junior suites usually have a small sitting area, not a separate room.

Double, queen- or king-size beds: In the United States and Caribbean, these terms are understood. If you're reserving overseas, ask for a large matrimonial bed, as "double beds" can be understood as two single beds.

Upgrades: Often honeymooners are given free upgrades, which means being moved to a higher category of room than you paid for. For example, you may be upgraded from an oceanview room to an oceanfront room or a junior suite.

sonal service and hospitality. Because the terms *inn* and *bed-and-breakfast* are often used interchangeably, you'll want to ask lots of questions to be sure you get what you want:

Architecture and decor: Is the inn a historic building? Is it decorated with antiques? Will your room have a fireplace? A canopy bed?

Accommodations: Will your room have a private bathroom? Bath or shower? TV? Phone? How private is your room? What size and types of beds are available? Is it air-conditioned? If you want a firm mattress or a queen-size bed, be sure to ask.

Meals: When is breakfast served? Is it a full breakfast or simply rolls and coffee? Is room service available? Are other meals available? What about snacks and beverages?

Amenities: What extras are included? Some inns provide guests with bicycles, canoes, beach access, or tennis courts. Others offer musical soirées or theme weekends. Many hosts will also help you to arrange other activities in the area, such as hot-air ballooning, shopping, and so on.

Other considerations: Is smoking permitted? Are pets? Can you pay with a credit card or check, or will you need cash? Are there other house rules? Most inns require a nonrefundable deposit, and many have minimum-stay requirements.

How do you find an inn? Some inns can be booked through travel agents, but you'll find many more listed through local tourist information centers or chambers of commerce. (You'll find listings, by destination, in Appendix B.) There are also many guidebooks, available in bookstores, that provide detailed descriptions and booking information.

Once you've picked your destination and decided on what type of accommodations you'd like, you'll need to arrange transportation. The next few chapters cover planes, ships, car rentals, and other transportation alternatives. If you're driving your own car, read the tips on "road romance" in chapter 5 and then skip to the chapter on packing.

CHAPTER 4

Getting There by Air

The excitement builds as you approach the airport, and your hearts speed up with anticipation. Airports are exciting places. Of course, they can seem like a maze, and what can seem even more like a maze is the tangled web of fares and routings.

Competitive pricing often means that even for fairly short distances, flying can be the least expensive way to go. However, the types of discounts and restrictions—not to mention the frequent flyer plans—are enough to make your head swim. And if you think that a direct flight means you'll go without stopping from here to there, think again (see "Learning the Lingo" in this chapter). Some of the routings are truly ridiculous.

This chapter will help you understand the system so that you can save money and avoid unnecessary inconvenience. For example, Jim and Diane's travel agent had booked them for three nights in Cancún, Mexico, then three nights in Cozumel, and then one more night in Cancún. Why were they flying back to Cancún for one night? Because their travel agent thought that they had to fly home from Cancún. In fact, the flights the couple was booked on all went to Cancún and then continued to Cozumel. So they had needlessly paid for tickets between Cancún and Cozumel. And worse, because their flight from Cancún was scheduled to stop in Cozumel, they would be going through all the trouble of flying to Cancún and switching hotels only to fly back to Cozumel the following morning. When I told them that, they were furious. They called their travel agent, who did some quick work and was able to switch their reservations at the hotel in Cancún for an additional night in Cozumel, where they would meet their flight home. Their travel agent should have known better, but had Jim and Diane asked if their flights were nonstop, *they* would have known better. So how do you make sure that you're booking the most direct flights at the best fares? To do this, you'll have to learn some basic facts.

First Class or Coach?

The first question you're asked when you inquire about an airline fare is usually "First class or coach?" First class can cost far more than double the price of an average coach fare, although not always. You're paying for increased leg room, free drinks, better food, and personal service. Many flights also offer business class, which costs more than coach but less than first class; the amenities are likewise in the middle. Drinks will be free but food service, although better than coach, will be less elaborate than first class.

If you opt for coach, your fare options multiply. The first fare you're quoted may be more than three or four times the fare you'll actually pay. The "lower excursion" fares (the name may vary) generally must be purchased between seven and twenty-one days in advance, and your trip must include a Saturday night stayover. (Most discount fares are nonrefundable, but you can usually change the dates for a fee.)

If you must pay full-fare coach, ask how much it will cost to upgrade to business class; it may be worth the small surcharge.

Finding the Lowest Fare

During recent years, fierce competition has prompted fare wars. Although the airlines have not technically lowered their fares, they often run sales in which you have a week or a few weeks to book at a low price. Some of these are widely advertised. Others are publicized only through joint promotions with supermarkets, charge card companies, or other "partners." You may find the fares advertised on radio or in newspaper travel sections. Sometimes, however, even travel agents are not advised of these fares, and they are often only available on a limited number of seats, so you have to keep your eyes open and book quickly.

A fairly new wrinkle in the airfare wars is the appearance of "niche" carriers. These airlines usually fly limited routes and schedules at rock-bottom fares. When a niche carrier begins offering low fares, the bigger airlines usually match them but with lots of restrictions, severely limiting the number of seats sold on each flight at that fare as well as the days of travel.

The smaller carriers often have no restrictions on when you can buy and how long you can stay. The drawbacks? You need to be sure they'll stay in business and that they have backup in case a plane is grounded for repairs. Some of these airlines aren't listed and can't be booked through the travel agents' automated systems, so you may have to do your own research.

༺༻ HONEYMOON FACTS ༺༻
Taking Flight

Almost 75 percent of all couples fly to their honeymoon destinations.

Source: Modern Bride Honeymoon Market Report

How do you find them? Watch the ads in the travel sections of major city newspapers. You can also try checking with the chamber of commerce, convention and visitors bureau, or airport manager in your city and at your destination to find out which airlines offer scheduled service. If you'd like to call the airlines directly, you'll find toll-free numbers for major carriers in Appendix A.

For low fares to Europe and the Orient, check out the offerings of consolidators (also known as wholesalers, bulk-fare operators, and discounters), which act as brokers. They usually run ads in newspaper travel sections, and many work with travel agents.

The downside? Although consolidators' tickets are usually on scheduled flights, sometimes they are not on the best-known airlines or the most direct flights. If your flight is delayed or you miss a connection, your ticket probably won't be honored by another airline. This could mean waiting a day or more for the next flight. Tickets are usually nonrefundable, you may not get frequent flyer mileage credit, and you may not be able to get seat assignments in advance or special food arrangements, such as for kosher or vegetarian meals. More important, this segment of the travel industry has had its share of frauds and bankruptcies. You can minimize your risk by paying with a credit card (the 2 to 3 percent fee you may be asked to pay will allow you to apply for a refund on your credit card if you don't receive the tickets you order) and by buying through a travel agent you trust who is familiar with consolidators.

Charter flights can also be a money-saving option. As with consolidators, use caution when purchasing charter flights. They can be less expensive than regularly scheduled flights, but not always. Some are discounted seats (called "blocked space") on regular flights with some added restrictions. Others use planes with more cramped seating. Often, you'll find longer check-in lines, a greater tendency to delays, and more schedule and price changes (without the right to a refund) than on scheduled flights. Why fly a charter? The price may be lower, and more important, doing so may be the only way to fly nonstop to your destination, saving you the inconvenience and time of changing planes. And sometimes charter flights are used with attractive package tours. How do you find them? Read newspaper travel sections and ask your travel agent.

Frequent Flyer Clubs

Whichever airlines you fly with, be sure to join their frequent flyer club—even if this is your first flight. Many airlines give you points just for signing up, and because there's no charge, you risk nothing by joining. Ask for an application form when you book your flight. You may be surprised at how quickly the miles add up to free trips or upgrades to first class. Some clubs also team up with charge cards, letting you accumulate miles for dollars charged.

Planning for Comfort

Unless you go first class, flying is not a pampering experience. But you can plan ahead to minimize your discomfort. Here are some tips:

Airports: Big cities often have several airports. If you have a choice, use the least-congested one. You'll have an easier time getting in and out of the airport.

Check-in: Most airlines ask you to check in at least two hours before an international flight and an hour before domestic departures. Although some travelers like racing through airports, I generally follow the airlines' advice and save my adrenaline for better purposes (like kayaking through rapids or hot-air ballooning!). However, even after passing through customs, immigration, and security, you'll probably have some waiting time before you can board your flight.

Before the flight: Unless you're flying first or business class or your travel agent has been able to arrange for you to use a special lounge, make yourselves comfortable at a bar or restaurant or stretch your legs with a walk. Some airports offer extensive shopping opportunities—duty-free if you're overseas—although you may end up paying top dollar. Also, bring a book or activity to keep you occupied while waiting to get on the flight (and while flying). Unless you're carrying on a lot of luggage, there's no real advantage to queuing up and being the first to board.

Seating: If you're not flying in business or first class, expect cramped seating. Some airlines offer more spacious seating than others, and your travel agent should have the latest information. Preselect your seats if possible. Travel agents have computerized seating configuration plans and can advise you. You and your fiancé will want to sit together, not sandwiched between other people. Request a window and aisle seat and you won't have people sitting on all sides of you. If there are three to the row you are in, the seat between you may remain

❧❧❧ *HONEYMOON TIPS* ❧❧❧
Learning the Lingo

On-time performance: Travel agents can tell you how frequently a particular flight is delayed more than fifteen minutes. Delays tend to occur at peak times and in busy airports.

Direct: Although direct flights stop along the way, you shouldn't have to change planes.

Nonstop: Nonstop flights mean what they sound like and are truly the most direct way to fly!

Bulkhead seat: Seats behind a cabin divider. These sometimes provide more legroom.

Seat width: The distance between seats as measured from armrest to armrest.

Seat pitch: The distance between seats from front to back. This determines legroom.

Seat configurations: Some planes are configured with all aisle and window seats. Others have as many as five seats side by side, which is obviously less comfortable.

Nonsmoking flight: No smoking is permitted on board at all.

Nonsmoking section: On flights where smoking is permitted, areas of the plane are generally divided into smoking and nonsmoking sections. If you can't stand the smell of smoke, ask to be seated in the nonsmoking section and specify that you also want to be far from the smoking sections of all three classes.

Special meals: In coach class, airline meals often deserve the jokes about them. Some are better than others, but many seasoned travelers opt to order special meals (there's no charge, but you need to reserve at least a day in advance). Options include vegetarian, seafood, kosher, and low-cholesterol meals.

Boarding passes: Try to get your seat assignments and boarding passes in advance. If you don't need to check luggage, you may be able to avoid waiting at a check-in counter when you arrive at the airport. However, even with boarding passes, you still need to check in when you get to the gate.

Nonrefundable tickets: If your plans change, you may not be able to get a refund for your tickets. Some airlines will allow you to change your travel dates for a fee; others will issue a refund if your doctor advises you not to travel (and confirms it in writing for the airline). Ask your travel agent about trip cancellation insurance.

empty; if not, most people are happy to trade a middle seat for a window or aisle. If you're stuck in a row with five seats across, be sure you have an aisle and the seat next to it. Taller people tend to like aisle seats. On some planes, bulkhead and exit row seats offer more legroom—on others, less. If you plan to watch a movie on your flight, you'll also want to consider whether your seat will afford you a clear view of the screen.

In flight: Wherever you sit, you'll be more comfortable if you wear non-constricting clothing that breathes (this means no pantyhose). Take off your shoes and raise your feet by resting them on luggage or blankets, protect your neck with an inflatable U-shaped pillow (bring one), and use an airline pillow to support the small of your back. Try to get up to walk and stretch every hour. Because the air aloft is especially dry, bring moisturizer for your skin, saline drops for your eyes (if you use contacts, consider wearing glasses in flight), and avoid dehydration by drinking plenty of noncaffeinated, nonalcoholic beverages. If you are congested, take a decongestant about an hour before the flight and again before the descent. Chewing gum, sucking candies, or yawning should clear or "pop" your ears. If not, close your mouth, pinch your nose, and breathe out gently to equalize the pressure.

Tell the world: Officially, airlines don't give honeymooners special recognition. However, everyone loves newlyweds, and if you mention your wedding when you check in for your flight, you may find yourselves waiting in the first-class lounge or even upgraded to business or first class. Tell your stewardess once you're seated on board, and you may find yourselves toasting with champagne.

In the next chapter, you'll find pointers on traveling by land—both on how to get to your destination and how to make the most of your honeymoon once you've arrived.

CHAPTER 5

Travel by Land

S hari and David love to discover new places by serendipity, so when they took off for Bali, they definitely planned on renting a car once they arrived. "Our travel agent suggested that since we weren't used to driving on the left and didn't speak the language, we should hire a car and driver, but we really wanted to be on our own," said David. "It worked out great. Each evening, we'd talk to our hotel concierge and chart out the next day's route. Then we'd read about the places we planned to visit. Of course, we did get a bit lost once or twice, but that was part of the fun. And we met so many people."

Elaine and Kevin, on the other hand, felt that driving around a strange place was not for them. "Driving is too much like work," said Elaine. "We wanted to see the island [Barbados], and we didn't want a tour with fifty people getting on and off at each stop. Our hotel recommended a private guide, and we liked her so much that we went out with her twice. She took us to meet the owner of a working plantation, gave us a real feeling for the history and politics of the island, and even packed a gourmet picnic for us and dropped us off for a few hours at a secluded beach."

Renting a car or hiring a private guide means that you can explore at your own pace without adhering to schedules. Depending on where you'll be honeymooning, guided tours, public transportation, and hotel shuttles may also be available. You may even decide to reach your honeymoon destination by train or bus. Your travel agent, hotel, or the tourist office can tell you what's available. In this chapter, you'll learn about these and other options and how to make the right choice for you.

Auto Excitement

There's little to match the excitement of hopping behind the wheel and being free to follow your whims as you explore new places. You might even consider renting your dream car—perhaps a snappy BMW convertible, a stately Lincoln Continental, or a sporty Porsche. If you have a special model in mind, ask your travel agent or car rental company if it is available. Otherwise, you'll choose a size/price category: economy/subcompact, midsize, or luxury. Specify any features that are important to you such as air-conditioning, cruise control, or a large trunk.

❦ *HONEYMOON TIPS* ❦
Road Romance

Cars offer you the freedom to explore and discover your own private places. Here are some suggestions to enhance the romance.

1. Have your hotel pack a picnic—or pick up fixings along the way—and find a scenic spot to enjoy your meal.
2. Ask your hotel concierge, the rental car clerk, and other couples for suggestions on romantic, secluded places.
3. Drive to a scenic overlook to watch the sunset. (Ask where local couples go.)
4. Listen to the local talk shows on the radio as you drive. In addition to current entertainment happenings, you'll be "visiting" with local residents!

Car Rental Realities

Paula and Andrew had planned to drive along the California coast for their honeymoon, but when they filled out the paperwork at the rental car counter, the clerk took one look at their licenses and told them they were too young. "You have to be twenty-five, but no one told us that. So there we were, old enough to get married, but too young to rent a car," said Andrew. "Fortunately, the clerk took pity on us, made some phone calls to competing companies, and found us a car we could rent. I don't know what we would have done otherwise. Our honeymoon would have been ruined."

Paula and Andrew were lucky. If you're under twenty-five, be sure to ask if there is a minimum age when making your reservations. For insurance reasons, many rental car companies won't rent to drivers under that age. Some will, but they add a surcharge.

You may be surprised to learn that rental car companies are increasingly checking drivers' records and refusing to rent to drivers with several convictions for moving violations or driving while intoxicated.

If you don't have a major credit card, it's worth getting one. Otherwise, you'll probably need a sizable cash deposit as well as prearranged approval. You'll also need valid licenses; if you're going abroad, you may need an international driver's license. Your local Automobile Association of America (AAA) office can provide you with one, even if you're not a member.

Additional charges can also add up to quite a shock. The low rates you see advertised in newspapers and magazines are often pumped up by a number of surcharges, some mandatory, some avoidable. These can include state and city taxes, airport fees (if you are picked up at the airport by a car rental company that isn't located on the airport grounds), mileage charges, and drop-off charges (if you aren't returning the car to the same location from which it was rented). Ask

ꙮ HONEYMOON TIPS ꙮ
Ways to Save

1. Comparison shop. Use toll-free numbers (see Appendix A) to call at least three companies and ask for the best rate as well as about special deals and promotions. Ask about additional charges and factor them in when comparing rates.
2. Check special rates: unlimited mileage rates if you plan to drive long distances; weeklong rates, often far less than daily rates, even if you're not staying a full week. Also, watch newspaper travel sections for special promotions and check with your travel agent about fly/drive and hotel/car rental packages.
3. Know whether you need to purchase optional insurance/waivers. Often, it's not necessary because you're already covered, so call your auto insurance agent and read your credit card terms to learn what coverage you have before you leave on your trip.
4. Check with clubs you belong to and your employer about discounted rates for members or employees, but don't assume these are the best you can do.

about any surcharges and factor them in when comparing rates. Some firms also ask for a refundable deposit, which may reduce the amount you can charge to your credit card during your trip.

Before You Go

When you fill out the paperwork for your rental, you'll face decisions about a set of optional charges for insurance and liability waivers, which you'll be asked to either accept (and pay for) or decline (and be responsible for damages in case of an accident). You can save as much as $20 a day by checking in advance to find out what coverage you already have.

Ask your insurance agent: What does my auto insurance cover when I rent a car? Does that coverage apply outside this country? Am I covered if the car is damaged in an accident or I'm hurt? What if other people are injured? Am I covered if the car is stolen or vandalized? What additional coverage might I need?

Read your credit card terms: What coverage is provided if I use this credit card to rent a car? Do you provide primary coverage, or do I still have to collect from my auto insurance company first?

Ask the rental car company: What insurance, waivers, and other options do you offer? What type of coverage is required for overseas rentals? Is it included in the rate? Is an international driver's license required? Are there lim-

---

❧❧ HONEYMOON TIPS ❧❧
Learning the Lingo

Collision Damage Waiver (CDW) or *Loss Damage Waiver (LDW):* Purchase this and the car rental company waives its right to hold you liable if your rental car is damaged or stolen. If you're not already covered or want to avoid reporting an accident to your insurance company, you should opt for this. The exception: in some states the liability is limited to a dollar amount that may be less than purchasing CDW for a week!

Additional Liability Insurance (ALI) or *Supplemental Liability Insurance (SLI):* These usually provide liability protection for $1 million. Your own insurance may already protect you. If not, this is important.

Personal accident insurance: This covers medical expenses and insures against death. Your existing health and life insurance may make this unnecessary.

Personal effects coverage: This offers limited coverage for personal possessions that are stolen from the car (never leave valuables in sight!) but usually doesn't include jewelry, cameras, and other high-value items. Homeowners or renters insurance usually makes this coverage unnecessary.

Extra driver fee: Now that you're married, this is one fee that will probably be waived. But because your driver's licenses will have different last names, be sure to say that you are married. (Say you're newlyweds and you may get friendlier service as well.)

---

itations on which countries we can drive through without purchasing additional insurance? Are there any other legal or insurance regulations we need to be prepared for?

Traveling by Train

In many areas, trains are the best way to get where you're going. You can relax and watch the scenery, get up and walk around, and even meet people as you go. In areas such as Alaska, California, and the Rockies, excursion trains take you through some of the country's most dramatic landscapes, whereas on the East Coast, trains often rival planes for city-to-city travel.

If you plan to do a lot of hopping around, a rail pass may also offer significant savings over airline tickets or point-to-point rail tickets. In the United States, Amtrak offers rail/hotel packages, regional "All Aboard" rates, and off-peak and other special fares. In Canada, VIA Rail offers similar service. Both can be booked by travel agents.

In Europe, trains connect most of the popular destinations—even small cities and resort areas—with reliable and convenient service. A variety of rail passes is

available, including single-country, regional, and all-Europe passes as well as flex-
ible passes that don't require your travel to be on consecutive days. Also check
out student and youth discounts. However, unless you'll be traveling quite a bit,
you may save money by buying point-to-point tickets. You may also want to
consider rail packages that include a rental car or bicycles once you reach your
destination. For details, call Rail Europe or the national tourist office of the
country you're interested in. (Turn to Appendixes A and B for contacts.)

Public Transportation

In major cities, the best ways to get around are walking or using public transportation or taxis. Many cities have tour buses that offer a good overall orientation and let you get on and off at major sites for a day for a fixed price. Also
check with the tourist office about city passes; these sometimes combine a transportation pass with free or reduced admission to museums and other attractions.

Many attractions in resort areas provide free hotel pickup and drop-off, and
some resort areas provide free shuttle service around the resort and to nearby
points of interest. Many even provide transportation to and from the airport.

In the next chapter, you'll learn about one of the most romantic and popular modes of transportation for honeymooners—cruising.

CHAPTER 6

Choosing to Cruise

*I*f cruising were a single destination, it would rank number one for honeymooners. The reasons are easy to understand; a cruise combines the magic of being at sea, the adventure of sailing into exotic ports of call without the hassles of packing and unpacking, and food that's every bit as bountiful as you've probably heard. Cruising created the word *posh,* which once stood for the cabins with the best views: Port Out, Starboard Home.

Most modern cruise ships are luxurious floating resorts that indulge and entertain you as they transport you to intriguing destinations. Theaters, restaurants, cocktail lounges, discos, casinos, health clubs, and swimming pools are all just a short walk from your cabin. Perhaps best of all, accommodations, airfare, and transfers as well as shipboard food, sports, and evening entertainment are generally included in a package price that is often less than you'd pay for a honeymoon on land. And after all the decisions of wedding planning, many newlyweds say they appreciate being pampered and not having to think about where to dine or dance or how much it will cost.

Of course, although most couples rave about their cruise experiences, cruising isn't for everyone. Some travelers find even the largest ships confining and don't like the regimentation of adhering to schedules for meals and shore excursions. And unless you splurge for a large cabin, you may be amazed at how cramped your quarters can be.

Picking a Ship

Your cruise experience will be largely determined by the sailing (ship, itinerary, and departure date) you choose. In this chapter, you'll learn how to pick the right ship for your tastes and interests. Here are some factors to consider before selecting a sailing:

Budget: Decide how much you want to spend and how long you want to cruise. Cruises can last anywhere from several days to several months. You may also opt to combine your cruise with a stay at a hotel. Your budget and time frame will help determine where you will cruise.

Ports of call: From Antarctica to Zanzibar, if a destination is accessible by water, there's probably a ship that goes there. The most popular destinations include the Bahamas, Bermuda, the Caribbean, Hawaii, and Mexico. Or how about a dreamy trip through the Greek isles or along the Nile or island-hopping in the South Pacific? And if you're nature lovers, consider exploring the Galápagos Islands of Ecuador, traveling along the Amazon, or cruising through Alaska's Glacier Bay. Once you've picked a part of the world, consider specific places you'd like to see. If you aren't familiar enough with geography to know where you'd like to go, think about what you'd like to do. Do you want to shop, bask on secluded beaches, scuba dive, or sightsee?

Time in port: Some couples are happiest on transoceanic crossings, where no port distractions interfere with the rhythm of life at sea. Others view the ship primarily as transportation. Most, however, prefer something in between. If there are places that you want to see, be sure that you have enough time to spend in your preferred ports. Will the attractions you want to see be open on the day (and hours) that the ship is in port? Don't forget to allow an hour to clear customs and an extra hour if your ship anchors and ferries passengers ashore instead of docking right in port.

Special interests: If you share a hobby—golf, tennis, jazz, or murder mysteries—you may want to see if there is a sailing timed for your honeymoon that caters to it. Some sailings feature onboard naturalists or historians as lecturers. Others have professional athletes as onboard pros. Snorkeling and scuba diving are popular island cruise experiences. Most ships provide exercise rooms; however, if you like a specific type of workout, find out exactly what equipment is available. "Exercise rooms" may mean anything from rusty stationary bikes to high-tech gyms with full spas. Many ships claim to have a track or lap deck, but runners should ask if they'll be dodging lounge chairs and slow walkers.

Ambience: Every ship has its own personality, and in the case of specially themed cruises, this can even vary from one sailing to the next. To see if a ship is for you, start by looking at the brochure and then call directly and ask about the specific sailing that coincides with your schedule. At first glance, all ships may seem perfect to you. But look more closely. Do you want to dress up for dinner every night? What is the average age of the passengers? What do the descriptions

---

ৎৡৣৡ HONEYMOON TIPS ৎৡৣৡ
Ways to Save

1. Check your newspaper's travel section to find listings for cruise discounters.
2. Use a travel agency that specializes in cruising. A cruise specialist can save you money as well as explain the differences among ships.
3. Book early. Some cruise lines have a policy of guaranteeing the lowest prices to those who book first.
4. Choose a less expensive cabin on a more deluxe ship. Your cabin will be smaller, but you'll have a more luxurious experience overall.

seem to stress? If there are children's programs, for example, there will probably be plenty of kids. See what amenities are listed and ask for specific information about features that are important to you. Is twenty-four-hour room service available? Does the gym have the equipment you want?

Cabin choices: Cabin prices vary greatly, depending on size, location, and view. Your cabin is likely to feel small, no matter what you pay. Know what you're paying for. Higher prices could mean a bathtub instead of a shower. Outside cabins cost more than inside cabins; the difference could be a tiny porthole or a balcony! Upper-deck cabins carry more status but often no real advantage in terms of size or view. More importantly, do your windows open to the early morning jogging track? Are you near a noisy elevator or the disco? If you're watching your budget, consider opting for a less expensive cabin on a better ship, where you'll enjoy better service and food.

Meals: On most ships, you'll make two decisions about dining before you even see the dining room: whether you want first or second seating and how many people you want to sit with. Then you'll be assigned to a table for the cruise. Meal hours vary by ship. Because most ships serve breakfast and lunch as continuous buffets as well as sit-down dinners, base your decision on the latter. First, or early seating, dinners are usually served at about 6:30 P.M.; second, or late seating, meals are generally served about 8:30 P.M. Most honeymooners prefer late seatings, which leave time to shower and relax after the day's activities. And although a table for two sounds romantic, many couples enjoy socializing with fellow passengers over dinner. You may even want to request a table with other honeymooners. If your dining companions are not compatible, simply ask the maitre d' to change your table.

Budget for extras: Although your major costs are paid for up front, be prepared for some expenses en route. On most cruises, you'll pay extra for drinks, wine with meals, tips, or onshore activities. Ship-organized tours can add up to $100 per port, but in many ports, you can easily hire a taxi and organize your own excursion for far less. While tips are voluntary rewards for service, plan to leave about $5 to $6 a day (per couple) for your room steward, the same for your dining room waiter, and about half that for your busboy. (Most cruise lines provide envelopes in which you can present your tips on the last day at sea.) Others can be tipped for special services at your discretion. The exception is ship officers and cruise directors—to show appreciation, write a note; don't tip. Also budget for beauty salons, pictures from the ship's photographer, massages, laundry, phone calls, casino stakes, gifts, and souvenirs.

Questions to Ask Yourselves about Cruises

Here are some topics to talk about that will help you pick the right cruise for you.

What's our budget? Don't be afraid to stick to a budget.

How long do we want to travel? Cruises range in length from overnight to several months. You may want to combine a cruise with a hotel stay.

Where do we want to go? If there's a part of the world you'd like to explore, cruising can probably get you there.

How much time do we want to spend in port versus on the ship? If you primarily want to relax, choose an itinerary with several days at sea.

Do we have any special interests that we'd like to share on the cruise? Some cruises feature sessions with sports pros, naturalists, or historians or create itineraries that cater to various special interests.

Do we prefer a more formal or a party-hearty ambience? Each ship has a definite ambience and many appeal to certain age groups. Ask!

Tips for an Enjoyable Cruise

Packing pointers: Your cruise line will send a suggested packing list. On most ships, be prepared to dress up for dinner almost every night. Keep in mind that cabins are small and you'll have to find room for your suitcases, so don't overpack. Soft-sided luggage is a good idea; it stows under your bed. You may also want to bring a foldable nylon bag for souvenirs. Don't forget passports, sunglasses, sunscreen, cameras, and film.

Shopping: Many ports offer duty-free or "in-bond" prices on imports such as perfumes, watches, jewelry, and electronics. This means that the country you're visiting has not charged an import tax; however, it doesn't mean there is no markup. You may be able to find better buys at home. Don't trust the advice of ship lecturers or guides, who sometimes earn commission on your purchases. If you plan to make major purchases, shop your local discount stores before leaving and bring the prices along.

Curing the queasies: Most modern ships have stabilizers that keep them from being tossed by the waves, but there will be some motion. If you feel queasy, watch the horizon, not the water. If that doesn't work, take a motion sickness pill. You can bring your own (several are available without prescription) or let the ship's doctor give you something.

Formalities: Depending on where you're sailing, you may need passports, visas, or even inoculations. Ask your travel agent or the cruise line.

If you can't decide where you want to go or if you want to visit many places in a short amount of time, cruising could be the perfect honeymoon for you. When you opt for a cruise, you are buying a "package" of meals, ports, and accommodations. However, cruises are not your only option along those lines. In the next chapter, you'll learn about other types of packages and how to evaluate them.

✧ CHAPTER 7

Package Pros and Cons

When their travel agent suggested they purchase a package for their honeymoon, Rachelle said that she and Nat almost walked out. "We had visions of being herded here and there and eating with masses of people. But it turned out that the package only included airfare, a rental car, and accommodations in exactly the hotel we wanted. Using the package, we were able to save over $300."

What Is a Package?

These days, the term *package* covers a wide range of options, from tours in which almost every minute is planned and prepaid to basic plans that include accommodations and perhaps a sight-seeing tour or daily breakfast. Honeymoon packages often include free upgrades when available (to a better type of room than you're paying for) as well as free use of specific facilities such as golf courses and tennis courts. Air/hotel packages often—but not always—cost far less money than what you would pay if you purchased each separately.

How can travel suppliers afford to do this? When hotels can project that some of their more expensive rooms will not be sold, they can offer free upgrades. In this case, the hotel truly loses nothing while giving you something of considerable value. In other cases, providing a package that includes a free car rental or sunset cruise is, in effect, a way of lowering the hotel rates (perhaps during a bad business period) without officially doing so. (And you can be sure they pay less for those services than you would.)

Many travel wholesalers and tour operators provide additional value because they purchase airline seats, hotel rooms, and other services in bulk and then pass some of those savings on to you. However, all packages are not good deals, and you need to evaluate what you're getting to know if you're truly saving any money. In this chapter, you'll learn about the various types of packages and how to evaluate them.

Types of Packages

Escorted package tours: If you're interested in doing a lot of sight-seeing and enjoy guided group tours, then an escorted package tour itinerary might be right

❦ HONEYMOON TIPS ❦
Ways to Save

1. Shop around. Ask your travel agent to show you a variety of packages. By seeing what features and service come at what price levels, you'll be able to identify good value when you see it.
2. Compare package rates with the lowest rates available directly from the hotel, airlines, and other components of the trip.
3. Know what's important to you and don't be drawn in by extras that you aren't interested in. For example, if a honeymoon package offers free watersports and tennis lessons but all you want to do is lie on the beach, then it may not be a good value for you.
4. Don't confuse low prices with good values. If a price is low, ask why. Then you can evaluate whether it is a good value for you. For example, Caribbean summer rates can be a good value; winter rates are higher because visitors will pay more to escape the cold northern winters. On the other hand, if you want a beachfront hotel, then a low rate on the hotel three blocks away is not a good value.

for you. On the plus side, you won't have to worry about making decisions about where to go, where to stay, and how to get there, and you'll have a guide on hand to enrich your experience. On the other hand, you'll be thrown together with people whose company you may or may not enjoy, and you may not always be doing exactly what you'd like.

Ask detailed questions about the hotels, meals, guides, and exact itinerary (see "Questions to Ask about Packages" in this chapter). You may be getting pre-planned menus with little choice or staying at so-called first-class hotels that turn out to be far from the center of town or the beach. Your itinerary may be focused on shopping stops where your guide gets commissions on purchases rather than on the sight-seeing that you would prefer. Although some guides are very knowledgeable, some simply read their commentary from a script.

You may also want to ask about who your traveling companions will be. What is their average age? Nationality? Are they smokers or nonsmokers? Will English be the only language used in guided tours, or will you have to sit through each explanation in a number of languages?

Independent tour packages: These tours usually include airfare, hotels, transfers, and perhaps a rental car and other extras or options. Here, the advantage should be money savings. The trade-off? You may not be staying in the hotel you want or get a room with a view, and your transfers may involve a long wait. Be sure your travel agent spells out in writing exactly what is and is not included. Be wary of packages that promise a specific hotel "or similar." That phrase can mean something very dissimilar from what you expect.

❧❧ HONEYMOON TIPS ❧❧
Learning the Lingo

Here are some commonly used terms to help you decipher what packages offer.

Add-on fares: Cost of air travel from your city to the city where the tour originates.

Transfers: Transportation between the airport and hotel.

Vouchers: Coupons issued by tour operators or travel agents for prepaid accommodations, tours, meals, and other services that are exchanged for the items you're entitled to.

Optional: Anything listed as optional means that it is available at an additional cost.

Conditions of sale or *fine print:* At the bottom or back of many brochures, in tiny "mouse type," you'll see the fine print. Be sure to read it. This determines exactly what you will and won't receive—in effect, the conditions of your contract.

Special interest packages: Golf, tennis, and scuba diving are a few examples of special interests that packages cater to. If you plan to use the services that are included, it's probably a good deal.

Honeymoon packages: These plans generally include a bottle of champagne, gourmet dinners, or romantic activities and often an upgraded room when available. Often they list "complimentary" use of facilities that are free to all hotel guests. To know if the package is a good value, you'll need to compare it to what it normally provided to guests and to any other discounted rates available at the hotel—and be sure that the extras are things you want.

If you evaluate your options carefully, you can probably find a package that will fulfill your honeymoon wishes—and save you money. Your best source of guidance is a good travel agent. In the next chapter, you'll find tips on traveling abroad.

Questions to Ask about Packages

Read the fine print in your brochure and all documents you sign, or you may find that you're not buying exactly what you thought you were. What follows are some things to look for in tour packages.

Exactly what is and isn't included in the package price? Are service charges, tips, and taxes included? These can add up to a sizable amount.

Which hotel(s) will be used? The fine print in some tour packages may state that the operator reserves the right to substitute "comparable" hotels. Some spell out exactly what this means, and others don't. Also, note whether you're guaranteed a particular quality of room. You should know where you're staying when you purchase the package.

Will there be any price or itinerary adjustments? Many tour operators reserve the right to adjust their prices and itineraries and don't provide full refunds even if you want to cancel because of their change.

What airline will be used, and is the airfare subject to change? If the airline is not specified, you may end up on a charter flight with less convenient routing and service.

Under what conditions are refunds provided? You should be able to cancel, perhaps paying a small fee, up to two months before departure. After that, there may be more severe penalties and, sometimes, no refunds provided. Trip cancellation insurance may be advisable.

When will we receive tickets and confirmations? There may be quite a time lapse between payment and receiving your travel documents. Be sure you are dealing with a reputable company, pay with a credit card, and receive a detailed receipt.

What happens if the tour operator stops operating or the trip is canceled? If your tour operator is a member of the U.S. Tour Operators Association (USTOA), your deposits and payments are insured. ASTA has a similar plan for participating tour operators. Don't take the tour operator's word for it. Check directly with USTOA or ASTA to be sure the company is still a member in good standing. Otherwise, paying by credit card provides some protection. Don't buy trip cancellation insurance from the tour operator; it won't help you if they go out of business. If you buy insurance, be sure it covers you if the trip doesn't operate, not just in case of bankruptcy. In many cases, companies cease operation without declaring bankruptcy.

CHAPTER 8

International Honeymoons

omparing wedding customs with the couple you met at a sidewalk café in
Paris . . . bargaining for a rug in Istanbul . . . learning to dance the hula in
Hawaii . . . the thrill of discovering new customs, navigating your way through
unfamiliar situations, and perhaps of trying to make yourselves understood in a
foreign language . . . to some couples, these are the joys of travel. And even the
difficulties (such as discovering that prices are not set and every purchase is an
exercise in bargaining) can be viewed as a stimulating—although at times trying—experience.

Of course, you don't have to deal with another language; simply pick a destination where English is either the official language (such as Great Britain,
Australia, Bermuda, the Bahamas, Jamaica . . .) or widely spoken (Mexican resort
cities such as Cancún or countries where English is part of the basic school cur-
riculum, such as Denmark and Israel).

And if you want to go abroad but the idea of eating different kinds of foods
and dealing with strange customs doesn't appeal to you, then stick to cosmopolitan cities or resort areas that cater to Americans. In most places, staying in
an upscale, American chain hotel will provide a familiar home base, where an
English-speaking concierge can help you get oriented.

Wherever you go, you'll find that even a small effort to communicate in your
hosts' language will earn you high dividends in goodwill. Make the word for
honeymooners or *newlyweds* part of your basic vocabulary, and you're sure to find
an even warmer welcome. Even in big cities such as Paris that are not known for
their friendliness to tourists, *jeunes-mariés* (French for "newlyweds," pronounced
jun-mar-ee-**ay**) are usually treated to big smiles. In this chapter, you'll find tips
on dealing with formalities, foreign languages, and health questions.

Formalities

Passport: If you're honeymooning in another country, chances are you'll
need a passport, which serves as international proof of your identity and citizenship. Many travel agents will handle the process for a small fee, but it's easy to get
one on your own, especially if you allow plenty of time.

In the United States, citizens can pick up a passport application form at any
U.S. passport agency, county clerk's office, or major post office. You'll need two

passport-size photos that have been taken within the past six months and an offi-cial birth certificate (with a raised seal) from the Department of Health where you were born (this can take six weeks or more to obtain by mail). Allow at least two months for your passport application to be processed. If you already have a pass-port, make certain it will be valid through your honeymoon. Many countries require that your passport be valid for at least six months beyond the date you plan to return from your trip. (For Canadian passport information see Appendix A.)

Maiden names: If you are leaving on your honeymoon right after your wedding, you won't have time to get a passport with your married name. Because the passport you bring on your honeymoon will be in your maiden name, you'll save a lot of confusion with airlines if you use that name to make your reservations. After you return, you can have your passport amended at no charge with your married name and new address.

Visas: Many countries require visitors to obtain a visa. Some issue these for a fee at the border; others require that you obtain these in advance from their embassy or consulate office. Your travel agent or airline can advise you. Many travel agents will also arrange to obtain your visas for a small fee.

Customs: At most border crossings, you'll pass through a customs check-point. Unless you're carrying a large amount of gifts or items that you'll be dis-tributing in the country you're visiting or traveling with much more camera or electronics equipment than seems normal for personal use, you'll probably whiz through customs upon arrival at your destination. If you plan to bring many gifts or other items into a country, contact a tourist office or embassy before you go to see if you need to make special arrangements.

When you return home, you'll have to declare all your foreign purchases and possibly pay some taxes. If you plan ahead, this will be easy. As you travel, collect receipts in an envelope for all your purchases and have it handy when you're returning home.

For more details, write for the booklet *Know Before You Go,* available from the U.S. Customs Service, or *I Declare,* from the Canadian Customs Service (see Appendix A).

Driver's license: If you're planning to rent a car, ask if you'll need an inter-national driver's license, which is basically a multilingual document that says you have a license. If so, it's easy to obtain one. Just bring your license and a passport-size photo to the American Automobile Association nearest you, and they'll pre-pare it for you on the spot.

Staying Healthy

For many people, changes in eating and sleeping habits can trigger the most common travelers' problem, diarrhea. The solution to this generally involves rest, an antidiarrhea medicine, and drinking plenty of liquids to avoid dehydration. If you're traveling to a part of the world where there are problems with sanitation, be especially careful about what you eat and drink.

Here are some general guidelines:

1. Drink only bottled water, preferably carbonated and in sealed bottles so you know it's truly clean. Use this water for drinking and even brushing your teeth.
2. Avoid ice cubes and drinks made with water or crushed ice. Alcohol doesn't sterilize untreated water, so mixed drinks must be made with sterile water. Stick with bottled sodas, wine, or beer.
3. Avoid fresh salads and raw vegetables washed with water. Stick with fruits and vegetables you can peel.
4. Never eat rare or raw meat and avoid buffets. Hot foods should be eaten hot; cold foods should be served cold. Food that cools or gets warm tends to gather bacteria.
5. Avoid dairy products, especially if unpasteurized.
6. Use your common sense. Don't buy food from that crusty old woman on the corner or eat in a restaurant that looks unclean.
7. If you get sick, see a doctor immediately and you'll probably head off more serious symptoms. If you have a bacterial infection, it's important to start treatment as soon as possible.
8. Check with your doctor or the Centers for Disease Control (see Appendix A) before you leave to see if any other precautions are advisable.

The Language Game

If you're visiting a non-English-speaking country, you'll probably enjoy learning some basics of the local language. And you'll find that your attempts to communicate in it will be very much appreciated. The easiest way to get started is to pick up a phrase book before you go. These books are organized by subject, which makes practicing simple conversations quite easy.

If foreign films are available at your local video store, try to find some in the language you're trying to learn. Consider watching the movies twice. The first time, read the subtitles and take in the story; then, since you know the story, watch at least part of the film as though it were an opera and enjoy the sounds of the words. It's a great way to get your ears attuned to a new language.

If you have the time and ambition, you may even want to take a basic language course. Some schools offer courses designed for travelers that give you some basics in several sessions or a weekend. There are also a number of self-instruction tapes and interactive computer programs available. As you learn the language, you'll feel more and more excited about your honeymoon.

Finally, if you're going to a place where the alphabet is different, then definitely try to get a simple language phrase book. By pointing to the correct word or phrase, you'll be able to order in restaurants, communicate in shops, and even ask for directions. You'll find that communicating without speaking the language is not as hard as you'd think—and lots of fun!

In the next chapter, you'll learn the best ways to exchange money and pay when traveling abroad.

CHAPTER 9

Money Matters

Kayla and Mike had left their wallets in their room while they were at the beach. "We should have used the hotel safe, but we figured we wouldn't be gone long," said Mike. "Besides, everyone seemed so nice, we couldn't imagine being robbed," added Kayla. When they returned from their swim, their key didn't fit. "The lock had been broken, but miraculously, nothing was missing. We figure the maid had come and scared off the would-be robber. We had a lot of cash, wedding gifts, and it was still sitting in the drawer. Were we lucky!" exclaimed Mike.

Because cash is so easily stolen and virtually untraceable and irreplaceable, carrying large amounts of it is never a good idea. And thanks to credit and bank cards and traveler's checks, you really need only limited amounts of cash.

Many travelers suggest setting out with about $20 in single bills for tipping and another $100 in five- and ten-dollar bills as a reserve—more if you're going to a country where U.S. dollars buy more than the local currency. Also exchange at least $50 to $100 into the currency of your destination in case you need cash before you can get to a bank. (A number of banks offer foreign currency exchange service; Reusch International offers currency exchange by mail—see Appendix A.)

The Best Ways to Pay

Traveler's checks are replaced if lost or stolen and can be obtained from most banks. Some banks and travel clubs offer free traveler's checks to members. Otherwise, you'll probably pay a 1 percent fee. You may also want to consider using American Express Traveler's Cheques for Two so that either of you can use the checks.

If you're going abroad, consider purchasing traveler's checks in foreign currencies. They're available from many banks, currency exchange services, and travel agents. Foreign currency traveler's checks will save you on exchange rates and fees, and you won't have to worry about where to exchange them. However, because you'll pay a fee every time you convert from U.S. to local currency, try not to purchase more than you're sure you'll need, and exchange leftover checks before you return home.

For the best exchange rates on cash or traveler's checks, head for a national bank; many have branches at international airports. Keep in mind that currency is bought and sold, just like oil, wheat, or any other commodity, and the prices fluctuate daily. And as with commodities, a handling fee and/or commission is charged for each exchange. That's why it's cost-effective to exchange only the amount you'll spend. Although exchange rates are generally posted, fees and commissions often aren't, so be sure to ask. You may decide to change your currency in larger increments if you're paying a fee for each transaction. Always keep your currency exchange receipts. In some countries, you'll need these to convert unused currency back to U.S. dollars.

In addition to banks, most major hotels and large department stores as well as exchange houses also convert currency, although you'll usually pay slightly more for the convenience. Small shops, taxi drivers, and street vendors in most countries are not set up to exchange U.S. currency or traveler's checks and will generally—and justifiably—charge a premium for their effort.

Major credit cards are widely accepted in most countries, especially in big cities. And by using a credit card, you won't pay a commission on exchanging your money. If the U.S. dollar is increasing in value against the currency of the country you'll be visiting, there's an additional advantage: the delay in processing (up to a week or two) means you'll benefit from the changing exchange rate. Of course, if the dollar's value is decreasing, the opposite is true.

Many credit cards can also be used to obtain cash advances. VISA and MasterCard can even be used at member bank automated teller machines (ATMs) to obtain cash advances. American Express issues its cardholders cash advances at any of its offices. Also check out the American Express Cash Now program. Be sure to check with your card issuer (call the number on your bill) before leaving to see if and where your card is valid. You'll probably need to be assigned a personal identification number (PIN).

Many small hotels, inns, restaurants, and shopkeepers do not accept credit cards. If you plan on using a credit card to cover most of your travel expenses, check ahead with your lodgings, and if you're going overseas, ask the tourist office of the countries you'll be visiting which credit cards are the most widely accepted.

Bank cards are becoming increasingly useful. If your bank is a member of the Plus or Cirrus network, you can use ATMs around the country and the world to withdraw cash from your account. And you'll get the best exchange rate—the interbank rate, which can be up to 5 percent better than the rate you would get from a bank or money exchange service. Ask your bank if it charges a transaction fee for overseas use. If so, you may want to avoid withdrawing money frequently in small amounts.

Be sure to check with your bank before you leave to see if you need a special (PIN) number or enhanced card and for a list of locations in the places you'll be visiting. Because the system is fairly new, don't rely completely on your bank card as a source of cash.

Before you go, make a list of traveler's checks, credit card numbers (and cancellation/reissue procedures), and if you're going abroad, a copy of the identification pages of your passports. Leave one set with a trusted friend or family member and carry a copy—separate from these items—when you travel. It will make these items easier to replace if they are lost or stolen en route.

Carry a pocket calculator, or better still, a currency converter, so you can quickly calculate prices in dollars. Many guidebooks and shops offer handy exchange rate tables; however, before using one, be sure it's not based on an outdated exchange rate. There are many types of compact currency converter devices. The best ones will let you set an exchange rate at the start of your trip; then all you'll need to do is enter the local price and see its U.S. dollar equivalent. Some also convert temperature, distance, weight, and international clothing sizes to U.S. equivalents.

Tipping

In most countries, good service is rewarded with a gratuity. However, in a few countries, especially in the South Pacific, tipping is frowned upon.

Some hotels and restaurants—especially in Europe and some parts of the Caribbean—automatically add a service charge to your bill, in which case you may want to leave small change or 5 percent, depending on the service and the type of establishment. Ask when making your reservations so you don't end up tipping along the way *and* paying the service charge on your final bill.

❦ HONEYMOON TIPS ❦
Tips on Tipping

Here are some basic guidelines in U.S. dollars. Generally, it's best to tip with the foreign currency equivalent. If service is exceptionally good, you may want to tip a bit more; if it is poor, a bit less.

Taxi drivers: 15 percent of the fare.

Bellhops, redcaps: $1 per bag.

Doormen: $1 to hail a cab.

Concierge: $2 to $10 for special arrangements; you can tip for each service or at the end of your stay.

Valet parking: $1 to deliver your car.

Chambermaids: $1 to $2 per person per day.

Waiters and bartenders: 15 to 20 percent of pretax price; in many countries, 15 percent is automatically added to your bill.

Washroom attendants: $.25 to $.50 or whatever the posted charge.

Group tour guides/drivers: Unless tip is included, tip $1 each for a full-day tour; $5 to $10 for a weeklong tour.

If you are honeymooning at an all-inclusive resort, tips are probably included. If so, no further tipping is required. In fact, at some resorts, workers can lose their jobs for accepting tips.

Avoiding Travel Scams

In recent years, the travel industry has been plagued by a number of scams. In general, if a deal sounds too good to be true, there's probably a catch.

There are two common types of travel scams. The classic rip-off begins with a phone call telling you that you've won a free trip. Then you are asked to give your credit card number or have a check or cash ready for a messenger the following day to cover the "processing fee," and you are told to pick three dates. You probably wait for "processing" only to find that the dates you want are impossible. So you keep trying other dates until one day there's no answer; the company has gone out of business. If you are persistent early on, you may be lucky—or unlucky—enough to actually take the trip. Then you may find yourselves in a room so awful that you'll agree to pay to "upgrade" to another hotel, which you could have booked far more cheaply on your own. So your free trip, if you get it, could cost you more than a legitimate package tour.

A more subtle rip-off comes as a result of deceptive advertising. An ad may highlight a low price for part of a trip. But it will be tied to a whole package that, if you're lucky, will be fairly priced—certainly not a bargain.

Of course, there are true bargains, but they can be difficult to evaluate. Restrictions, special conditions, and small-print add-ons can make the final price much higher than you'd expect. Or worse, the company you're dealing with may be a fly-by-night fraud that will take your money and disappear before you are even scheduled to travel. The American Society of Travel Agents suggests you be aware of the following warning signs:

1. The price seems unbelievably favorable.
2. You're notified by mail or phone that you've won a contest you haven't entered.
3. A telemarketer pressures you to make an immediate decision and give your credit card number or have a check ready for a messenger the following morning.
4. The seller is not willing to give her full name and the company name, street address (not just a post office box), and phone number.
5. The seller wants you to commit money before receiving complete information about the offer, including the total cost, terms, and conditions *in writing*.
6. Travel suppliers, such as airlines and hotels, are not listed by name (only by vague descriptions such as "major airlines" or "first-class hotels").
7. The "free" offer is linked to a required purchase or fee to join a club or cover administrative costs.

8. You or your travel companion must purchase additional travel services at unspecified costs.
9. You must wait sixty days to book your travel dates but must pay a deposit or make a purchase immediately.

If you are suspicious or get hooked, get in touch with the American Society of Travel Agent's Consumer Affairs Department at 703-739-2782, the Federal Trade Commission at 202-328-3650, your state's attorney general, or the local FBI office. If you paid by credit card, contact your card issuer to see if you can dispute the charges. Federal law generally places the burden on credit card companies for delivery of goods charged on their cards.

Travel Insurance

If you need to cancel or interrupt a trip because of a major illness or death in the family, you can lose thousands of dollars, especially if you've prepaid your entire honeymoon. That's where trip cancellation insurance comes in.

If you purchase a policy from a travel insurance company, not the cruise line or travel supplier, your policy usually also covers your investment in case a travel supplier defaults or goes out of business. Be sure that the policy covers operator "failure" or "default," not just bankruptcy, because sometimes companies stop providing service without declaring bankruptcy.

Always read the fine print. Some policies exclude certain conditions, such as a medical problem that you were being treated for at the time you bought the policy. Some also exclude injuries from certain sports and congenital conditions.

Budgeting for Romance

Marcia and Vito were saving for a house. They had budgeted $2,000 for their honeymoon and didn't want to splurge beyond that, but they wanted to get to Italy. By shopping for the lowest airfare and staying in small hotels outside the big cities, they were able to go to Italy and keep within their budget. "The hotels were very intimate, not luxurious, but friendly. Actually, they had more personality than some of the fancier, more expensive hotels," said Marcia. "We also saved money by having picnics instead of always going to restaurants. Then, we splurged on a few great meals, but at lunchtime when the prices were much lower than at dinner. It was even better than my dreams."

Unless you have unlimited funds, it's important to set a realistic budget. Start by discussing how much you plan to spend. Like Marcia and Vito, most couples can find ways to fulfill their dreams without bankrupting their future. Once you've agreed on how much you can afford, talk about how you want to allocate your funds. Marcia and Vito felt that going to Italy was more important than staying in the most luxurious hotels. Other couples opt to be pampered at a luxury resort closer to home. You'll find that it's not how much you spend but how you allocate your funds that counts. Remember, you don't have to be a millionaire to create rich honeymoon memories. You may want to make copies of the following budget worksheet so that you can try out different scenarios before you settle on the final budget for each category.

Bring a copy of your final budget on your honeymoon and check along the way to see whether you are over or under budget. If you're spending too much, you'll be able to catch yourselves before you go too far. And if you're not spending as much as you thought, you'll know that you can afford to splurge on an elegant dinner or perhaps a fine keepsake of your wedding trip.

In the next chapter, you'll find pointers on packing for your honeymoon.

Your Honeymoon Budget

Fill in your total budget first. Then, as you start gathering information on destinations, use this planner to compare options.

Transportation

Major transportation (air, cruise, car . . .)   _____
Airport transfers   _____
Tips   _____
Rental car   _____
Gas/tolls   _____
Taxis, buses   _____
　　Total Transportation   _____

Accommodations

Basic rate   _____
Taxes, surcharges, tips   _____
Extra services (laundry, hairdresser . . .)   _____
　　Total Accommodations   _____

Meals

Breakfast　　$ _____ per day × _____ days =   _____
Lunch　　$ _____ per day × _____ days =   _____
Dinner　　$ _____ per day × _____ days =   _____
　　Total Meals   _____

Entertainment

Sports equipment rentals/purchase   _____
Theater/concerts   _____
Nightclubs/casino gambling   _____
Tours, admission to attractions   _____
　　Total Entertainment   _____

Extras

Shopping/gifts and souvenirs   _____
Snacks/drinks   _____
Other   _____
　　Total Budget   _____

ℰℛℰ CHAPTER *10*

Packing for Romance

"**I**t was 9 P.M. We'd just finished unpacking, and Charlene asked me to go buy her some aspirin," said Leon. "I thought, 'Great, our first night together and she has a headache.' But I returned to find our hotel room glowing with candlelight, a bottle of champagne on ice, and decorations from our wedding around the room. I can't believe that with all the details of the wedding, she thought to organize this, too. It was one of the most beautiful surprises of my life."

Packing for romance is easy. In this chapter, you'll find practical suggestions on how to select your honeymoon wardrobe and bring everything you need—including some romantic flourishes—without overpacking.

The Packing Game

Experienced travelers try to pack exactly what they'll need—no more, no less. It helps to think of packing as a game. You lose one point for each item you bring but don't use (three points if the unused item takes up lots of space or is heavy); subtract three points for any hard-to-find items you forget to bring and one point for any other forgotten items. Give yourself a point for packing a sensible first-aid kit and five points if everything fits into carry-on luggage. If you are traveling in your own car, then you needn't subtract any points for bringing extra items if you organize them well.

Why the emphasis on packing light? The most important reason is that although you'll sometimes find porters and bellhops to carry your bags, you will often be left to handle them yourselves. Enough said? Frequent flyers usually pack only carry-on luggage so that they won't have to entrust their bags to the airlines, risking loss—temporary or otherwise—and pilferage. Although the airlines have improved their baggage handling, there still is a fair chance that you'll arrive at your destination without your bags. Finally, there is the aesthetic joy you'll feel in the precision of having brought just the right items.

The Basics

Whether you decide to play the "efficient packer" game or not, the key to bringing what you need is advance planning. I view this as a four-step process:

1. Find out what the weather is likely to be.
2. Think about what types of activities (sight-seeing, lounging at the beach, going out to a fancy restaurant) you're planning to enjoy and make a rough day-by-day itinerary.
3. Decide what you want to wear for each activity and make a head-to-toe clothing list for each one, including shoes, jewelry, undergarments, and accessories.
4. A few weeks before your trip, post a piece of paper on your wall in the morning and as you get ready to get dressed, write down each item you use (toothbrush, shampoo, moisturizer, hair dryer, comb . . .). Keep the list posted so you can add items as you think of them.

Plugged In

If you don't have a drip-dry hairstyle or like to touch up your clothes with an iron, you'll want to check ahead with your hotel to see which items they provide.

Hair dryers are standard in many hotel rooms; irons are usually available on request. Some hotel rooms have coffeemakers; if yours does not and you like coffee before you're out of bed, you may want to bring a small coffeepot to avoid having to wait for—and pay for—room service every morning.

If you're going abroad, be sure to inquire about the voltage and whether converters are provided. Even if you're not bringing any personal appliances, you may need a converter, for example, if you have a video camera with rechargeable batteries.

Packing Light

It's your honeymoon. You want to look your best every day. Of course, you'll pack your favorite outfits. But even for a two- or three-week honeymoon, you don't need to fill a trunk to always have something fresh and special to wear. In fact, staying away longer doesn't necessarily mean packing more. You can pack the same amount for one week or three weeks. How?

❧❧ HONEYMOON TIPS ❧❧
Pack a Surprise

Bring a romantic gift such as massage oils, a book of love poems, perfume or cologne, silk bathrobes, or lingerie. Buy a new outfit and don't wear it until your honeymoon.

Do laundry at the hotel. Either let the hotel handle it or hand wash.

Bring easy-care fabrics. Washable silks—especially shirts and underwear—generally dry wrinkle-free in a few hours. Some treated cottons never wrinkle and dry overnight. For cold-weather destinations, silk long johns add a lightweight, warm layer to your clothing and are hand washable and quick-drying.

Pack coordinates. Clothes that mix and match with each other let you create new looks with a few versatile items.

Staying Wrinkle-Free

You don't want to spend your honeymoon ironing, but traveling tends to crumple clothes, and you're not into the just-rolled-out-of-bed look. What can you do? The first step is picking the right fabrics. Silks and wools can be shower steamed to smooth out wrinkles (hang the items in the shower where they won't get wet, close the bathroom door, and let the hot water run until the bathroom steams up). Many synthetic fabrics never wrinkle.

If your clothes are not crease resistant, take heart. It's not only what you pack but how you pack as well. Every frequent traveler seems to have a special method to minimize wrinkling. Here are a few basic principles:

Place heavy items, such as shoes and toilet kits, at the bottom so they don't press down on clothing.

If clothing is rolled carefully without folds, it will usually unroll wrinkle-free on arrival. This is especially good for tee shirts.

If you're not bringing a garment bag, clothes that tend to wrinkle can be laid out neatly, with plastic between each layer, and then either folded gently around a sweater or laid out and placed carefully into the suitcase. If you're packing a garment bag, placing rolled items in the corners helps prevent shifting.

Your clothes are less likely to wrinkle if you pack your suitcase full enough so that they won't have room to shift much en route but not so stuffed that they get crushed. Use plastic bags to fill in some empty spaces that may be taken up with souvenirs on the way home.

Once you arrive, unpack so you have time to get any wrinkled items pressed. Most wrinkles will disappear if you hang your clothes in a closed, steamy bathroom.

Carry It On

If you are flying, be sure you have one bag that you never check. That bag should contain your passports, visas, and other travel documents as well as tickets, confirmations, and vouchers. Money, credit cards, cameras, jewelry, and other valuables should also be kept with you. Also carry on your glasses, prescription medication, and a change of clothes in case your suitcases are delayed as well as books, magazines, and games to play in flight. Some couples also like to bring their wedding gift list, address book, and stationery so they can write their thank-you notes en route.

Romantic Flourishes

Just back from a long day of sight-seeing, Hugh called Amber to join him in a bath. "Our hotel room had a gorgeous marble whirlpool tub, and he was sitting there in bubbles—he had thought to pack my favorite bubble bath!" said Amber.

"I had decided to bring the bubble bath on our honeymoon about three weeks before we left," Hugh explained. "We were so stressed out that every night, we were taking these bubble baths together, and it was really nice."

Whether you decide to bring a taste of the familiar, as Hugh did, or to set a romantic mood with candles and champagne, like Charlene, it's fun to think ahead and pack for romance. Negligees and silk pajamas, a cassette or compact disc player with your favorite romantic music—or perhaps, a portable radio so you can pick up local programs, scented candles . . . these are just a few ideas. Use your imagination to add the ingredients for a romantic surprise to your packing list, and you'll be set to create honeymoon memories to last a lifetime.

In the next chapter, you'll find tips on taking great honeymoon photos.

❧❧❧ CHAPTER 11

Picture Perfect

"We've been married twenty-five years, and we still love looking at our honeymoon pictures," said Cesar. "They bring back those feelings of excitement and the romance of starting a new phase of life together."

Your honeymoon hotel, the nice taxi driver who was your guide for a day, the sugar birds who shared your breakfast every morning . . . photos capture moments that will help you relive the magic of your honeymoon for years to come.

Getting Equipped

If you don't already have a camera, you'll probably want to bring a simple-to-operate model for your honeymoon. You don't need a fancy camera to take memorable photos. Many of the new point-and-shoot models require no technical knowledge and offer far more flexibility than you might expect; some have telephoto, wide-angle, and zoom lenses built in that allow you to frame a photo exactly as you'd like.

Don't wait for your honeymoon to try out a new camera. Shoot and develop at least one test roll before you go. That way, you can be sure the camera is working properly, and you won't have to figure out how to use it while you're trying to have a good time.

Bring plenty of film and an extra set of batteries. In many vacation areas, film is expensive, and in some places, you may not even be able to find the film or batteries you need. Also bring your camera's operating manual, a lens brush and lens tissue with some cleaning fluid, and a small notebook and pen to record your shots.

You may also want to bring prepaid processing mailers, which you can buy along with the film. Then, as you complete each roll, you can drop it in the mail, and your photos may even be waiting for you when you return home. (Don't plan on this if you are going to a country where mail service is uncertain.)

Honeymoon Photos

"Can you believe we shot ten rolls of film on our honeymoon and don't have a single photo of the two of us?" asked Holly. "From our pictures, you'd never know we were on a honeymoon."

❧❧ *HONEYMOON TIPS* ❧❧
For Your Scrapbook

With a little planning, you can return with photos that truly capture the joy of your honeymoon.

1. Take pictures everywhere. Keep a small camera with you so that you can take pictures whenever you want.
2. When you do something romantic—take a ride in a horsedrawn carriage, go to a scenic overlook, take a sunset cruise, and so on—have your camera handy and ask someone to take your picture.
3. Capture your hotel on film. Ask your bellhop to take a photo of you when you arrive in your hotel room. If your hotel has a grand entrance, have someone photograph the two of you standing in front of it. Take a picture of the view from your room.
4. Take candid photos of each other. Photograph each other relaxing in your room, writing postcards, sleeping, shopping.
5. If a place is special to you, photograph it several different ways and get someone to take a picture of the two of you there. If you make friends, take photos with them. Will you rent bicycles? a car? a sailboat? snorkel equipment? Pose together and ask someone to take your picture.
6. If your camera has a time release, set up photos with the two of you even when no one is around. Be imaginative, setting your camera on a bureau or a table to frame a photo of the two of you.

It's easy to believe—and quite common. Many couples spend their honeymoons taking pictures of each other and never think of asking anyone to take a photo of them together.

Equally frustrating is seeing the perfect shot and having left your camera back at the hotel. Bring your camera wherever you go. If you carry a big camera bag with lots of equipment and get tired of lugging it, consider adding a small camera to your array of equipment. That way, if you are going for a long hike or even a short walk, you can always have your minimodel at the ready. If you don't want to buy an extra camera, consider purchasing a one-time-use camera. They come in many models and are also useful for special situations, such as taking underwater and panoramic shots.

You don't have to put your camera away just because it's raining. You probably won't go back to that spot on a sunny day, and besides, rainy-day pictures can be quite interesting. My favorite honeymoon photo was taken on a rainy walk along the Seine in Paris.

Don't be afraid to take photos of people. Most are quite happy to have their pictures taken as long as you ask first. In some places, you'll be asked for a tip. Use your common sense. If you're in a market taking a picture of your spouse making a purchase, then the fact that you made a purchase should be enough.

Otherwise, you may want to give a small tip or offer to take their names and addresses and send them a copy of the photo.

Tips for Taking Pictures

You've probably noticed that some people take very interesting photos, while other people's shots are boring. What makes the difference is not the camera but the photographer. Too often, someone sees a gorgeous scene, picks up the camera, and, barely looking through the viewfinder, snaps a shot.

Here are some guidelines to help you take more interesting honeymoon photos:

Pick a subject. If you are in a market, you may want to photograph a vendor, your spouse looking at a colorful display, or a small child. If you try to cram all these images into one photo, you'll probably have a confusing mishmash.

Frame your subject. If you are shooting a person, get close enough to fill the frame.

Notice what else is in the frame. Is there a pole growing out of someone's head or five people around the person you are focusing on?

Try different compositions. You may want to reframe your shot so that as little as possible distracts from your subject or so it is not directly in the middle of the frame. Or shoot the same subject from different perspectives.

Get the two of you into your pictures. How? Frame them yourself and then ask a fellow photographer/tourist to take the shot. Or try to find a table or ledge at the right height, focus, and set a timer. (Don't try this in a busy area where someone could snatch the camera.)

Notice how the light hits your subject. Generally, it's not a good idea to shoot into the sun. Notice what is in shadow. Photographers often find that early morning and late afternoon light can make a subject more interesting.

Think about the colors in your shots. Professional photographers have stylists who often dress their models in basic colors because they stand out. Try wearing bright shirts in contrasting colors for a day of sight-seeing and see how you jump out of your photos!

Use the flash carefully. Be sure that your subject is within the range of the flash. Also, try to shoot at an angle (not directly into someone's eyes) so that the flash does not reflect back into the camera.

Pick your film. Do you want slides or prints? Some films are made for indoor light sources; others work best in sunlight. Also, pick your film speed based on the lighting conditions you expect. Faster-speed films (such as ISO 400) are best for low-light conditions and capturing action but produce grainier photos. It's generally better to use slower-speed films (ISO 25 to 200) unless the lighting is too dim.

With a bit of careful planning, you'll have a honeymoon album that will help you share your wedding trip with friends and family and relive happy memories for a lifetime. In the next chapter, you'll learn how to bring back more tangible honeymoon memories.

CHAPTER 12

Memories to Go

One of Gina's favorite honeymoon memories is quite tangible: a lapis lazuli ring from Hawaii. "The color of the Pacific," said her husband when he picked it out for her. "Each time we look at that ring, it brings back happy thoughts."

Some of your best memories may also be triggered by your honeymoon purchases. Because many destinations are known for their shopping opportunities, you'll probably want to make at least a few special acquisitions. Here are some tips to help you shop like seasoned pros.

How to Find a Good Buy

Start out by doing some research about the places you'll be visiting. Read travel articles, guidebooks, and brochures before you leave to see if there are major purchases you might like to make while there. Once you've decided on possible purchases, check out the cost and quality of these items in your local stores and discount outlets so that you'll know when you're getting a good buy abroad.

Never be misled by "sales." As you know, "*X* percent off" is relative and doesn't always mean a good buy. Another buzzword that is often taken to mean "bargain" is "duty free." This simply means that the local government is not charging an import tax on the given items coming into its country. The resulting price might be lower than you could find back home, but not necessarily. And if you're making a lot of purchases, you may have to pay U.S. duty upon your return. Check on the latest U.S. Customs regulations before you leave if you plan to go on a buying spree.

Overseas Tax Refunds

Take advantage of the tax refunds that many countries offer visitors. Before you leave, check with the tourist office to see if value-added tax (VAT) refunds are available and how they work. In some countries, the refund can be 25 percent or more, but you'll have to follow certain rules, which include purchasing minimum amounts, showing your passport, filling out some paperwork, and sometimes allowing extra time at departure to have the paperwork validated by a customs agent. Some countries will not issue refunds if you open your purchase before you've left the country. Try to avoid getting your refund by mail in a foreign currency check; it can cost more to process than its face value. Your best bet is to have the store issue a charge-card credit, but you may be able to get a cash refund (for a service charge) at your port of exit.

Buyer Beware

Travelers can be easy targets for scams, so be wary of making major investments abroad in such commodities as silver, gold, gems, handmade rugs, and the like unless you know a lot about what you are buying or are shopping at an internationally reputable store that honors returns. The same goes for letting a merchant mail prepaid purchases home for you. Using a credit card may provide some protection if your purchase is not delivered.

It's also a good idea to shop around before making a major purchase. There's nothing worse than walking into a shop and seeing the item you just bought selling for half the price you paid. My rule is to check out at least three shops before making a major purchase. Be very suspicious of prices that are good only if you purchase on the spot. You won't know if the price and quality are favorable until you've shopped around. Also be wary of recommendations from guides, who often suggest expensive, "touristy" shops and sometimes get commissions for sending you.

Learning to Negotiate

Bea and Stuart complained that everyone in the crafts market was trying to take advantage of them because they were tourists. "They are trying to charge us outrageous prices," Stuart explained. "They think we're too stupid to know better, but I've seen some of these things in gift shops for half the prices they're quoting."

No one had told Stuart that the merchants didn't expect him to pay the prices they were asking. In many countries, bargaining is a way of life and of socializing—sometimes in the shops as well as the markets. Bargaining is an art and can be lots of fun.

In many countries, the starting price will be more than double what the merchant expects. Don't be offended. If you're interested in buying, tell the merchant the price is too high or make your own "absurd" offer. If all else fails to bring the price down to what you'd feel comfortable paying, walking away slowly and regretfully may get you your price. If your price is met, however, you should be prepared to make the purchase. Otherwise, it is like a breach of contract.

༄ HONEYMOON TIP ༄
How to Haggle

1. Start by checking out quality and prices in a fixed-price store if possible.
2. Ask a few merchants for their best price before you begin making any offers.
3. Decide how much the item is worth to you and then go back to the merchant with whom you want to make a deal.
4. Ask again for the best price. Then make an offer somewhat lower than your bottom line. If you're confident your offer is fair, stick to it. You'll probably get the item at the price you want. If no merchant sells the item at your price, you're probably offering too little.

If you have no idea of what the price should be and want to shop around, try asking the merchant for his or her best price and then say you'll think about it. The merchant may drop the price further. Don't feel you have to buy unless you make an offer that the merchant accepts. Often, you'll be asked how much you want to pay. Be honest. Say you need to shop around and ask for a card so you can return. You may even want to make a note of the item and price on the card.

Finally, if you don't want to spend your time shopping and bargaining, you can shortcut the process by knowing what you want to pay, offering a bit less, and then coming up to your price and holding firm.

As you practice, you'll develop your own techniques. Listen to other people's experiences and you'll get a sense of the country's customs. You may also want to start out by perusing the fixed-price department stores. There, you'll get a general idea of cost and quality. This can help you bargain more intelligently in the markets.

Most important, keep things in perspective. Don't let yourselves get paralyzed by worrying over a few dollars. It's more important to bring back something you'll really enjoy than to get the best price. Try to purchase something special. It doesn't have to be expensive. Paintings, sculptures, wall hangings, and even mugs or salt and pepper shakers can become cherished keepsakes. Did you like the local music? Pick up a tape. Did you enjoy the cuisine? A cookbook and some local spices will let you return to your special place in spirit whenever you please. Or purchase the bathrobes from your hotel as a warm reminder of your honeymoon.

CHAPTER 13

Imperfections in Paradise

As with your wedding, you want your first night as a married couple to be perfect, to feel like a fantasy come true. Your friends may even have bought you special lingerie to help make it special. The truth? Many couples are so tired from their wedding that they are happy to simply go right to sleep. Don't worry if you or your new spouse feel that way; you'll have plenty of nights together in the future!

Here are three other honeymoon myths that often put unnecessary pressure on couples.

Myth One: No matter how nervous you are, you shouldn't dampen your partner's pleasure by putting off lovemaking. Communication is the key, not only to a good marriage but also to a happy sex life. If you're nervous, sometimes simply saying so helps the feeling go away. If you're tired, perhaps a nap will make all the difference.

Myth Two: The groom should take charge of planning the honeymoon. A honeymoon is for the two of you, and it should be planned by both of you.

Myth Three: If things don't go as planned from the start, it shows that your life as a married couple is jinxed. Most people don't actually say this, but many feel it. In truth, many happy marriages have started with a series of honeymoon fiascos.

The Right Attitude

Sometimes, attitude can make all the difference. Adam and Yvette had planned to do all kinds of outdoor activities during their honeymoon in Hawaii. However, it rained almost every day they were there—very unusual for Hawaii. The first day, they went to a museum. The next day, despite the rain, they wanted to go rafting along the coast, but they were told it was too stormy. They noticed some kayaking brochures and ended up taking a beautiful (wet) trip up a river instead. Another day they went hiking and reached a mountaintop in time to catch the dramatic sight of rain clouds blowing in. They even rented all-terrain vehicles and went on a hair-raising trip through the mountains—in the rain. It certainly wasn't the sunny trip they'd planned. They're dripping wet in all of their photos, but they had a great time.

Roz and Lou, on the other hand, weren't looking for adventure, and at one point they weren't sure if they would survive their honeymoon. Driving to their honeymoon cottage, they got caught in a blinding snowstorm. Finally, they inched their way to a motel—to find it was closed. Back on the road, their car had to be towed out of two snowbanks. Forty years later, they still keep in touch with the friendly tow truck owner who felt so bad for these hapless honeymooners that instead of charging them for the second tow, he invited them to stay with his family until the next morning when the roads were plowed. And they still laugh about their first night in the cabin, when Lou came out of the bathroom dressed in his nightclothes: thick woolen socks and a hat.

A sense of humor and a bit of flexibility can go a long way on a honeymoon—and in general. Of course, it won't replace careful planning. But if you've read the previous chapters, you should be well on your way to a wonderful honeymoon!

How Would You React?

Your wedding and honeymoon will probably be even more special than you can imagine. Even if you have lived together for years, making a formal commitment to each other often engenders a depth of emotion you never would have thought possible. It is a time to build memories that will always be a wellspring of romance. Keep in mind, however, that no matter how carefully you plan, no honeymoon can be 100 percent perfect. But couples who have weathered hurricanes and more mundane disasters—lost luggage, missed planes, or hotel reservation mix-ups—say that these experiences brought them closer together. "Having gotten through this, we figured the rest of our marriage would be a breeze—and for the most part, it has been!" said Angie, who got so sick on her honeymoon that she had to fly home.

Of course, even the most carefully orchestrated honeymoon may include unexpected and not-so-pleasant experiences. Here are a few examples of planning gone awry. Think about how you would react, and then see what seasoned travelers would do.

1. You had ordered the resort's "romantic evening" package: a private dinner brought by room service to your oceanfront terrace, accompanied by the sound of the sea. You hadn't planned on having ringside seats for the Mexican fiesta going on just a few steps from your second-floor terrace. Would you
   a. Call the front desk and complain bitterly because they hadn't warned you?
   b. Be angry but realize that this was just bad luck and nothing could be done?
   c. Be upset with yourselves for not planning better?

     d. Although initially disappointed, decide to enjoy the entertainment, dance cheek to cheek on your terrace, and congratulate yourselves that you'll have best view of the fiesta fireworks at the end of the evening?

     e. Make the best of the evening but still feeling the hotel owes you something for not warning you about the fiesta, you call the general manager the next morning, explain the situation, and ask for a complimentary room service dinner as compensation?

2. You're enjoying a romantic dinner in your private villa, cooked and served by "your" chef, when suddenly you see flames in the kitchen, and your quiet evening dissolves into a tumult of sirens and firemen. There's no damage, except to your romantic dinner. Would you

     a. Try to get the chef fired immediately?

     b. Feel that this was par for the course?

     c. Chide yourselves for not checking the stove for grease earlier in the day?

     d. Take pictures so you could laugh with your friends?

     e. Speak to the duty manager after the excitement subsides and politely ask for a complimentary dinner in the best restaurant?

3. You've just traveled for fourteen hours. You're tired. You have confirmed reservations, but the hotel says you'll have to wait five hours before they'll have your suite ready. Would you

     a. Scream and demand that they provide you with a room immediately?

     b. Not be surprised? This is just your luck, after all. Would you wait in the lobby, angry but resigned?

     c. Blame each other for not calling from the airport to reconfirm?

     d. Check your bags and go sightseeing?

     e. Ask to speak to the manager, explain your situation and ask for a temporary room where you could take a nap?

4. Your travel agent has booked you into a hotel that has definitely seen better days. You don't want to stay at this hotel, but you have already prepaid your entire stay. Would you

     a. Yell at the desk clerk and demand to be switched to a better hotel?

     b. Wonder why this kind of thing always happens to you and then relax and decide to stay there?

     c. Blame yourselves for not asking your travel agent more questions?

     d. Check in and then buy flowers to brighten up your room and air freshener to get rid of the musty smell?

     e. Call your travel agent immediately and ask for help?

5. Your flight is delayed by six hours, and you know you're going to miss your cruise unless you can get on another flight. You're told there is no flight they can put you on. Would you

     a. Scream and demand that they find you another flight?

     b. Think, why me? and settle back to see what happens?

     c. Blame yourselves for not allowing time for mishaps?

     d. Head for the bar and sip margaritas while you write thank-you notes for wedding presents?

     e. Call your travel agent, explain the situation, and see what can be done?

6. You bargain for an unusually beautiful necklace in a foreign marketplace and agree on what you feel is a fair price. The clerk writes up the charge slip for a higher price. You notice the difference. He says that he made a mistake and that this is the correct price. Would you
   a. Grab the charge slip, rip it up, and storm out?
   b. Angrily figure that the negotiations weren't fair but pay the higher price anyway?
   c. Know that it's like breaking a contract for the merchant to renege on an agreed price but sign for the new price anyway because you don't want a hassle?
   d. Shrug and decide you don't mind paying the difference?
   e. Tell the clerk calmly that you won't pay any price other than the one you agreed upon and demand that he rip up the slip immediately and rewrite it for the agreed-upon price?

There are no right or wrong answers, but your answers do reveal a lot about how you react to adversity and how happy you'll be. If you answered *a* or *b* to the above questions, you probably often feel that the world is out to get you.

If you chose *a* for most of your answers, your righteous anger may not only get in the way of having a good time but will also make you less effective unless you can channel that anger constructively. How? Make sure you are speaking to the right people—those who can help. Go right to the top—the general manager, a supervisor. Then try to state unemotionally what was done wrong and ask for what you think would be fair reparation. If yelling makes you feel better, do so only after you've tried to settle things calmly.

If you chose *b* for many of your answers, you probably often feel unlucky but believe that what happens to you is totally beyond your control. That isn't always true. Although no one may be to blame, that's not the issue; finding a remedy is. Learn to ask for help effectively. Of course, sometimes all you can do is accept the inevitable. If you are sure this is the case, then why not try to take a positive slant. (See *d*.)

If you often chose *c* for your responses, you're probably the type who thinks you should be in control even when you can't be. Recognize that especially when traveling, some things are truly beyond your control and that often no one—least of all you—is to blame, but you can certainly try to remedy the situation. (See *a*.)

If you often chose *d*, you'll probably always have fun, but you may sometimes adapt to things you don't have to. This attitude is most useful when there is no remedy and no one to blame. For example, what happens if you planned to bask on a beach and it rains for the first four days of your honeymoon? Unless you planned your trip during the rainy season and your travel agent assured you that it was always sunny at that time of year, there really is no one to blame and nothing that can change the situation. Then it's up to you. Do you sit around and complain, or do you find something you enjoy doing?

If many of your answers were *e*, you're probably a pretty savvy consumer. You don't get rattled. You go right to the person who is authorized to help you, and you try to get them to work with you to remedy the situation. Of course, you may not always be able to get instant satisfaction, but you'll certainly have the best chance. Combine that with the upbeat attitude of *d* and some of *a*'s controlled anger, and you'll sail through your trip—and life—happily.

Effective Complaints

A lawyer recently told me he was going to sue a travel agent because he'd been lied to and overcharged for a diving package. He explained that he and his wife had decided to go at the last minute—booking about two weeks before departure. The package he was offered included airfare, hotel accommodations, and daily diving. The agent said that because space was tight, he should book immediately if he really wanted to go. The price sounded expensive. He asked the agent to call the hotel directly and see if there were any less expensive packages. The agent claimed to have checked and said this was all that was available. However, once at the hotel, the lawyer learned that he would have saved about $500 had his travel agent booked directly with the hotel rather than a tour operator. He called the agent when he returned home. "It isn't our agency's policy to check directly with a hotel," he was told. Furious, he took his complaint to the agency owner and offered to split the difference rather than go to court. He received a check for $250. "If they hadn't outright lied to me, and then defended their lack of service rather than apologize, I would not have felt so wronged," he explained. "But I was ready to go to court, just to prevent them from doing this to anyone ever again."

Of course, as a lawyer threatening to sue, he commanded instant respect. However, honeymooners also have tremendous power. Honeymoons and destination weddings are the most talked-about trips that the majority of people ever take, and suppliers know that if you are satisfied, you will become the source of one of their strongest advertising tools—personal recommendations. Some resorts depend almost totally on repeat business and word-of-mouth referrals.

The key to effective complaining is knowing who to complain to and what to ask for. If you aren't finding satisfaction, don't wait to call your travel agent, especially if you are having a problem with an airline, car rental, or hotel reservation. Most travel agents have twenty-four-hour help lines for you to use after office hours.

For example, when Connor and Fay learned their flight would be delayed for hours, they were afraid they would miss their cruise. The airline agent said there was nothing she could do. So did her supervisor. Connor and Fay called their travel agent, who was able to get them on a competing airline's flight.

Similarly, when Hal and Zoe were given a hotel room that smelled musty, the desk clerk refused to change it. They demanded to speak to the hotel manager, who agreed that the room was not acceptable, apologized, and moved them into a oceanview suite.

❧ *HONEYMOON TIPS* ❧
Five Steps to Successfully Lodging a Complaint

1. Before complaining, decide what you would like done to remedy the situation.
2. If you don't find satisfaction right away, ask for a supervisor or manager.
3. Still no results? Call your travel agent. Other possible allies: the local visitor's bureau or chamber of commerce.
4. Keep notes of whom you spoke to and when, in case you decide to follow up when you return home.
5. When you've done all you can, relax and get on with enjoying your honeymoon.

The moral: don't assume that a situation can't be remedied, and don't wait until you return home to complain. Once you've accepted the service (or lack thereof), it's too late for a remedy.

If you handle the problem yourselves, be sure you talk to someone who has the authority to make a decision. Usually, that will not be the first person you'll be referred to. Often, you'll need someone with the title of supervisor or manager. If you still aren't happy with the result, your travel agent should be able to help you. Most important, don't let yourselves get caught up in a situation; do what you can and then relax and enjoy your honeymoon. Years from now, you'll probably laugh at these moments.

PART TWO

Planning a Destination Wedding

CHAPTER 14

About Destination Weddings

*M*ary's parents have avoided seeing each other for ten years. Michael's parents are in the middle of a bitter divorce. The idea of trying to bring everyone together for a wedding seemed too painful for all concerned. So when Michael and Mary got engaged, they considered going to city hall. "But that seemed to downplay the importance of our wedding," said Mary. "I could just imagine us waiting in line at city hall, then going through a perfunctory ceremony and coming home to eat leftovers. It seemed so sad." Then they read an article about destination weddings. "We knew immediately that would be the perfect solution," she said. "We didn't have to involve our families, yet the ceremony would still be very special. Instead of a wedding reception, we held an informal housewarming with our friends and visited separately with each of our families after we returned."

Kim and John had been living together happily for four years, but they almost lost each other forever when they decided to get married. John comes from a large, traditional family. To him and his family, a wedding means a large reception that allows his hundred-plus "close" family members to celebrate with them. Kim has a small family whose idea of a wedding is an intimate, elegant affair. Further complicating matters, John's family is Catholic and Kim's is Jewish, but neither Kim nor John is religious. Kim felt a civil ceremony would be the perfect compromise. John's family insisted on a church wedding. Because of all the prodding by their demanding families, their wedding became an issue that wouldn't go away, and the phrase "If you loved me, you would . . ." became so common in their arguments that finally they split up. A few months later, determined to return to their prewedding planning bliss, they decided to elope. "We had already planned our honeymoon in Jamaica and as an afterthought, we asked our travel agent if we could get married there. It turned out to be easy to arrange, and it worked out perfectly," said John. "We didn't tell anyone until we returned home. We didn't know how they'd react, but Kim's parents threw a small dinner party for us, and my parents proudly introduced us as husband and wife at my family's annual July 4th barbecue."

Maria and Ricardo considered having a big wedding celebration, but as they began discussing the details, they found themselves trying to please everyone but themselves. "We realized what we really wanted was a ceremony where we could focus on each other, not on all our friends and family and the hoopla of a big wedding, and since we were footing the bill ourselves, cost also was a factor," said Maria. "We had planned to honeymoon in Hawaii, so we decided to get married there, too. It was very romantic. Our ceremony was on a promontory overlooking the beach, with the sound of the surf in the background. We exchanged floral leis and after the ceremony, we were serenaded with the 'Hawaiian Wedding Song' and sat down with our minister and witnesses for wedding cake and champagne. It was just perfect. And best of all, it only cost about $600!"

Pros and Cons

As you can see, if you're considering a destination wedding, you are not alone. In fact, according to the latest *Modern Bride* survey, about sixty-five thousand couples a year are now planning their weddings away, a number that is growing every year.

Of course, most of the two and a half million couples who get married every year want a traditional wedding attended by friends and family. The costs and travel time involved in destination weddings almost always mean fewer guests, and if you feel rooted in a community, you may want to celebrate your wedding there. However, complicated family situations, different religions, and conflicts over wedding styles and who should attend are among the reasons couples opt to marry away. It's a way of removing a wedding from sticky situations and the world of "shoulds" and casting it in a new, romantic light.

The expense and time-consuming tasks of wedding planning are also factors for many. With the cost of an average wedding running about $17,000, some couples decide they'd rather use the money for a down payment on a home or some other project. But while they want to save money, they still want a memorable wedding.

Many modern couples want their marriage ceremony to be personal and private. "At a big wedding, the celebration and your guests become the focus of attention. I wanted our wedding to be for us . . . intimate and personal," said Daniel, explaining why he and Anita decided to plan a destination wedding.

✺❧ WEDDING FACTS ✺❧
The Price of Marriage

The average couple spends $17,470 on a traditional wedding, including about $1,000 on bridal wear, $7,000 for the reception, and $1,090 for photography.

Source: Modern Bride Research

Most destination weddings include a limited number of guests—often none. Some couples even plan a destination wedding as a way of limiting a guest list without offending anyone. Steve, a professional athlete, felt that if he got married in his hometown, he'd have to invite his whole team. "Between the team and our families, it would have been a big bash, not the romantic ceremony we dreamed of. So we decided to invite only our immediate families and go to Bermuda."

Whether it's a determining factor or not, almost all couples who get married away say that one of the biggest, and often unexpected, bonuses is being able to focus on each other. "All my friends had big weddings, and they all say the same thing: 'It's a blur; it was over so fast.' They all say we did it the right way. It was just the two of us, and we didn't have to worry about anything. The hotel took care of all the details. We were like guests at our own wedding and truly enjoyed every second of it," agreed Suzanne and Richard.

On the other hand, some couples, irresistibly drawn to the romance of getting married in some exotic locale—perhaps a tropical beach or a European castle—want to celebrate their marriage with large wedding parties. Those with enough money have been known to book whole resorts. But even couples of more modest means who have family and friends scattered over wide geographic areas have found that a destination wedding can be a wonderful—and surprisingly affordable—way to bring everyone together, often for a long weekend of events. In the following chapters, you'll learn how to plan a wedding that helps you achieve your priorities.

Getting Started

From the moment you announce your engagement, you'll begin getting input from family and friends on the type of wedding they think you should have. Emotions often run high during this period on all sides. You'll certainly want to consider the feelings of those you care about, but as Kim and John learned, it may be impossible to satisfy everyone. You'll save everyone a lot of stress and hurt feelings if the two of you agree on the type of wedding you'd like *before* you begin discussing your plans with other people.

For many couples, planning a wedding is their first big step toward creating an identity as a couple. It may be the first time you'll have to balance the demands of each other's families in addition to each other's wishes. Add to that the stress of handling all the decisions, details, and logistics that go into planning a marriage ceremony and celebration, and you can understand why, for most couples, the engagement and wedding-planning period is a roller coaster of emotions. All the more reason for the two of you to let everyone know that you are in charge from the beginning.

You'll have lots to consider. Start by asking yourselves the questions under the heading "What's Your Wedding Style?" in this chapter to help set your priorities. Then, turn to the relevant chapters for ideas on where, when, and how to plan the various aspects of your wedding trip.

✿✿✿ *Stress Control* ✿✿✿
Talk to Each Other First!

You can save a lot of hurt feelings if you give yourselves time to develop a clear idea of the type of wedding the two of you want before discussing your ideas with friends or family. If you seem sure of what you want, others tend not to get as involved in trying to influence the outcome or to feel slighted by your decisions.

Keep in mind that what makes a wedding truly memorable and glorious is the love it symbolizes. Don't let budgetary limits or special family situations make you think that your wedding ceremony and reception can't be meaningful and unique. As you'll see in the following pages, some of the most touching and beautiful weddings have been arranged on the tightest of budgets and have accommodated some of the most unusual demands and desires.

What's Your Wedding Style?

Before you begin discussing the following questions together, each of you should take the time to think through and write answers on your own. Then discuss your answers together and come to agreement on the key points before you begin your actual planning.

1. What are your primary reasons for choosing a destination wedding? Keep those reasons in mind as you make your plans. It's easy to lose track of your priorities. For example, if you want to get away from family tensions, don't involve your families in your planning.
2. What kind of ceremony do you want? Do you want a religious or civil ceremony? Are there rituals, traditions, or personal vows you want included in the ceremony? (See chapter 17 for some ideas.)
3. Are there friends and/or family members you would like to have present? Can they afford to attend? Can you afford to pick up the costs? If either of you has children, will they be present? (See chapter 19 for ideas on how to include your children and still have a romantic wedding and honeymoon.) How many guests would you like to have? (See the next chapter for tips on handling these questions without hurting anyone's feelings.)
4. Do you prefer a private ceremony without guests? If you want a wedding where you can focus only on each other, then this is for you.
5. What kind of reaction do you anticipate from your families and friends? How will you present your plans? If they disapprove, will you still be comfortable with your decision? If you think they'll feel hurt, present your deci-

sion carefully so they understand and support it. If you want them to feel more included, consider having a celebration party where you share your photos and/or video after you return. (See chapter 21 for some ideas.)

6. How will you celebrate after you've exchanged your vows? If you're not inviting any guests, consider planning a special dinner for that evening at a restaurant with a romantic ambience and perhaps a quiet dance combo.

7. Do you want a reception? Some couples have parties when they return and dress in full wedding regalia. You may find your parents are eager to host a reception for you. Or you may opt for an open house or an informal party. (See chapter 21.)

8. What is your budget? Set a budget for your destination wedding before you start planning and then try to work within it. (Turn to the budget chart in this chapter to see what types of items you should figure on.) If you're on a tight budget, there are many inexpensive honeymoon/wedding packages; some hotels even include the wedding as part of your honeymoon. (See chapter 16.)

9. Do you have a date in mind? If you're inviting guests, pick a time that is convenient for most people and far enough in advance for them to plan to join you. Also, keep in mind that flights and accommodations are generally more expensive around major holidays.

10. Do you have a setting in mind? Do you want to be married on a tropical beach, in a historic church, or at a European chateau? These are just a few of your options.

11. How do you want to dress? Most couples who get married away wear formal wedding attire. Others opt for more casual or locally influenced styles. (See chapter 17 for some unique options.)

Destination Wedding Checklist

Soon after Engagement

- Determine your budget and the kind of wedding you want.
- Decide on the size of your wedding and the degree of formality.
- Consider where you would like to have the wedding.
- Send for information on legal requirements, wedding sites, and wedding packages.
- Visit a travel agent.
- Learn what types of ceremonies and special locations to hold your ceremony and/or reception are available.
- Ask about consultants who can help you comply with marriage regulations and arrange for an officiant, photographer, flowers, and the like.
- Set up a folder for contracts, notes of conversations, and other wedding information.

- Check on what documents your home state requires for remarriage if either of you has been divorced or widowed.
- Shop for your wedding attire.
- Sign up with a bridal gift registry so that when people ask what you want for a wedding present, your parents or friends can refer them there.
- Draw up a guest list.

After You Select Your Destination

- Negotiate a rate for the ceremony, reception, and honeymoon if all will be held at the same hotel; make sure to have contracts that spell out all the arrangements you agree on.
- Invite any relative(s) or friend(s) you'd like to have in your wedding party. If they are able to be there, discuss attire.
- Reserve a block of rooms and negotiate a group rate for guests who will attend, either at your hotel or nearby.
- Have a backup plan in case it rains, if you plan an outdoor wedding.
- Make your plane reservations.
- Be sure you have valid passports, visas, and inoculations where required.

Six to Four Months before the Wedding, If Inviting Guests

- Finalize your guest list.
- Mail a letter to everyone you'd like to attend informing them of your plans, including information on special hotel arrangements, rates (if guests are paying their way), and if you like, brochures on the destination so guests have time to clear calendars and make arrangements.
- Order invitations, announcements, and stationery.
- Finalize arrangements for the ceremony and reception, including location, caterer, music, cake, and so on.
- Confirm your arrangements with the photographer and videographer.

Two Months before

- Mail invitations.
- Select attendants' gifts.
- Buy wedding rings and have them engraved.
- Shop for travel clothes.

One Month before

- Send wedding announcement and picture to local newspapers.
- Have your final dress fittings.

One Week before

- Review final details with the hotel, photographer, videographer, florist, musicians, and others involved in the wedding. Arrange to meet with your officiant before the ceremony.
- Make certain that everyone's wedding attire is in order.
- Plan guest seating if needed.

Destination Wedding Budget

Depending on the size and style of wedding, these are the costs you should budget for. If you have a wedding package, check to see which of the ceremony, reception, flower, and service fees are included.

Bride's Attire

Dress   _____

Headpiece and veil   _____

Special undergarments   _____

Jewelry   _____

Shoes   _____

Groom's Attire

Tuxedo, suit, other   _____

Shoes   _____

Ceremony

Location fee   _____

Officiant fee   _____

Marriage license   _____

Translations/processing fees and the like   _____

Flowers   _____

Reception

Location fee   _____

Food   _____

Beverages   _____

Wedding cake   _____

Music   _____

Decoration/flowers   _____

Other   _____

Tips and taxes   _____

Transportation

To ceremony   _____

Between ceremony and reception   _____

After reception   _____

Flowers

For ceremony

_____

Bridal bouquet

_____

Attendants' flowers

_____

Mothers' corsages

_____

Service Fees

Bridal consultant

_____

Other

_____

Wedding Parties

Engagement party

_____

Rehearsal dinner

_____

Other hosted events

_____

Gifts

Maid of honor

_____

Best man

_____

Bridesmaids

_____

Groomsmen

_____

Other

_____

Photography/Videography

Formal portraits

_____

Wedding album

_____

Parents' albums

_____

Extra prints

_____

Video

_____

Extra copies

_____

Stationery

Wedding invitations

_____

Announcements

_____

Thank-you notes

_____

Personal stationery

_____

Postage

_____

Other

Wedding rings

_____

Celebration party for friends and family back home   _____

Souvenirs for guests   _____

Garter   _____

Bags of rice or seeds to toss after ceremony   _____

For travel and accommodations costs, refer to your honeymoon budget.

In the next chapter, you'll learn how to create a guest list that will minimize hurt feelings, plan an extended schedule of wedding events, and announce your wedding to friends and associates. And if you think you have to pay for everything yourselves, read on.

❧ CHAPTER 15

Simple Ceremonies, Grand Gatherings

Mel and Samantha are both widowed and quite well-off financially. Each has adult children from previous marriages who were delighted to hear of their plans to get married, so they decided to turn their wedding into a three-day celebration/family gathering. They invited 150 people to Maui and planned tours, picnics, and other group activities—and picked up the whole tab, including over $100,000 in expenses at the hotel alone. After three days, they took off on a trip around the world.

But you don't have to have an unlimited budget to turn your wedding into a reunion for family and friends. Betsy and Gary couldn't afford to pay for everyone, but they did want to spend several days with their friends and family, who now lived scattered from Florida to Montreal. For their wedding, they chose a cottage colony in Bermuda. Guests paid their own way; all stayed at the same hotel. "Except for the wedding and celebration dinner, we planned nothing," said Gary. "Since we all stayed at the same hotel, we naturally ended up spending lots of time with everyone around the pool, breaking off occasionally in small groups to go into town or sightseeing. It was a great vacation and reunion for everyone. After three days, we said good-bye and moved across the island to another hotel so we could be alone." And the cost? "Just a bit more than our honeymoon would have been."

However, most couples who opt for destination weddings bring their friends and families in spirit only. If you want an intimate ceremony just for the two of you, then make it clear from the start that you are not inviting anyone. "Since no one came with us, no one felt slighted," explained one groom.

A wedding ceremony for two can be every bit as special as a grand gathering. "I couldn't imagine anything more romantic. We exchanged our vows in front of a grand castle in the middle of the Swiss alps," said Dora. "The minister was terrific. We had written our own vows, and he incorporated them into the ceremony. And my bouquet was a beautiful arrangement of wildflowers that Greg gathered from the surrounding fields!"

Your Guest List

Keep your priorities in mind as you decide who, if anyone, will accompany you on your destination wedding. You may want to share your wedding day with a few immediate family members and/or close friends. Perhaps you'll invite just one or two best friends to come as witnesses, or maybe only your parents and siblings.

You'll probably be limiting your guest list simply by having a destination wedding, because many people won't have the time or money to join you. Most people won't feel snubbed if you think of expanding your guest list in terms of circles of friends and family: parents, siblings, first cousins, a few best friends each, and so on.

Consistency is the key to keeping everyone happy. For example, if you have two siblings and only invite one, the other will almost certainly feel hurt. Similarly, if the groom's parents are invited, the bride's parents will expect to be included as well.

Some couples have no desire to limit their guest lists. Their destination weddings are grand affairs with hundreds of guests; planning an affair like this is much like planning a traditional wedding—with the added logistics of getting everyone there and finding accommodations.

Who Pays for What?

Although in many cultures, the bride's family covers most of the expenses for the wedding and reception, in some cultures, the wedding bill falls to the groom's family. These days, however, there are no fixed rules—especially when the wedding is removed from the bride's hometown setting. Often, with a destination wedding, especially one where no guests are invited, the couple foots all or most of the bill. However, some couples are surprised to learn that one or both families want to contribute, either to the wedding and honeymoon trip or to a reception upon their return.

If you are inviting guests, you can set things up so that they pay their own way. However, be prepared for some disappointment and hurt feelings if some people can afford to come and others can't. Discuss in advance what you will do if some of the people closest to you truly can't afford to join you. Some couples offer to pay for their immediate families; in other families, parents may pay for your siblings to attend or vice versa. Or one set of parents may host the entire affair. Sometimes, there is no simple solution. "My parents wanted to come, but we realized that Alan's parents couldn't afford to join us, so we decided not to invite anyone," said Bethany.

Although you and/or your families will probably host most of the events, you might consider offering your guests a package rate that includes group activities as well as accommodations if your funds are limited. All-inclusive resorts and cruise ships, where activities and meals are included for all guests, make budgeting simple.

Unless you want everyone to stay at the same place, it's considerate to include a choice of suggested accommodations—including campgrounds—and costs with your invitation. Information on attractions in the area is also useful. If a travel agent is handling the arrangements, he or she can usually provide discounted group rates as well as information packets for you and your guests at no charge.

The Long Weekend Wedding

If your wedding will be attended by family or friends who don't see each other often, you may want to spend several days together and then officially begin your honeymoon. Many couples plan several days of "events." Some hold their wedding the day after they arrive; for others, the wedding is the grand finale.

Gloria and Manny invited thirty-six guests to a resort complex on St. Thomas, where they owned a vacation condominium. "We took care of all the arrangements. Our travel agent sent our guests plane tickets along with a brochure about the resort and the island and a resort map on which we circled the 'Landers party' area on the beach. This was not only where we held our ceremony, but where everyone hung out during our stay," explained Gloria. "We also planned two great outings. After our wedding ceremony, we chartered a boat for a sunset/dinner sail. And the next day, we all sailed over to a deserted beach for snorkeling and a picnic."

Margaret and Ross offered their guests a more structured itinerary. Both are Americans of Scottish ancestry, so they decided to get married in the small Scottish town that Margaret's family had left more than a century ago. They were joined by thirteen family members, ranging in age from small children to grandparents. For most, it was their first trip abroad. "Margaret and I arrived a few days early to finalize the arrangements at the church and to pick a restaurant where we could celebrate after the wedding. We had also set up two days of touring.

☙ STRESS CONTROL ☙
Use a Travel Agent

If you're inviting guests to your destination wedding, engage the services of a good travel agent to coordinate everyone's travel arrangements. The service costs you nothing and takes all the details off your hands.

✎✎ *WEDDING TIPS* ✎✎
Ask for Group Rates

Most cruise lines and hotels will offer your group attractively reduced rates if you are bringing ten or more guests for several days. Some hotels will even throw in your wedding arrangements and a simple reception if your party is spending several days at their resort.

After that, everyone split off in their own directions. It worked out really well," said Ross.

Rob and Christine, who were married in Lake Tahoe, began their celebration with a welcome dinner on Friday. Rob's parents hosted a brunch the following day, and on Sunday they were married in a lakeside chapel, with a reception afterwards.

All-inclusive resorts, packages, and cruises simplify matters further; you won't have to worry about dealing with bills for each meal and activity. And like Gloria and Manny, by designating an area for your group to hang out, you and your guests can get together without making formal plans. One caveat: if you and your guests are staying at the same hotel and many of them plan on staying after your official gathering is over, you'll probably want to take off on your own, perhaps to another resort or area or on a cruise, for some time alone. The next chapter will outline things to consider when picking a destination for your wedding.

If possible, when inviting your guests, provide them with information about costs and a schedule of events (with suggested attire). A good travel agent can help you plan activities and meals for the group, provide you with brochures for your guests, and help coordinate the arrangements for your wedding.

Group Settings

When considering where to stay, think about how much togetherness you want with your guests. For the ultimate in intimacy, small groups can rent a large villa or two neighboring villas, complete with cook, chauffeur, and maid; doing so can be more economical than hotel accommodations. If that seems like too much togetherness, you might choose to stay at a different hotel than your guests and get together only for specific events. Staying at the same hotel or resort, where you can enjoy time together and apart, is the simplest and most popular arrangement.

Picking a Date

Valerie and Ian had planned to get married on the anniversary of their first date. However, Ian's department was slated to be audited at that time, and they had to shift their dates. Then Valerie was asked by her boss not to take more than two days off unless she waited another month. Their best man and maid of honor also had time constraints. Ian and Valerie are no exception; many couples are surprised to find that picking a date for their wedding is one of the hardest decisions they'll have to make.

Remember that your guests will probably be joining you—and away from home—for several days. So in addition to juggling the demands of your own jobs, you may want to check with your most important guests to find out if they have any time constraints. Try to plan far enough in advance so that people can budget for the expense and set aside the time to join you.

The seasonality and availability of your planned destination may also be a consideration. If your dream is to get married at a cozy ski lodge, you won't want a summer wedding (unless you're headed for the Southern Hemisphere). On the other hand, in locales such as the Caribbean, where most people go to escape the winter cold, you may want to go "off-season," when you'll find increased availability and lower prices.

Invitations

If you're inviting guests, you'll probably want to send written invitations. Your invitation will also help signal the type of wedding you're having. If you're planning a black-tie event, you'll want to send out formal invitations. You can order these from stationery stores, specialty shops, or department stores, where a consultant will show you a variety of styles and help you with the wording. You can also order formal invitations by mail. You'll find mail-order firms among the advertisers in bridal magazines—most will send you samples, along with suggested wordings. Some resorts will also provide you with invitations.

Along with your invitation, it's considerate to include information about accommodations, and—if guests are expected to pay their own way—prices, along with response cards.

The next chapter will provide guidelines on picking the right wedding site.

CHAPTER 16

Picking a Place

Catrene and Blake were paging through a bridal magazine and looking for wedding ideas when they saw a photo of a couple getting married on a beach. "When we saw that picture, we looked at each other and hugged!" said Catrene. "We knew we had to get married on a beach like that! And who could be upset with us for exchanging our vows in a way that would be meaningful to us?"

To Angela, on the other hand, getting married at a castle in Europe was the only way to start her happily-ever-after. "I felt like a fairy-tale princess, especially when Max and I rode off in a horse-drawn carriage!"

Sometimes, a shared hobby becomes the focus of a wedding ceremony. Scuba enthusiasts Josh and Elaine had already planned their honeymoon—featuring a scuba diving trip through the Bahamas—but hadn't figured out where to hold their wedding. Then they saw an ad for underwater weddings in the Florida Keys. "Everything fell into place," said Elaine. "You know, our friends thought we were kidding until they saw our wedding video. Then they all said how beautiful and romantic our ceremony was."

Everyone's idea of a romantic wedding setting is different. For some, it's a tropical beach. Others dream of exchanging their vows in a quiet mountain chapel or a historic church. Yachts, ski slopes, sky diving . . . or Walt Disney World, with Cinderella's Castle in the background . . . whatever your wedding fantasy is, you can probably find a way to arrange it.

Making It Work

Some fantasies are far easier to realize than others, but with a little creativity and flexibility, you should be able to create the wedding you want. For example, if your hearts are set on a country that makes it difficult or impossible for Americans to marry legally, you might consider getting legally married at home and then having your "real" ceremony at your dream destination.

Keep your priorities in mind as you evaluate possible wedding sites. If you're too busy to spend much time on wedding arrangements, then you may want to hire a wedding consultant or pick a place with an on-site planner who can handle all the details. To combine economy and romance, consider an all-inclusive honeymoon that includes your wedding. In some destinations, arranging a wed-

---

☙☙ **STRESS CONTROL** ☙☙
Get It in Writing

Once you've agreed on your arrangements, the hotel or establishment should confirm everything in writing. If you're bringing a large group, you may be asked to pay a deposit based on a minimum number of guests at an average per person cost.

---

ding is as easy as getting married at your local city hall; other places practically require an expert to get you through all the red tape.

Resorts That Do It All

Across the country and around the world, you'll find hotels and resorts that will happily handle all the details of planning your wedding. Many resorts in the Caribbean and Hawaii have devoted wedding coordinators who will discuss your wishes with you by phone, confirm everything in writing, and then make the arrangements. Often, you'll have your choice of several beautiful settings around the resort and can finalize your wedding site choice once you arrive. Be sure that the coordinator will be responsible for handling all of your arrangements so you won't need to speak to caterers, florists, and the like.

You'll also find countless hotels within the continental United States that are well equipped to help you arrange a complete wedding, from ceremony to reception. Wedding chapels in popular wedding/honeymoon destinations such as Gatlinburg, Tennessee, and Las Vegas, Lake Tahoe, and Reno, Nevada, stand ready to arrange your ceremony at a moment's notice. Other favorite wedding/honeymoon destinations include Walt Disney World, whose FairyTale Weddings division can arrange weddings from small and simple ceremonies to elaborate, fanciful affairs.

The most popular place for offshore weddings is Hawaii, where beaches, seaside chapels, and lush tropical gardens are among the popular settings. The U.S. Virgin Islands, Jamaica, Bermuda, St. Lucia, and the Bahamas are among other popular wedding sites. Many resorts have at least one full-time wedding planner on staff; several have their own wedding chapels. Other resorts can refer you to local wedding coordinators.

Free and Almost-Free Options

Some resorts will provide you with a simple wedding ceremony if you stay a minimum number of days with them. For example, SuperClubs resorts (a chain of all-inclusive hotels that includes the Grand Lido and Boscobel resorts in Jamaica) will arrange for an officiant, two witnesses, your wedding license, and a simple celebration with champagne and wedding cake at no charge. (Photography and videography are available for an additional fee.) Sandals Resorts (in Jamaica and several other Caribbean islands) offers wedding packages that include video and a photo album starting at about $500. Because they make it so easy for Americans to marry there, many Jamaican resorts average several weddings a day!

Many hotels and resorts offer preset wedding packages, often with a menu of options. You'll see their ads in bridal magazines. Send for their literature, but don't feel that you are limited to what they spell out. Most will happily try to accommodate your wishes.

Beyond Resorts

Resorts are not the only places for a destination wedding; there is a whole world of fantasy locations. In some countries, such as Scotland, arranging a wedding is simple enough that some couples even handle all the details on their own, although most engage the services of a wedding consultant. However, if your hearts are set on marrying in a country with lots of formalities attached to weddings, such as Italy, be prepared for tangles of paperwork. Unless you have an enormous tolerance for red tape and enjoy the process of working your way through a bureaucracy, engage the services of a wedding coordinator or a travel professional.

In the next chapter, you'll learn more about getting married abroad, including some ideas on incorporating local touches into your ceremony.

Questions to Ask about the Site

Wedding planner: Is there one person who will handle all the arrangements? Will that person be there on our wedding day?

Wedding site: Where will the ceremony be held? If it is outdoors, is there a backup plan in case of inclement weather? Will ours be the only wedding that day?

The ceremony: Who is available to perform the ceremony? Will we meet with the officiant in advance? Can we personalize the ceremony? Are there special touches you can suggest?

Packages: Are there standard wedding packages? What does each include? What extras might we want that are not included?

Reception site: Where will the reception be held? Can we see photos of functions held there? If the site is outdoors, what happens if it rains? Will other hotel guests have access to the area? What size group can the space handle? What types of special touches are available? At what cost?

Reception rates: What are the per-guest price ranges? What does that include? How much should we budget for taxes and tips? Other extras? Do prices vary with the time of day and day of the week or month?

Food: How will food be served—buffet style? Served from trays by waiters? Or on preset plates set in front of diners? What is the ratio of waiters to guests? (One waiter to ten to twelve guests is about right for seated gatherings; one to fifteen or eighteen, for buffets.) Is wedding cake included? How will it look and taste?

Drinks: How will drinks be charged? You may be able to pay by consumption or have an open bar for a cocktail hour or longer, paying a per-guest fee per hour. Will you serve mixed drinks and premium brands? Will drinks be brought to guests or served at the bar?

CHAPTER 17

Making Sure Your Marriage Is Legal

Kisha and Darrell arranged their own wedding in Bermuda. "The tourist office sent us a brochure that explained everything," said Kisha. "We set it up ourselves by phone. It was unbelievably simple."

Tiffany and Victor, on the other hand, ended up getting married after their honeymoon. "We thought we had everything arranged to get married in Italy," said Tiffany. "We even had notarized translations of our paperwork. We knew we'd have to do *some* paperwork in Rome, but after spending a whole day running around trying to get all the authorizations we needed, we decided to give up, enjoy our honeymoon, and get married at our city hall back home."

Depending on where you decide to get married, the formalities can be minimal or a practically full-time job to work through. Why the difference? The basic rule for getting married abroad is quite simple: to be legally married under U.S. law, your wedding ceremony must comply with the laws in the place you decide to marry. In some countries, the requirements are few. In others, you'll have to bring translated, certified documents and stop at as many as three different offices once you arrive at your destination.

What's Required?

How do you find out the law of the land in the place you intend to marry? In the more popular wedding destinations, the tourist offices can provide you with information (see Appendix B).

If there is no tourist office in the country where you'd like to marry, you can contact its consular office. Most countries have consular offices in New York City and embassies in Washington, D.C., which are listed in phone directories. The U.S. State Department is another good source. It can provide you with a list of U.S. consular offices abroad as well as marriage requirements. If you are divorced or widowed, bring proof that you are free to marry, such as a death certificate or divorce decree. You may also need to comply with a waiting period—which could be anywhere from twenty-four hours to six months or more—

before being legally free to marry. Some countries require that you be in the country for that amount of time; in other countries, you can get a waiver or comply by doing some paperwork by mail.

Religious Ceremonies

In some countries, a religious ceremony must be preceded by a civil ceremony; in others, the religious ceremony is legally binding. Each religion also has its own rituals and requirements. For a Catholic wedding, you'll need to bring your confirmation and baptism papers as well as a letter from your parish priest confirming that you have been through pre-Cana counseling and requesting that the marriage be performed in another church. (Some priests will also perform weddings in nonchurch settings, but you'll need special permission.) Plan to work directly with the priest who will marry you as well as your parish priest to get the necessary documentation.

Similarly, to perform a Jewish wedding, most rabbis will ask for a letter or phone call from your hometown rabbi. They may also have certain religious requirements that could be more or less orthodox than your own practices.

Your best bet is to check out the legalities and then talk to your own cleric about the best way to arrange a religious ceremony abroad.

Personalizing Your Vows

"The resort took charge of our whole wedding, and everything was perfect— except for the ceremony itself," said Arielle. "When the minister asked if I promised to honor, obey, and serve, I almost didn't say 'I do'; then, I thought Ike's vow would be the same. But Ike had to promise he'd protect and provide for me. And the minister went into a long dissertation on what marriage meant that had nothing to do with our ideas. I wish we'd thought to discuss our ceremony with the minister in advance."

Like Arielle and Ike, many couples who get married away from home let the resort arrange everything—including their wedding ceremony. Even if you don't feel the need to write your own vows or ceremony, you may want to make sure that your ceremony reflects your ideas and feelings. This is the one detail that you must take care of yourselves.

Some religious traditions allow for a great degree of personalization. Others have a tightly prescribed ritual. Still, most officiants are happy to accommodate requests to personalize your ceremony. Many keep a library of suggested readings from which a couple can choose and are willing to incorporate spiritual poems, hymns, or Scriptural passages into your wedding ceremony.

Try to speak with your officiant as early as possible. Then you can begin thinking about what you would like your ceremony to include. You may want to

---

✣✣ STRESS CONTROL ✣✣
Wait to Wed

Don't plan to get married the day you arrive, even if it's legally possible; give yourselves at least a day to unwind and some leeway in case of travel delays.

---

use your own words to express your feelings about love and marriage. If so, be sure to write them down and practice them.

Local Touches

When Lara and Ken got married in Acapulco, they brought 140 guests. Their theme was the *paloma* (dove). Each guest received a small Mexican onyx box with a dove design, and one of the highlights of their wedding celebration was a traditional Mexican "fireworks," a multistory wooden pinwheel that slowly ignited into a design that incorporated their names in a heart and was topped off by a dove.

Wherever you decide to marry, you can make your wedding more special by incorporating some local customs as well as special foods, music, costumes, and transportation. For example, in Hawaii, you'll probably be adorned with floral leis. Some Hawaiian ministers bless couples with Hawaiian chants and water-sharing ceremonies, and your music may be played on a ukelele. In Mexico, you may have a mariachi band and wear a decorative rope or necklace that symbolically unites you as part of the ceremony.

In Bermuda, couples traditionally plant a tree and have bride's and groom's cakes, while in Fiji, you may be transported to your ceremony in a festively decorated canoe. Ask the tourist office, your hotel wedding planner, and your officiant for ideas of local customs you can incorporate into your ceremony.

Expert Help

Convention and visitors bureaus and tourist offices are excellent sources of information. (See Appendix B.) Many even provide you with brochures on getting married and lists of local consultants and hotels and other sites that specialize in arranging weddings.

You can also ask about U.S.-based tour operators that offer wedding-planning services. Some of these have good local contacts who can help ensure that all goes smoothly.

❧❧ *WEDDING TIPS* ❧❧
Evaluating a Consultant

It's hard to trust someone you may know only from phone conversations to plan your wedding. Want some reassurance? Ask for references and check them out. Check with the Better Business Bureau, tourist office, or chamber of commerce to see if there have been any complaints (or compliments) registered.

Some travel agents are also quite knowledgeable about arranging weddings and can advise you about resorts and tour operators that are equipped to handle weddings.

What's the easiest and most economical way to plan a destination wedding? Often, it's letting someone do it for you. At many resorts, a wedding director will handle all the details, advising you about legal requirements such as blood tests and any documents you'll need to bring and often arranging for the marriage license as well.

If you're getting married abroad without the help of a hotel's wedding planner, you may want to engage the services of a professional who specializes in arranging weddings abroad. You'll probably pay an hourly rate or a set fee. Expect to pay a minimum of $500. Ask the tourist office of the country where you're planning to marry for suggestions.

Before making any commitments, ask for references. Then, be sure all of your arrangements are clearly spelled out in writing.

Questions to Ask about Legalities

Residency: Is there a waiting period or residency requirement? These can be six months and more, and some countries only allow citizens to marry there.

Before you arrive: Do we need to file any papers, post banns, or go through any premarital preparation programs before the wedding?

Documents: What documents will be required? These might include U.S. passports, authenticated birth certificates, health records, divorce decrees, and even proof of economic solvency. Must these be translated? Notarized? Who can legally do this?

Wedding sites: Can the wedding be held outside? Some religions, the Catholic Church in particular, frown on weddings being held outside of a house of worship. (Weather is also a consideration.)

Remarriages: Are there any special requirements for those who are divorced or widowed? Sometimes there is a waiting period. You'll probably need to provide an authenticated and translated divorce decree.

After the wedding: Once married, how do we obtain a copy of the marriage certificate? If you're marrying abroad, experts often recommend that you have it authenticated by the U.S. consular office in the country where you marry.

Medical exams: Is any type of medical examination required? These might include blood tests or physical exams, which sometimes must be performed in the country or municipality where you will marry.

Officiant: Who will perform the ceremony? Does he or she have any requirements? Will he or she marry people of different faiths? Will the ceremony reflect our beliefs? Can we personalize our ceremony?

Religious ceremonies: Is a religious ceremony legally binding? In Mexico, for example, clergy do not perform legal marriages; you must have a civil ceremony first, which can be followed by the religious ceremony.

CHAPTER 18

What to Wear

Carrie and Neil wanted to be married on a tropical beach at sunset, with Carrie dressed in full bridal regalia and Neil in a tuxedo. "It was just the two of us, the minister, and two witnesses. I was afraid I might feel silly in my wedding gown . . . on the beach, and without a wedding party . . . but it was so romantic," said Carrie. "And I couldn't imagine getting married dressed any other way. It just wouldn't have seemed like a wedding!"

Vanessa, who also chose a tropical beach for her ceremony, dressed more informally. "Stu and I had both been married before with big formal weddings. This time, the wedding was to be for us—intimate and in our own style. We had decided to get married informally in Jamaica, so I brought a wide-rimmed white straw hat and a white linen dress. But the day we arrived, we went to the market where I picked out a white cut-work dress—they're really simple and beautiful, and it was great to be able to wear something local. Stu had brought a white shirt and white slacks from home and we picked up a bright woven sash and a straw hat for him as well. Looking at our pictures, we're really happy we made the choices we did."

Traditional or unconventional, formal or informal, what you wear for your wedding should be meaningful to you. It's something you're sure to remember for the rest of your lives. And through your pictures, so will your family and friends—even if they are not at your ceremony.

Your wedding is an important event, no matter where it is held and who attends. And there are no rules about what should be worn. You can wear white, whatever your age or marital history. If your wedding fantasy includes wearing a flowing bridal gown, there's no reason not to—whether guests attend or not.

You can also opt to dress casually, perhaps with just a hint of bridal lace. Draw from local styles or create your own. This is *your* wedding!

Here are some ideas and some tips to help you find your own personal style.

Bridal Gowns

If you decide to purchase a traditional wedding gown, you'll find that they come in a wide range of styles and prices. The average bride spends about $850 for her dress, $170 on her headpiece, and $50 for shoes.

ᏬᎦᏬᎦ STRESS CONTROL ᏬᎦᏬᎦ
Carry Your Gown

Don't check your wedding clothes with the airlines; have them packed and carry them on—what if your bag is late or lost?! And don't assume you'll be able to rent a tuxedo; reserve one—or better still, bring one to be sure.

To get an idea of what kind of gowns you like, page through the major bridal magazines and see which manufacturer's looks you are attracted to. (Bridal manufacturer's ads usually include listings of stores in your area that carry their lines.) Tear out pictures of any gowns or special features (necklines, fabrics, styling) that you like. If you want a particular gown, having the magazine's name and issue date will help a store locate the gown you want. Even if you don't find the exact dress you want, the pictures will help an experienced bridal shop salesperson understand what you prefer. You can also get some great ideas at local bridal shows.

Finding Your Gown

Allow yourself time to enjoy the process of shopping for your gown as well as for alterations. Bridal gowns are ordered to the nearest size and then altered to perfect fit, so be sure the dress can be ready when you need it. Experts recommend you begin shopping about six to eight months before your wedding. However, don't despair if you don't have that much time. Joselyn was able to find her gown just a week before she flew off to get married. Said Joselyn, "The stress was almost unbearable, and I kept looking for just the right dress. Finally, I decided to pick something—even if it wasn't perfect. Fortunately, I found a sample gown I loved—and it fit!"

When shopping for a gown, bring shoes with the heel height you plan to wear so you can be measured for the right length. Also, do your hair as you want it to look when you try on headpieces and veils to get a good idea of what is most becoming. Decide roughly how much you'd like to spend in advance and tell the salesperson your budget so she can show you dresses in your price range. Don't let yourself be talked into impetuously splurging. If you take the time to check out several stores and try on a lot of dresses, you're sure to be happy with your decision.

A bridal gown is a major purchase. You'll probably be asked to leave a nonrefundable 50 percent deposit when you order and to pay the balance before your final fitting. Alterations usually are not included in the price. Be sure you understand the terms and refund policies before leaving a deposit.

If you don't want to own your gown, you may be able to borrow one from a family member or friend. There are also a growing number of shops across the country that rent bridal gowns and formal evening wear. You might also consider purchasing a used gown from a vintage clothing store—be sure it's in good condition and don't assume it can be repaired unless you yourself know how to fix it.

Dressing with a Sense of Place

Rebecca and Zachary wanted their Cancún wedding to reflect some of the feeling of Mexico. So in addition to hiring a mariachi band, they went to the local market and bought Zachary a white shirt and bolero-type pants like the ones worn by Yucatecan men. He added a colorful sash. For Rebecca, they picked out an embroidered white dress and a broad-brimmed white hat.

In the more formal setting of Bermuda, Luther "went local" in dark blue Bermuda shorts . . . with knee socks and a jacket and tie. He had planned to wear a navy blue suit, said June, "but we saw someone formally dressed in shorts, and the idea was so novel and unique to us that we just had to buy Luther an outfit. And then we thought, 'why not wear it for our wedding ceremony?!' "

The inspiration for your wedding attire can come from many places. For some, like Luther and June, the idea is spontaneous, while other couples hit the books, looking for ideas on local customs as well as styles. Tourist offices can also be good sources of information.

Often, wedding planners will provide you with suggestions for local garb. Eva and Craig, who were married in Fiji, were offered the option of dressing in traditional Fijian attire by their resort's wedding coordinator. "They actually supplied us with the clothes," explained Eva. "I wore a beautifully adorned dress of tapa cloth (pressed mulberry bark), and Craig wore a grass skirt. It was very exciting."

For some, a sense of place has little to do with culture. Michelle and Jonah met on a scuba diving trip and are both avid divers, as are many of their friends. So, when they were trying to think of what they could do to make their wedding special, an underwater wedding ceremony seemed a natural. But Michelle still wanted to wear something bridal. Her solution? A white lace bathing suit with a small ballerina skirt and a headpiece and veil. She sewed small weights into the ends of the veil so it would fall neatly around her. Jonah wore the bottom part of a knee-length wet suit and a black-and-white bow tie. Nondiving guests watched the ceremony from a submarine.

Dana, who also had an underwater wedding, wore a wedding gown. "It just wouldn't have seemed like a real wedding ceremony without it," she said. "Of course, I found an inexpensive used wedding gown for the ceremony, but I bought a new one for our reception."

Couples have gotten married on the ski slopes with their ski poles wrapped in lace, in Victorian garb in a hot-air balloon, and dressed as Cinderella and Prince Charming at Walt Disney World. There are no rules, so let your garments express your fantasies!

❧❧ CHAPTER 19

Bringing the Children

J ulio and Luciana were married on a great broad lawn, with the Caribbean Sea in the background. "After our vows, we danced a pas-de-trois with Cesar, my five-year-old son, who spontaneously said, 'I love you.' It was an unforgettable moment," said Luciana. "We knew then that getting married away—without any guests—was the right decision. And since Cesar was, in fact, going to have to live with this marriage, we felt he should be a part of the wedding as well. Without all the distraction and nervousness of planning a big wedding, we felt better able to use the wedding and honeymoon to heighten our sense of being a family."

Felice and Wayne also wanted an intimate wedding. "We had planned a family trip to Hawaii, and it occurred to us that getting married there would be just perfect," said Felice. "In our minds, Wayne's six-year-old daughter was part of the marriage, too, so we started calling our wedding a 'family-starting ceremony.' She wore a princess gown, and we presented her with a necklace as part of the ceremony," said Felice. "We loved that it was just the three of us."

Shandra and Troy, on the other hand, invited fifty close friends and family members to their Walt Disney World wedding. "We wanted our wedding to be an important event for everyone and had planned to make Erin, my seven-year-old stepdaughter, the flower girl so she would feel a part of everything," said Shandra. "The minister had an even better idea; he suggested we extend our vows to include her. In the ceremony, after Troy and I exchanged our vows, the minister turned to Erin and told her how important she was in the relationship and asked for her commitment. I placed a Mickey Mouse watch on her wrist and the three of us held hands as the minister discussed the meaning of family and blessed us. Everyone was deeply moved. No matter how often we tell Erin how much she means to us, I think no words will ever have the impact that including her in the vows did."

Family-Starting Ceremonies

Whether they have grand weddings like Shandra and Troy or intimate ceremonies like Felice and Wayne, couples with young children from previous marriages often want to make them a major part of the wedding. Many include the children in the ceremony itself. Grown children may actually fill the role parents usually do and "give their parent away." Adolescents may offer readings, and younger children may be flower girls and ring bearers.

A growing number of couples are also creating vows for their children, and many wedding officiants include a segment on the importance of everyone's contribution to the new family. Some ask the children to promise to do their part to create a happy, harmonious family and to say "I do" as they exchange a symbol of acceptance, either with their stepsiblings or a stepparent.

The symbol may be a ring, or the whole family may exchange something specially designed to be worn as a lasting symbol of their unity. For example, Avril and Emmett exchanged wedding rings, and then their entire family presented each other with engraved gold pendants.

When young children are involved, many couples use something they know the child wants. Mickey Mouse ears, watches, a pretty bracelet or cuff links, even flowers . . . whatever symbol your child will appreciate can be used.

Preparing Your Children

Be sure your child feels comfortable with his or her role in the ceremony and has a chance to practice in advance. Don't force participation. If your child has negative feelings about your union, your wedding ceremony certainly is not the place to work these out. In fact, if the feelings have not been dealt with, you might be embarrassed to find your child "acting out" instead of participating.

Darlene and Junior, who have four young children between them, took everyone for several months of family therapy when they decided to get married. "It gave the kids a chance to say all of the things that were on their minds . . . things like 'I wish you'd go back with mommy' and 'We want our real daddy.' Although some of it was hurtful, we felt it was the only way we could ever be happy together," said Junior. "When Darlene and I decided to get married, we really did feel as though our families were getting married. But if we had tried to have them take part in the ceremony before the therapy sessions, we would have had a mutiny."

❧❧❧ *WEDDING TIPS* ❧❧❧
Vows for Children

Couples with children from previous marriages who want to create the sense of a new family being formed through their union can ask their officiant to help create a "family ceremony" in which everyone exchanges vows—and perhaps rings or another symbolic item—as they say "I do" to joining the new family.

ꙅꙮ STRESS CONTROL ꙮꙅ
Easing Anxieties

Your children will worry about what your marriage will mean to them. You can ease everyone's anxiety by anticipating questions about how your relationship will affect them at the time you announce your engagement. What impact will your marriage have on their living arrangements or visiting schedules? What should they call their new stepparent? What, if anything, will you expect of them? Reassure them that they won't be competing for your affection with your new spouse. Understand that they may be disappointed as their hopes, perhaps unconscious, that their natural family will reunite are dashed. Don't be surprised at negative reactions, even from grown children. A remarriage often stirs up anger that seemed resolved years ago.

Honeymooning with Kids

Laurel and Darren had a wedding in their home town but brought their children—each had one from a previous marriage—on their honeymoon at the Boscobel Resort in Jamaica. "People ask what kind of honeymoon we could have with an eight- and ten-year-old. But if we'd left them home, we would have felt guilty and missed them. And we wanted them to feel as though they were getting married, too. We had gone on plenty of outings together, but this was the first time we'd gone away as a family. We thought it would be a good way for the kids to get more comfortable with each other—on neutral ground—in an exciting new place. It was lots of fun. But we also chose Boscobel because of its terrific children's program; after all, it was our honeymoon, and we wanted some time alone—we had plenty—while they were having a ball with the other kids."

Like Laurel and Darren, many couples view taking a "honeymoon" with their kids as a way to help bond together children from previous marriages into a new happy family.

Randy and Alison were afraid their children would feel excluded from their new relationship if they didn't come on their honeymoon. "We felt it was important to show the children that, in a sense, our wedding was also theirs. So it seemed natural that we all celebrate afterwards with a trip," explained Randy. "We figured we'd have lots of time to be alone in the future."

On the other hand, many couples feel that they need time to celebrate their marriage before returning to the complicated realities of their blended families.

"Kids on a honeymoon?" said Maria. "That's a contradiction in terms. John and I felt our honeymoon was a time for us to focus on each other and our relationship. And we felt it was important for the children to understand that we had a relationship apart from them."

Brad and Susan solved the problem by taking two wedding trips—back to back. After a wedding in which Susan's children—aged seven, nine, and thirteen—took part, their entire wedding party spent two nights at the Mount Washington Hotel in New Hampshire, where they were married. Then their children spent a week with family friends while Brad and Susan honeymooned on Cape Cod. "It was important for us to have some time alone after our wedding. And we felt the kids should do something special, too. It was also a way for the kids to see that something important had happened in our relationship. After spending a week on our own, we picked up the kids and drove to Hyannis for our first real family vacation."

Take Two Trips

Although a "Brady Bunch" trip can help incorporate children into a new family, the downside, according to Robert Keroack, my psychotherapist husband, "is that it blurs the boundaries between the couple's relationship and their relationship with their children. Planning two separate trips helps the children understand that there is couple time and family time."

Of course, unlike Brad and Susan, not everyone can take two trips back to back. Some plan their family trip right after the wedding and wait several months for their honeymoon; others take a long weekend honeymoon and then collect the children for a family trip.

Time for Everyone

If you're planning to take just one trip—a "family honeymoon"—you may want to follow the example of Laurel and Darren and opt for a resort or cruise ship sailing that has an extensive children's program. Check out Club Med (look for one with Mini- and Baby Clubs), Hyatt (with Club Hyatt and Rock Hyatt for children and teens), and all-inclusive resorts, such as Boscobel Beach in Jamaica, that specialize in family vacations. Walt Disney World has some children's programs, and many resorts have children's programs during school holidays.

These programs allow you to have time alone and still vacation with your children. And while you're enjoying your time alone, you'll know your children are having good times of their own and won't feel left out.

✤ CHAPTER 20

Photography and Videography

T'yrone and Rose asked their resort to hire both a photographer and a video-grapher to capture their wedding on film. "Since none of our relatives or friends would be there to witness our wedding, we felt it was essential to have good photos and a video," said Rose. "In some ways it made our ceremony even more important, since people would be focusing on it without distraction, and somehow I think people expect something they watch on a screen to be more perfect than reality. We were very lucky. The hotel found us good people, and we were very happy with the results."

Avi and Rita were not so lucky. "The hotel's photographer lost the negatives, so we were faced with the choice of restaging the event or having only the unprofessional photos that a few of our guests took," said Avi. "It worked out okay. The photographer had us pose again for some portrait shots in our wed-ding clothes. We combined those with our friends' candid shots of our ceremony and created a great album. To make us feel better, the hotel upgraded us to a suite for the rest of our stay, so we were pretty happy after all."

Finding a Professional

Although you can interview photographers and videographers by phone and check out their references, if you're like most couples who get married away, you'll simply trust the hotel wedding coordinator to make a good choice for you. And that's usually a good decision. After all, many wedding coordinators handle hundreds of weddings a year and get to know the styles and strengths of local photographers and videographers. Some hotels even have on-site profes-sionals. And because their reputation rests on the results, most hotels are very careful about who they hire and recommend.

On the other hand, in some destinations, there may be only one—or no—local professionals to choose from. Or you may want a style of coverage that the local professionals are not equipped to provide. Some couples actually fly in the photographer or videographer they want. Several of Sirena's friends had used the same videographer, and she loved their videos. "He truly captures all the emotions and excitement and does more than just film the ceremony. Another friend recently got married away, and her video reminded me of one of those carnival pictures where you stick your head into a cardboard set. There were snippets of her and her husband, but mostly we were watching empty scenes of the island and the resort with some hokey background music. I wanted someone who would focus on us."

Of course, you don't have to fly in a professional to feel confident about your choice of photographer or videographer. Even if your wedding package includes photography and videography, you may have some input into the final product.

If you are making your own arrangements and a wedding coordinator is helping you, you can ask for several recommendations. You can also get referrals from Professional Photographers of America. (See Appendix A.) Ask for examples of their work. Most reputable professionals have some kind of background kit and sample work they can send, as well as references from satisfied couples. (You can check with the local Better Business Bureau to see if any complaints have been registered.) Don't be turned off if their references are wedding planners or caterers; some don't want former clients bothered by phone calls from couples they don't know.

Questions to Ask Photographers

When calling photographers and videographers, here are some basic questions to ask.

Are you available on my wedding date? If your date is set, then ask this question first. Also ask how long the studio, photographer, or videographer has been in business.

Who will actually be shooting my wedding? Many studios use different photographers or videographers; some can tell you in advance who they will send. If possible, talk to the person who will be assigned to you and get references for that person, not the studio. You'll be spending some of the most memorable hours of your lives with that person, so it should be someone with whom you feel comfortable.

How much time will you spend with us and during which hours? What types of pictures or video footage will you take? These questions should help you get a sense of the type and style of coverage you'll get.

Are you familiar with the location where we'll be getting married? Some places of worship forbid videography or artificial lights. Do you know if any permits are required? This is not the photographer or videographer's responsibility, but often they will be quite familiar with the site and can help you make the arrangements.

What is the payment schedule? Most professionals require a deposit to hold the date, with an additional payment on your wedding date and final payment upon delivery of the albums or videos. Also inquire about the cancellation policy in case your plans change.

Are there any additional charges we should expect (overtime, photographic assistants, travel time)?

How long after the wedding can we expect to see the final product?

What can we do to help you do the best job for us?

What wedding packages are available? Most photographers offer packages that can include a wedding album and parents' albums, with a specific number of prints. Find out exactly what is included—how many photos and what sizes. Ask about the types and quality of albums. You may even want to see samples. Ask if there is a charge if you want to keep the proofs and what the charge is for additional prints. You'll also want to know who keeps the negatives. If the photographer does, ask how long they are saved and if there is a time limit on ordering additional prints at the quoted price.

Standard videography packages generally include a studio-edited video that lasts two hours or less. Some provide a specified number of copies or the option to buy copies at a set price. Some packages also include a ten- to fifteen-minute highlights tape. These can often be personalized with a thank you or greeting to the person you are sending it to.

Here are some specific questions for videographers:

What options are available, and what equipment will you use? Multicamera coverage, remote-controlled cameras, and unmanned (no remote control) cameras are among the options. If you are not inviting guests, you'll probably opt for more simple coverage; for example, you won't need a second camera to pick up guest reactions during your ceremony.

What kind of microphones will you use? Ideally, there should be a wireless mike on the groom (it's hard to hide a mike on a gown, and the groom's mike should pick up the bride's words). The cleric needs a microphone, and if you're using a reader's pulpit and musicians, they'll also need microphones. The sound system needs to be high quality, or you may end up picking up radio-transmitted police calls!

How will the tapes be edited? What special effects will be used? How much canned footage of the destination is used, and how much is shot of us? What will the soundtrack be? If you have some favorite music, ask if you can supply a tape or CD so it can be incorporated into your video.

Is the unedited master available for purchase? The videographer owns the copyright, although the subjects must give permission for the work to be released (unless you negotiate a "work for hire" agreement, which is usually expensive and unnecessary). Most videographers' contracts include a clause allowing them to pull segments for demo videos to show prospective clients.

How can we get extra copies? The copyright prohibits you from making copies. Explained Roy Chapman, publisher of *Wedding Videography Today*: "If copies are not made from the master and done properly, tapes are degraded and aren't a fair representation of the videographer's work. If you want copies, spell out the price in advance. Many videographers store the master and edited version under optimum conditions and charge for copies."

Questions to Ask References

When calling references for photographers or videographers, here are some questions you might want to ask:

How did you find him? If they're related or friends, then call another reference.

Was the photographer or videographer unobtrusive? Was she professional in behavior? How was she dressed? How did she relate to you and your guests?

Did the final product fulfill your expectations? Do you feel it captured the emotions and all the special moments? Was it of the quality you expected? How promptly was it delivered? Were there any unexpected fees on the final invoice?

Is there anything you would have done differently or any advice you would give us about working with this person?

Choosing a Photographer

What makes one photographer a better choice for you than another? First, good technical ability should be a given. Look to see that the photos are clear and not too exposed or too dark.

✻✻ WEDDING TIPS ✻✻
Spell It Out

Once you've selected a photographer and/or videographer, everything should be detailed in writing. Include the name of the photographer or videographer, not just the studio. Indicate the precise hours they'll work, overtime charges, and all the details you agree on.

Second, photographers have different styles. Classic wedding photography creates portrait-style, posed shots with soft romantic lighting; avant-garde wedding photographers take a more candid, photojournalistic approach; and some photographers combine the two styles. There is no right or wrong. Look at albums of friends and families to see which style appeals to you. Then, look at a prospective photographer's work to see if it is in line with the style you prefer and ask about his or her philosophy of wedding photography.

Ask to see complete coverage of a single wedding, and if you can, call the person whose wedding you saw as a reference. (Unscrupulous photographers have been known to send out samples that are not their own. This is a good way to discover them.) Decide if you like the way the photographer captured the event. Does it reveal the emotions? Were all the important pictures taken? If you like a photographer's work, then you'll probably want to speak with him or her in further detail.

Planning the Photos Ahead of Time

Some couples draw up a detailed shot list; most leave it to the photographer. Your photographer probably has shot hundreds of weddings and will have a basic list in mind. He or she may also know your wedding site very well and be able to suggest some beautiful settings for posed shots. However, you'll probably want to discuss the types of shots that will be taken—and where and when—so you can have some input.

"Let the photographer know if the bride doesn't want the groom to see her before the ceremony, so he can plan accordingly," said photographer Monte Zucker of Monte, Clay and Associates in Silver Spring, Maryland. "If you're having more than a handful of guests, it's a good idea to make a list of special people and appoint a bridesmaid or usher to point them out to the photographer. It's also important to anticipate things like whether your divorced parents should be in the same photograph or shot separately with their spouse. And you and your photographer should agree on a time schedule. The biggest mistake couples make is not allowing time for the photography. They think everything will just happen. If you want classic images, ask your photographer how much time he'll need before and after the ceremony to create the kind of images you want. You'll probably need to allow a few hours."

Videography

"We got married by ourselves on a beach; the video was meant to share our ceremony with our families," said Corinne. "But the videographer did much more than film our ceremony. He spent a few hours with us the day before the wedding shooting us doing things around the resort and talking to each other. Now, whenever we feel ourselves drifting apart, we pull out our wedding video, and like magic, we remember why we got married," said Corinne. "It's like watching a love story about ourselves! Every time I listen to Gavin explain how he first knew I was the one for him, I get tears in my eyes."

Luke, on the other hand, says watching his wedding video makes him seasick. "My friend offered to shoot it as a wedding gift, so we said 'Sure.' But it looks like it was shot during an earthquake—and worse, you can't hear what anyone is saying."

Videos, like photographs, come in a wide range of styles and quality. Some videographers provide you with an edited version of your ceremony mixed with some stock footage of the destination. Others spend hours filming you and then create an edited chronology that might begin with childhood photos. Some take a romantic tone; others inject humor, perhaps interspersing shots of celebrities who appear to be talking with your guests. Some videographers use a lot of special effects; others feel these can be distracting from this very personal celebration and will make the video seem dated when you watch it in the years to come.

Choosing a Videographer

Some wedding packages include videography; if so, don't assume that you can't have a more elaborate video than what's provided. Find out exactly what you'll be getting. If you want something different, you may find that the videographer can accommodate your wishes for an additional fee, or you may be able to use a different videographer.

This section will give you an idea of what's available; when interviewing and checking references, it will help to have some sense of what style you like. As with a photographer, try to see a full wedding video (not just a sampling of clips) and speak with references before engaging anyone's services.

❧❧ *WEDDING FACTS* ❧❧
What It Costs

The average couple spends about $1,100 on photography and about $480 on videography.

Source: Modern Bride Research

Whatever the style, the video should demonstrate certain basic skills. Says Roy Chapman, "Most people watch enough television to know intuitively when a video is good." Basically, it comes down to three things:

1. Look for good camera work. Images should be steady (not jumping around), clear, and in focus. Careful composition should include close-ups, medium shots, and long shots. Subjects should be well framed—not cut off at the forehead or feet.
2. Listen for the sound quality. You should be able to clearly hear the couple exchanging their vows, as well as the officiant's and other readers' words and the music. If the sound is uneven, there is a problem; probably, mikes weren't used on all the important sound sources. Look to see that the audio is coordinated with the visuals.
3. Watch for skillful editing. The video should capture and hold your interest. If long segments are boring, then the video hasn't been edited well. Also watch for special effects and see if they are used well or are an unwelcome distraction.

Here are some of the options you may hear videographers offer:

Multicamera coverage: Many videographers focus one camera on the couple taking their vows, a second on the minister, and a third to catch the ambience of the setting and guests' reactions. If you're having a large wedding, this could be a good option.

Remote-controlled cameras: Some religious settings don't allow a videographer on or near the altar but will permit an unmanned camera, which may even be camouflaged with flowers. Remote controls allow a videographer to control the camera movements from a distance.

Studio editing: There are three basic kinds of editing. The best videographers use *studio editing,* which means they bring their tapes back to the studio to edit after the event. *In-camera* editing, where the video is "edited" as it is shot by rewinding over boring spots, and *live switching,* using several cameras and switching between them as the footage is being shot, leave little room for creative organization of the images or special effects.

Creative editing techniques: New options are popping up all the time. By shooting people in front of a "blue screen," anything can be added as a background. Or stock footage of famous people can be dropped in so they appear to be attending your wedding and mixing with you and your guests.

Many videographers also use multi-image screens. For example, they might film the bride and groom afterwards talking about the wedding and then fly their image into a small corner of screen as narrators. Or multiple images might show different people's reactions to the same event on a single screen. Dissolve shots, where one image melts into the next, can be used to add a romantic feeling.

Some videographers will also add personalized messages at the beginning or end of your video. Some couples send out thank-you videos—eight-minute highlight tapes with a message such as "Thanks for being a part of our special day" for each member of the wedding party.

Planning the Video Ahead of Time

If you are using a videographer suggested by your hotel, chances are that the person will know the possible wedding locales very well. "Take advantage of that knowledge and consult your videographer before selecting a site," suggested Russell Polack, general manager of Aqua Sun Videos in Jamaica, a company that creates more than three thousand wedding videos a year for couples at Sandals and other area resorts. "If you know you want a sunset wedding with the ocean in the background, we know where to shoot it so the light and setting will be just right."

Bring any background music and photographs that you would like incorporated into the video, he added. These might include childhood shots, pictures from an engagement party, and any other special moments you'd like to have included.

Consult with your videographer in advance about available enhancements such as special effects, extra copies, and personalized editions, he suggested. "We often shoot couples having dinner or breakfast in bed, on a sunset cruise, and enjoying other activities around the resort and add them to the wedding video."

If possible, view the video before you depart. "We turn our videos out in twenty-four hours so clients can view them before they leave. That way, we'll know you're happy and can correct any problems."

Take care of the video. Make sure the tab is pulled to prevent erasure and carry it through security; X rays sometimes damage videos, he cautioned.

If you're getting married overseas, be sure that the video will be provided in the right format. North America uses NTSC systems; Europe uses PAL, noted Polack.

The next chapter will give you some ideas of how you can share your wedding with friends and family once you've returned home.

Personalizing Your Video

Cannon Video Productions, run by John Goolsby, has been producing wedding videos since 1986. Here are some of the ways this award-winning wedding videographer creates his "love stories."

1. Go behind the scenes. "I often shoot the bride in curlers, the groom picking up his tux. Then, they get to see each other's excitement building. I also like to capture informal moments such as the rehearsal, when people are clowning around."

2. Share the past. "Before the wedding, we sit in a pretty spot, and I have them hold up pictures and tell each other about their childhood. Later, I scan the pictures in and overlay their voices."

3. Relive your courtship. "I film each one separately asking: What first attracted you to him or her? When did you first realize you were in love? What do you like most about him or her?"

4. Make a family keepsake. "I interview family and friends, get their names, relationship, and then have them tell stories about the bride or groom. If it's a grandparent or parent, I might ask them about their courtship and wedding."

5. Include the honeymoon. "I interview the couple talking about their honeymoon and combine that with shots of them on location."

6. Use meaningful music. "You can either use music indicative of the locale or favorite pieces."

7. Run credits at the end. "Some couples offer messages to relatives who helped a lot or as a tribute to a parent who passed away. Others tack on separate messages at the beginning or end for special people and send them a video in a keepsake box."

CHAPTER 21

After-the-Wedding Celebrations

Sue and Frank flew off to the Caribbean for a private wedding, but they also wanted to share the event with friends and family later. "We planned a 'beach party' for a month after we returned so we could have our photos ready to show. We rented a large pool, hired a reggae band, and served barbecued chicken and ribs. With snow piled high and temperatures well below freezing outside, it was great fun! One of my friends said it was the best wedding he'd ever had the pleasure of not attending," said Frank.

Alvin and Charmaine had a formal reception at a local hotel when they returned from their underwater wedding. "Scuba diving is our passion. When I read about a place in the Florida Keys that does underwater weddings, I knew that was how we had to get married. But Charmaine wanted a 'real' wedding reception. Our solution: we flew down for our underwater ceremony, honeymooned on a live-aboard dive boat in the Bahamas, then had our reception back home," said Alvin. "We had our wedding video playing on a continuous loop so everyone could see our ceremony. Not the traditional order of things, but everyone loved it."

When Kelly and Erin returned from their wedding in Austria, they had three wedding parties. "Each of our parents hosted a small family gathering when we came to visit, and our best friends surprised us with a small welcome-home party," said Erin. "We had thought about having some kind of reception but hadn't made any plans. We were totally surprised and really touched by all the parties. Our wedding was like a fairy tale come true; celebrating with our friends and families afterwards really meant a lot to us."

After a destination wedding, most couples want to have some kind of celebrations with friends and family. Some, like Alvin and Charmaine, want a true wedding reception, complete with a wedding cake and formal wedding attire. Others, like Sue and Frank, prefer a more informal celebration. And like Kelly and Erin, many couples with geographically scattered families and friends decide to host—or are lucky enough to be treated to—a series of small gatherings.

✨ *WEDDING TIPS* ✨
Sharing Your Wedding

Show photos or a video to share your wedding ceremony with guests at an after-the-wedding celebration.

Choose Your Style

Planning an after-the-wedding celebration requires the same basic decisions as planning a traditional wedding reception—or any party. Here are some questions to discuss with each other before you begin planning:

1. Do you want a formal or informal celebration? Your options range from a traditional wedding reception, minus the ceremony, to a casual get-together at your home. You could dress in your formal wedding attire (who says you only wear a wedding gown once!) or, like Sue and Frank, wear bathing suits.
2. Who will you invite? Decide how big a party you want and then create your guest list accordingly. (See chapter 15.)
3. Where will you hold the party? If friends and family are scattered or an unpleasant divorce between parents makes it difficult for you to invite everyone to a single gathering, you may want to consider having several separate get-togethers. You might ask each of your parents to invite close relatives over to meet your new spouse. Or you might decide to celebrate with a few close friends and relatives at a favorite restaurant.
4. Do you want to have a theme? Some couples plan receptions that mirror their wedding sites, tying in decor, music, and even food.

Once you've decided on the type of celebration you want, read chapter 16 for planning tips. You'll find additional helpful information in the book *Wedding Celebrations* by Cele Goldsmith Lalli and Stephanie H. Dahl. (See Appendix A.)

Wedding Announcements

Even if you don't have a reception or party, you may want to send wedding announcements to professional associates, relatives, and friends to let them know you are married and, perhaps, have a new address. Some couples hesitate to send announcements, fearing recipients will resent being asked for gifts; announcements are not requests for gifts, however, and the recipients should not feel any obligation to send one.

You can order wedding announcements from the same sources as wedding invitations. Announcements are worded similarly to wedding invitations, except you'll substitute "have the pleasure to announce" for "requests the pleasure of your company."

You may also want to enclose "at home" cards to let friends and associates know your new address. If you are taking your husband's name, the wording should be

After the first of May
10 Park Avenue
Fort Lee, New Jersey 07631

If you intend to keep your name, the wording should be

After the first of May
Alyce Raines Stephens
and
Thomas Donald Dillon
will reside at
10 Park Avenue
Fort Lee, New Jersey 07631

Gifts and Registries

Although people are not expected to give you wedding gifts unless they are invited to your ceremony and reception, many people probably will, so it's a good idea to sign up at the bridal registry of your favorite stores. There's no charge to register, and you'll be more likely to get gifts you really want.

Your choices will be recorded in a computer and updated as purchases are made. Register for items in a wide range of prices so people can select gifts that fit their budget.

How will guests know where you're registered? Many will ask you, your parents, or your best friends for gift suggestions; the registry is a good answer.

CHAPTER 22

Renewing Your Vows

*W*hat could be more romantic than a wedding? For many married couples, it's reaffirming their commitment to each other with a formal exchange of vows in an exotic location.

In fact, romance was exactly the reason why Juliane and Roland decided to renew their vows. While on their honeymoon in the U.S. Virgin Islands, they saw a wedding in a small chapel overlooking the sea. "It was so beautiful that we wished we could get married all over again," said Juliane. Five years later, they decided to do just that—right there—in a private ceremony. "I'm really glad our first wedding included everyone important to us, and I think it was right that we exchanged our vows publicly. But this time, we really wanted to focus on the feelings we have for each other," she said.

Pete and Marie, on the other hand, viewed their vow renewal as the symbol of a new start. They had been married for almost eighteen years. Over the years, they had grown apart and almost divorced. But after a year of counseling, they felt they understood and loved each other even more than when they had first married. Pete was looking for a way to symbolize a new era in their lives. They had planned a beach vacation, and in the brochures, he read about a vow renewal package. "Perfect!" he decided, and "proposed" to Marie with a diamond neck-lace. She agreed, and they had a private ceremony by the beach.

Overcoming a serious crisis or illness often brings a desire to celebrate. For Stella and Jesus, a car accident made them realize how fragile life can be. "When I got out of the hospital, we wanted to celebrate being together again," said Jesus. "Our eighth anniversary was approaching, so it seemed like a good time to renew our vows."

A reaffirmation may also be the chance to have the big wedding party you couldn't afford when you first got married or the church wedding you never had. Perhaps you want to commemorate a landmark event such as an important anniversary.

Ellen and Aaron, who worked in their family business, knew their parents' fiftieth wedding anniversary was coming just around the time that they all would be attending an industry conference in Maui. Many of their parents' business friends would be there as well. "Our parents had never had a true wedding; they'd gotten married at city hall. We decided to surprise them with an anniversary party that would be the wedding they never had," said Aaron. "We told them we were taking them out for a fancy dinner and to dress up. Ellen went shopping with Mom and persuaded her to buy a gorgeous white dress. And in addition to their industry friends, we secretly invited several couples who are their very close friends, and we arranged for a minister to perform the ceremony. Somehow we were able to keep it a secret. It took a lot of effort to pull it all together, but it was worth it all, just to see their faces when they realized what was happening!"

Legalities Aside

Renewing your vows away from home is as romantic as a destination wedding—with one important advantage: in a vow renewal ceremony, you are not bound to comply with the legalities of a true wedding.

This gives you the freedom to renew your vows in countries such as France, Aruba, and Tahiti, where it would be almost impossible to get married.

All constraints are off, too, when it comes to the actual ceremony. You can write your own vows and even recite them yourselves with no officiant. Or a respected family member or close friend can do the honors.

Although most religions have no formal ceremony, many priests, rabbis, ministers, and other clergy have created special ceremonies for couples who wish to renew their vows. If you opt for a religious ceremony, your clergy may bless your rings—either your original wedding bands or new anniversary rings—or some other symbol you wish to exchange.

If you're exchanging your own vows, you may want to exchange new rings or perhaps some other symbolic items. Some couples have exchanged necklaces or watches; others feel no physical symbols are needed. (If you'd like ideas on ways to include your children in the ceremony, turn to chapter 19.)

Formal Affairs

A vow renewal ceremony can be a small personal commemoration or quite formal. Men often wear a tuxedo, and women may wear a gown, carry flowers, and even wear a hat or headpiece with a small veil.

You can set the tone for your guests with your printed invitations. For a formal ceremony, the wording might be

The honour of your presence
(if a religious ceremony)

or

The pleasure of your company
is requested at the reaffirmation of the
wedding vows of

Mr. and Mrs. John Smith
on Saturday the eighteenth of November
at six o'clock
at Hotel ABC
Sunny Spot, USA
Reception immediately following the ceremony

R.S.V.P.   *Black Tie*

Private Ceremonies, Public Celebrations

As with destination weddings, some couples may opt to renew their vows privately, perhaps in an exotic locale, and then have a reaffirmation party . . . either with friends who fly to join them or when they return home.

Guests are not expected to bring gifts, but many will. Some couples request that guests make donations to a favorite charity rather than bring gifts.

Sharing Memories

For many couples, a vow renewal, like a wedding, symbolizes more than their commitment to each other; it also reaffirms their place as a couple in their community and is a chance to recognize some people for the important parts they've played in the couple's happiness. The following are some ways you can let your honored guests know they are a special part of your celebration:

- Invite them to participate in the ceremony itself through readings.
- Acknowledge the importance of your friends and family within the context of your ceremony.
- Display your wedding album and guest book. This is especially fun if many of your guests attended your wedding.
- Create a video/photographic presentation of major events in your lives over the years, including photos of as many people present as possible.
- Plan a party with a nostalgic theme. Dress in "period" clothing; play music that was popular when you got married, and have a first dance to "your song."

You'll find the information on destination weddings helpful in planning a vow renewal trip (see chapters 14–20). When you're ready to select a location, turn to the next section for profiles of the most popular places for destination weddings, honeymoons, and vow renewals.

PART THREE

The Top Honeymoon Destinations

A Snapshot View

A Sense of Place

"Every place sounds so wonderful," I am often asked, "how does anyone ever chose a place to honeymoon?" In fact, for most engaged couples, the hardest part of planning a honeymoon is narrowing down the choices and picking just one destination. Once you've decided where you want to go, the rest of the decisions seem to fall into place.

The purpose of this section of the book is to help you sift through the multitude of destinations that vie for your attention by giving you a feeling for some of the most popular honeymoon destinations—what you can do there as well as the types of accommodations, transportation, and restaurants you can expect to find.

But the destinations covered here are by no means a comprehensive look at the world of honeymoon settings—they are just the most frequently visited. Want a less traditional wedding trip? Perhaps your honeymoon might be a good time for a trip to Israel, where you might combine your sight-seeing with some R&R at a Dead Sea resort. Or maybe your dream is to cruise along the Nile and see the pyramids. Or how about a wildlife safari? Kenya and South Africa both have excellent facilities. You may want to visit the Taj Mahal in India or discover a world untouched by "modern civilization" in Papua, New Guinea. Closer to home, in Central America, think about a jungle trek in Costa Rica or in Belize, where the scuba diving is world class.

And don't forget the treasures of the Far East. You can cruise through China, exploring while enjoying the comforts of your ship. Hong Kong and Singapore combine exotic settings with excellent shopping opportunities and some of the world's best hotels. In Thailand, you can hide away at an exclusive seaside resort and then brave the fascinating bustle of Bangkok. On Indonesia's tropical island of Bali, luxurious beach resorts are a short drive from traditional mountain villages and stunning temples. For secluded beaches, head for Langkawi, a group of ninety-nine islands off the coast of Malaysia. Take a luxurious two-day Eastern & Oriental Express journey across Malaysia, sampling regional customs and cuisine. A few intrepid couples—with more time than most of us can muster—have even used their honeymoons as an opportunity to circle the globe.

Whole guidebooks have been written about each of the destinations described here, so it is beyond the scope of this book to try to provide you with complete information about any one destination. The descriptions are designed to give you enough of a sense of each destination to know whether it is a place you would like to honeymoon. Once you've chosen a place, you'll want to send for more information and, perhaps, pick up a guidebook or two. The tourist offices, excellent sources of information, are listed in Appendix B.

If you haven't already done so, you may want to start by reading the first chapter of this book and completing the exercise entitled "Finding Your Honeymoon Style." As you get into the details of setting up your trip, the first section of the book is there for you to refer to as needed. Happy planning!

CHAPTER 23

The Caribbean, the Bahamas, and Bermuda

Silky sand beaches lapped by warm, turquoise seas, an underwater world where flamboyantly garbed fish parade through vibrant coral gardens, water sports at your doorstep and rum punches on your terrace . . . all basking in tropical sunshine fanned by refreshing trade winds . . . no wonder the Caribbean is the premier honeymoon spot for American couples.

But deciding to honeymoon in the Caribbean is only the first in a chain of decisions. Next you need to pick an island, and each has its own enchanting blend of languages, culture, ambience, scenery, and facilities. There are jungle-cloaked isles ringed with mountain-rimmed coves and flat sand atolls with deserted strands that stretch for miles; cosmopolitan cities where the nightlife continues until dawn, and areas that seem lifted right out of Europe. And there are whole islands where the only footprints will be your own. Your choice of accommodations is equally varied: from simple guesthouses to elegant villas to lavish resorts abounding in sports, dining, and nightlife options. We'll start with some general notes, then provide an overview of the most popular and romantic islands of the Caribbean as well as of the Bahamas and Bermuda, arranged alphabetically.

Sports: Coral reefs encircle many of the islands, to the delight of divers and snorkelers. Most island resorts also offer sailing, windsurfing, waterskiing, kayaking, deep-sea fishing, and tennis. On some islands, you'll find championship golf courses and horseback riding.

Memories to Go: On most islands, you'll find woven baskets and hats and funny tee shirts. Islands such as Jamaica and St. Lucia also fashion resortwear from local batiks and silk-screened fabrics. Mahogany furniture, pewter, pottery, wood carvings, and paintings as well as wooden salad bowls and embroidered napkins are among the other craft items you may find on some islands. In the markets, be prepared to negotiate. Many islands offer duty-free shopping on imports.

Cuisine: Each island has its own special foods. On the lusher islands such as Grenada, Jamaica, St. Lucia, Trinidad, and Tobago, you'll probably find more varieties of fruit, vegetables, and spices than you've ever heard of. Island chefs combine them in surprisingly delicious combinations. For example, in Jamaica try jerk pork or chicken, heavily spiced and barbecue-smoked over pimiento wood, usually served with rice and peas (pinto beans). In the Bahamas, conch or grouper "fingers" are served with peas 'n' rice. Fried plantain, callaloo (a leafy, spinachlike veggie), fish and fungi (cornmeal and okra), and pepperpot (stew) are other typical dishes in the region. Most of the islands offer continental cuisines as well as unique nouveau cuisines that make creative use of local produce.

In Puerto Rico, you'll taste the Spanish influence in dishes such as asopao (rice with chicken or shellfish prepared as a hearty soup) and empanadillas (crescent-shaped turnovers filled with lobster, crab, conch, or other items).

In the French West Indies, gourmet French cuisine is easy to find, while the Dutch West Indies reflect their diverse heritage in dishes such as rijsttafel, a multicourse Indonesian feast; keshi yena (cheese stuffed with chicken and herbs); and sopito (fish soup). Most of the more developed islands also have the major fast-food chains represented.

Lodgings for Lovers: This region has a wide range of accommodations options. You'll find resorts that cater to the super-rich—some on private islands—and villas that come complete with maid, chef, and chauffeur. There are also condominiums and cozy cottages, grand convention/vacation hotels as well as posh intimate inns and simple guest houses with no air-conditioning or television that may charge as little as $25 a night. All-inclusive resorts come in a vast array of styles and price ranges, from action oriented to elegant.

Climate and Clothing: Year-round temperatures generally average between 75 and 80 degrees—and about 5 degrees cooler in the mountains—except in Bermuda, where winters are springlike. Costal areas are generally drier than the mountains. Rainfall varies by island but generally comes in short spurts during the rainier months: May, June, September, and October. You won't need dressy clothes unless you dine at the more formal resorts.

Getting Around: Many resorts have vans to meet you at the airport. Taxis on most islands are readily available and reasonably priced: however, on many islands, it's a good idea to agree on the fare in advance with your driver. If you plan to rent a car, keep in mind that on some islands driving is British-style, on the left, and that the mountain roads can be scary.

Formalities: On most of the islands, U.S. and Canadian residents don't need passports, but must show proof of citizenship: a birth certificate, voter's registration card, or driver's license with photo.

ANGUILLA

This sliver of an island, sixteen miles long and three miles wide, began attracting well-heeled vacationers just over a decade ago, when the first small luxury hotels were built. Now, the island boasts some of the most expensive, laid-back, and luxurious hotels in the Caribbean—with fine food to match. You'll also find a few moderately priced properties, but so far, no big chain hotels. In addition to the hotels, the draw is the island's beautiful white-sand beaches, and reef-protected waters, which are ideal for snorkeling. As you'd expect, water sports of all sorts are available here. Many hotels also have tennis courts, and some have gym facilities.

It doesn't take long to feel like you're in the know on this island; just head over to Johnno's beachside bar, where you can listen to music and learn the latest gossip. For local artwork, stop at the Devonish-Cotton Gin Art Gallery, which features the work of Courtney Devonish and other artists. When you're ready for "civilization," hop on a ferry to Marigot on St. Martin, less than twenty minutes away.

Especially for Lovers

- Take a boat to Sandy Island, a palm tree–shaded isle across from Sandy Ground, where you can snorkel and enjoy secluded strands. Or head out to one of the other islands or explore one of the seven underwater wrecks.
- Watch the fishermen pull their colorful, handhewn skiffs ashore at Island Harbour and then wave down the launch from Scilly Cay, a private island where you can swim, snorkel, or sip rum punches while your lunch—lobster, crayfish, and chicken—is grilled to order.

ANTIGUA

No high-rise hotels, no bustling cities, little nightlife to speak of . . . that's why many honeymooners are drawn to Antigua. What this island does have is great beaches (365 of them, boasts tourism literature) and clubby resorts with plenty of water sports and unobtrusive service that have attracted many families for generations. Join the yachting scene at Nelson's Dockyard, headquarters for British admiral Horatio Nelson in the eighteenth century. Here you can admire the yachts and poke around the dockyard's restored buildings, which serve as shops, museums, and restaurants. For a true getaway, take a day trip to Antigua's tranquil sister island, Barbuda, and visit the Frigate Bird Sanctuary.

Especially for Lovers

- For a great party, spend Sunday afternoon dining and dancing to live steel band music while enjoying stunning views of English Harbour at the Lookout Restaurant on Shirley Heights.
- When you're in a sociable mood, lively Dickinson Bay is the beach to be at, filled with vendors, beach bars, and sunbathers.

ARUBA

On this island, you could be busy day and night. Miles of dreamy white-sand beaches line the west coast, complemented by a string of lively resorts with casinos, showrooms, and nightclubs. Almost every water sport imaginable is available along the beaches. Underwater visibility ranges up to one hundred feet, and several sunken freighters keep divers interested. There's also golf, tennis, and horseback riding through the countryside and along the beach. Shoppers enjoy browsing through the pastel-colored Dutch capital of Orangestad. High-rise hotels line up along Palm Beach; toward town, beaches sport more laid-back, low-rise hotels. North of Palm Beach, strong tradewinds make for world-class windsurfing conditions. For secluded coves and large stretches of solitary desert, head for the east side of the island.

Part of the Kingdom of the Netherlands, Aruba is one of the more developed and prosperous Caribbean islands, and its people are known for their genuine hospitality. Although the official language is Dutch, almost everyone also speaks English as well as Spanish and Papiamento, a blend of Spanish, Dutch, and Arawak Indian.

Especially for Lovers

- Take a Jeep safari into the Cunuco (countryside) through stark hills dotted with cacti, wind-bent divi-divi trees, and immense boulders.
- Spend an evening at the opulent Alhambra Casino and Bazaar, where you can spend your winnings in the charming back alleys of the Bazaar and catch a revue at the Aladdin Theatre.
- Check out the Bonbini Festival, which takes place 6:30 P.M. every Tuesday evening at the courtyard in Fort Zoutman. You'll hear traditional Aruban music, see colorful dancing, and taste island cuisine.

THE BAHAMAS

Water so clear that you can see coral and fish as though through air. Sugary white- and pink-sand beaches . . . more than seven hundred islands and islets full of them. Do you want your beaches in combination with gambling, nightlife, and duty-free shopping? Head for New Providence Island, home to the capital city of Nassau and the resorts of Cable Beach and Paradise Island, or Grand Bahama Island, home to Freeport and Lucaya. More laid-back resorts and rustic beachside inns await on the friendly Out Islands. Each of these islands has its own special attractions. Some are known for their sport fishing and others, for diving; some have full-service resorts complete with golf and tennis, while others are pure hideaways with little organized activity and just a few tiny inns or guesthouses for accommodations.

Especially for Lovers

Nassau

- Take a horse-drawn carriage tour through the historic downtown area, with its pastel-painted Georgian buildings.

- Stroll through the Versailles Gardens, and the authentic fourteenth-century French Cloisters, reassembled stone by stone, at the Ocean Club on Paradise Island.
- Tango with Lady Luck in the casinos at the Atlantis Paradise Island or the Nassau Marriott Resort on Cable Beach; then catch one of their flamboyant shows.

Freeport/Lucaya

- Swim with trained dolphins at the world-class Underwater Explorers Society, where you can also join scuba and snorkel expeditions. Unique to Grand Bahama Island, the program allows the dolphins to come and go as they please.
- Create your own scent at the Perfume Factory at Freeport's International Bazaar and then shop for duty-free imports there and at the Port Lucaya Marketplace, where you'll be entertained with music and dancing.
- Catch one of the colorful Bahamian shows with fire-eating goombay dancers and junkanoo drummers at one of the hotels and then try your luck at a casino.

The Out Islands

- Sightsee underwater. Dive through the Thunderball Grotto, near Staniel Cay in the Exumas, the site for underwater excitement in the film *Thunderball,* starring Sean Connery. Near Marsh Harbour in the Abacos, meet Pickles, a six-foot moray eel who likes to play with divers. Experienced divers can explore Andros's Great Barrier Reef, the third largest in the world.
- Sail out from Marsh Harbour to island-hop through the Abacos, one of the world's great sailing destinations. Or rent one of the Green Turtle Club's motorboats, provisioned with picnic fixings, and find yourselves a deserted cay for the day.
- Follow in Ernest Hemingway's wake and battle for marlin and other big game in Bimini. Then swap fishing tales and look at Hemingway memorabilia at the Compleat Angler Hotel bar, one of the writer's favorite hangouts.

BARBADOS

Snap a photo by the statue of Lord Nelson in Trafalgar Square. Make friends at a polo game or cricket match. Enjoy afternoon tea or go for a drive—staying on the left side of the road, of course—along the rocky hills of the "Scotland District." This prosperous, small (twenty-one by fourteen miles) island, sometimes referred to as Little England, packs in a bevy of British-toned pleasures. From the powerful swells that pound the cliffs of the Atlantic coast to the east to the gentle Caribbean that laps pink-tinged sands on the west coast, you can swim and snorkel in azure seas, play tennis and golf, and enjoy all the water sports you can think of. Divers can explore a number of shipwrecks—about two hundred surround the island, many sunk by pirates in the sixteenth and seventeenth centuries. The Berwyn, with its shallow end in just eight feet of water, is ideal for snorkelers and divers alike. Or explore the depths on an Atlantis submarine trip.

Barbados is known for its gracious service and small, tony hotels that snuggle around lovely gardens and along palm-lined beaches. Many offer complimentary water sports and afternoon tea. "Rooms" are often separate cottages or suites; many properties feel more like intimate English country manor houses than hotels. There are also rental villas, apartments, and guesthouses priced as low as $20 a night. The island is also known for its haute cuisine; an annual culinary competition fosters high standards, and the island attracts top chefs from around the world.

Especially for Lovers

- Immerse yourselves in island lore and food at the twice-weekly pageant held Thursday and Sunday evenings at the Barbados Museum and experience the elegant side of colonial life in Barbados during a visit to the 300-year-old Sunbury Plantation House.
- Check *The Visitor* paper to see who's performing (try to catch Spice, a popular local band); then take an afternoon nap and get set for a rollicking late-night party. Habour Lights and After Dark are among the popular spots.

BERMUDA

Pastel-painted, white-topped homes, hibiscus-lined roads, pink-tinged sands, multihued waters, and rock-framed coves make Bermuda a photographer's dream. British-toned and proper, Bermuda is more formal than most of the region; men must wear a jacket and tie at many restaurants, and "proper attire" is required for tennis and golf. Bermuda also limits the number of cars on the island (one per family, none for rent) and cruise ships in its ports to maintain its tranquil, dignified ambience. Mopeds are the most popular mode of transportation, but taxis, ferries, and buses are also available.

With eight golf courses, Bermuda boasts more golf courses per square foot than anywhere in the world. You can play golf and tennis during the springlike winters as well as summer. Reef-sheltered Atlantic waters warmed by the Gulf Stream, plentiful tropical fish, and shallow areas create ideal conditions for scuba diving and snorkeling in summer. And year-round, shop for quality British and European imports, such as Irish and Scottish wool sweaters, china, and perfumes and Bermudian artwork.

Especially for Lovers

- Explore quaint St. George, the former capital. Photograph each other in the stockades, browse along the historic streets, and stop in St. Peter's Church, which boasts the longest continued use in the Western Hemisphere. Then head across the island to the Royal Naval Dockyard. Its historic stone buildings now house museums, boutiques, and the Bermuda Arts Centre, which exhibits works by Bermudian and foreign artists.

- Bicycle or hike along the Railway Trail, a traffic-free path on former railroad beds. On the East End, it borders the sea and passes by small coves that are ideal for a scenic break.

BONAIRE

Already acknowledged as one of the top scuba-diving destinations in the world, visitors are increasingly discovering Bonaire's allure above the water. Divers rave about the abundance and diversity of corals and fish. (All land and water from high tidemark to 200 feet deep has been set aside as an underwater preserve.) Nondivers enjoy Bonaire's relaxed ambience as well as sailing, waterskiing, windsurfing, kayaking, and wildlife watching. In addition to the island's five thousand resident flamingos, you can see parakeets, colorful iguanas, and 190 species of birds at Washington/Slagbaii National Park, a 13,300-acre wildlife sanctuary fringed by beautiful beaches. Kralendijk, the tiny capital, preserves its Dutch charm while offering local crafts and imported goods.

Especially for Lovers

- Take a boat over to Klein Bonaire, a small, uninhabited offshore island, where you'll enjoy empty beaches and fantastic underwater sights.

BRITISH VIRGIN ISLANDS

True escapists rave about this cluster of about fifty islands—only sixteen of which are inhabited. They're ideal for those who want to discover private white-sand beaches backed by steep green hills, where the nightlife is low-key, television and radio are oddities, sailing is the best way to get around, and the snorkeling and diving are superb. Although they are a bit less accessible than some islands, you'll find some of the Caribbean's toniest resorts here, including several private-isle resorts.

Especially for Lovers

- Charter a sailboat—with crew, of course—and go island-hopping at your own pace, while the crew takes care of the logistics.

CAYMAN ISLANDS

Most people remember the Cayman Islands from their starring role as a tax haven in the movie *The Firm,* but this trio of islands—Grand Cayman, Little

Cayman, and Cayman Brac—has long been on the wish list of divers. Most honeymooners stay in Grand Cayman, the most developed of the three. Grand Cayman is the top of a huge sunken mountain and offers some of the best wall dives around. At Stingray City, divers and snorkelers can frolic with the rays. Beach lovers rave about Seven-Mile Beach, which offers a number of hotels and condominiums. Across the road, the Hyatt Regency Grand Cayman boasts a Jack Nicklaus–designed golf course, tennis, and fine water sports facilities. More verdant Cayman Brac, named for its limestone cliffs (*brac* is Gaelic for "bluff") is just twelve miles long and has two laid-back beach resorts as well as condominiums. Little Cayman, even smaller, has several small properties.

Especially for Lovers

- Get close-up views 150 feet deep without getting wet on an Atlantis submarine trip. Underwater weddings can also be arranged. You can dive and your guests can watch, or you all can stay dry together.

CURAÇAO

If you're looking for a beach resort island with lots of shopping and sight-seeing, Curaçao could be for you. Its varied cultural background is reflected in its people, architecture, cuisine, and shops, which carry items from around world, generally at prices well below list. The Dutch architecture is most striking in Willemstad, the capital. Here, narrow-gabled townhouses that seem lifted right out of Amsterdam have adapted to the Caribbean with pastel colors. Many of the old Dutch fortresses and plantation homes are open to the public; several have been converted into restaurants and guest houses. Curaçao also boasts the oldest continuously used synagogue in the Western Hemisphere. You also can hike or drive through a large wildlife preserve and snorkel and dive through coral reefs and shipwrecks.

Especially for Lovers

- Drive to the north side of the island, where you can discover secluded cove beaches backed by steep cliffs.

DOMINICA

With little nightlife and few beaches, organized sports, or fancy hotels, Dominica is as far off the beaten track as you can get. This island appeals mainly to those who want to hike through tropical rain forests filled with unique species, swim in freshwater lakes, commune with nature, and become immersed in local culture. Temperatures range from 70 to 90 degrees along the shore but can be in the mid-50s in the mountains. Rainfall is frequent, especially in the mountains, even during the February-through-July "dry" season.

Dominican Republic

Fun-loving and hospitable, this island is home to the merengue and some of the lowest-priced resort vacations in the Caribbean. Santo Domingo, the capital and first permanent European settlement in the New World, has superb Spanish architecture, while the resort areas of La Romana, Punta Cana, and Puerto Plata offer secluded strands as well as active and elegant resorts. In addition to water sports, you'll find some unusual activities: Club Med features circus training, Punta Cana Beach Resort offers horseback riding, and Casa de Campo offers polo and two eighteen-hole golf courses, designed by Pete Dye. And Altos de Chavon, a re-creation of a sixteenth-century European city near La Romana, is also an artists' colony.

Especially for Lovers

- Shop for amber and gold jewelry and handmade Dominican furniture and decorative items—great buys that make wonderful honeymoon souvenirs. Dust off your high-school Spanish; outside of the resorts, you'll want a few phrases for bargaining and getting around.

French West Indies

If you feel like you're in France as you sit in a café or brasserie, buy imported perfumes and fresh-baked croissants, and admire the chic fashions in the islands of the French West Indies, you've got good reason to. Except in St. Martin (page 129), English is not widely spoken. The islands are actually *départements* (states) of France, and their currency, language, food, and uninhibited topless sunbathing will keep reminding you that you're in France. Of course, there are differences: the glorious beaches and the African influence, evident in the local patois, music, and unique Creole cuisine.

Perhaps the most French of all is tiny St. Barthèlèmy (only eight square miles in area), better known as St. Barts. Most residents are blue-eyed, fair-skinned descendents of the first settlers, who came from Normandy and Brittany. In the village of Corossol, you'll still see women dressed in traditional white bonnets weaving straw hats and baskets, while the small port city of Gustavia brims with cafés, restaurants, and duty-free boutiques. A short hop from St. Martin, St. Barts maintains its reputation as a haunt for the rich and famous. Some of its small, often exclusive hotels are villas built into the lush hillsides or along its silky sands.

In pretty Martinique, villages, cities, and resort areas peek through verdant jungle like oases of luxury, while beaches shaded from volcanic gray to white rim the island. Lacy balconies reach across the narrow streets of Fort-de-France, shops sell elegant French imports, and a crafts market vends the works of local artisans. Fourteen rhumeries around the island create rum from the island's sugarcane; all offer tours and tastings. The liveliest hotels are around Pointe du Bout. Trois Ilets also has an eighteen-hole golf course designed by Robert Trent Jones, Sr.

Guadeloupe is actually two islands connected by a bridge. On volcanic Basse-Terre, you can climb still-steamy Soufrière. Grand Terre is smaller, flatter, and home to Point-à-Pitre, the busy main city, and Gosier, the resort center. Guadeloupe is also an easy starting point for visits to several unspoiled nearby French islands, including Les Saintes and Marie-Galante.

GRENADA

Quiet coves and sandy beaches surround this lush green island. Inland, mountains cultivated with nutmeg, cinnamon, clove, cashew nut, ginger, and other spices earn Grenada its nickname: the Spice Island. Hiking and water sports are favorite activities. Guided walks to Annandale or Concord Falls in the Grand Etang Preserve take you into Grenada's rain forest, where you may glimpse elusive monkeys and colorful birds before rewarding yourselves with a dip in the cool pools beneath the scenic falls. Grenada is also known for its small, reasonably-priced beachfront hideaways and personalized service. There's also an all-inclusive resort as well as rental villas and cottages.

JAMAICA

There are two Jamaicas for honeymooners these days: the all-inclusive resort enclaves where all that you could want is provided within the confines of the resort and the diverse sights and accommodations (including villas, complete with cook, maid, and chauffeur; exclusive deluxe hotels; and inexpensive guesthouses) of the Caribbean's third-largest island. Most hotels are clustered along the north shore: Montego Bay boasts an international airport and some of the most popular resorts. Two hours drive east, Ocho Rios's resorts and rental villas nestle into verdant mountainsides while at the west end of the island, Negril's long beach retains its flower-child ambience despite a handful of all-inclusive resorts.

Wherever you stay, be sure to dive, snorkel, or take a glass-bottom boat ride over coral reefs that lie a short distance from much of the shoreline. Some of the best of these surround Booby Cay, a small island off Negril named for the birds that breed here and that was a setting in the movie *Twenty Thousand Leagues under the Sea*. Few couples leave Jamaica without climbing Dunn's River Falls. It's not a place to commune with nature but still beautiful—and fun. Come early to beat the crowds.

Especially for Lovers

- Raft down a lazy river. Sit back on a bamboo raft for two as a raftsman poles you downstream, past farmers herding their flocks to the river to drink, children splashing around, women doing laundry along the shore, and other rafts selling cool drinks. Take the three-hour trip down the Rio Grande near Port

Antonio, or start out from Martha Brae's Rafters village or Mountain Valley rafting, near Montego Bay.

PUERTO RICO

This small (100 by 35 miles), sophisticated island offers honeymooners a surprising diversity of experiences. With its classy casinos, splashy high-rise resorts, Spanish Colonial district, and lively beaches, San Juan attracts the lion's share of visitors. Evenings come alive in a swirl of salsa rhythms, sunset cruises, sizzling clubs, and big-name entertainers, and you won't feel out of place in your dressiest cocktail attire. The cobblestoned streets of Old San Juan, a sixteenth-century walled city, are lined with shops, art galleries, sidewalk cafés, and night spots.

Yet head out of San Juan *en la isla,* as islanders say, and you'll find upscale, self-contained resorts, quaint inns, and Spanish-style villas as well as ancient Indian ritual sites, charming Spanish-flavored cities, and beaches where you can be totally alone. The island's interior, bisected by the Cordillera Central mountains, is dotted with small *paradores* (inns). Scuba diving and snorkeling are fabulous in Vieques, Culebra, Fajardo, La Parguera, and Aguadilla. Surfers praise the northwest coast. Golf, tennis, and water sports are available at many resorts.

Looking for souvenirs? A vibrant art community ensures that in addition to clever tee shirts and straw hats, you can find some real treasures: paintings, sculptures, and local handicrafts such as *santos* (carved wooden figures of saints), hammocks, masks, pottery, weavings, delicately worked lace, and string instruments as well as designer clothing.

As the airline hub of the Caribbean, Puerto Rico is the region's most accessible island. Spanish and English are both official languages.

Especially for Lovers

- Just thirty-five miles east of San Juan, the vast El Yunque is the only tropical rain forest in the U.S. National Forest system. Stop by the visitor center for information about hiking trails and flora and fauna. On the way back to San Juan, stop at popular Luquillo Beach and the nearby string of food kiosks.
- Vieques and Culebra, two small nearby islands accessible by plane from San Juan or by ferry from Fajardo, are known for secluded beaches, coral reefs, fresh seafood, and quiet ambience. If you go, don't miss a night ride through Vieques's Mosquito Bay to see the phosphorescent waters.

ST. KITTS AND NEVIS

A two-island member of the British Commonwealth, these islands are known for their tranquil, bucolic ambience. Wreathed in sugarcane plantations and tropical greenery, the islands' thirty hotels include ten gracious, small inns—many in converted plantation houses. On St. Kitts, the tourism action centers along the white-sand beach of Frigate Bay, where you'll find an all-inclusive resort, a casino, an eighteen-hole golf course, and plenty of water sports facilities. Tours through the interior rain forest offer the chance to see exotic vines, wild orchids, and other colorful flowers. Smaller and even sleepier, Nevis is ringed by pretty white-sand beaches and a new luxury resort, with a Robert Trent Jones II–designed eighteen-hole golf course, gourmet restaurants, and all the sports facilities you could want.

ST. LUCIA

St. Lucia—only fourteen by twenty-seven miles in area—has enjoyed a fame more in proportion to its beauty than its size. Tranquil coves with idyllic beaches ring the island, and lush vegetation cascades down the twin peaks of the landmark Pitons into the verdant rain forests of the interior, where tropical flowers seem to pop out of the deep green foliage. If you've seen *Superman II,* you may recognize this exotic setting: it was here, between the half-mile-high Pitons, that the hero picked the perfect flower for his love, Lois Lane. Considering its beauty, you might expect throngs of tourists, but aside from a few luxurious resorts, the island is still so pristine that people come from neighboring islands to "get away from it all."

There are officially 500 miles of roads, but only 281 miles are paved. Often you'll feel more like you're on a trail than a road. Driving is British style, on the left. Car rentals are available (you'll need to purchase a local license), but you may prefer to hire a taxi; drivers are usually trained guides who can share island lore as you go. Boats are another great way to tour the island. Chartered and party boats head out from the capital, Castries, to visit the picturesque village of Soufrière, stopping at a secluded beach en route. Don't miss a trip to the nearby smoldering volcanic crater of La Soufrière, nicknamed "the Drive-in Volcano," where you'll see pools of black-sulfur spring water and yellow-green steam vents. Then, follow the example of eighteenth-century French royalty and soak in the "curative" mineral waters (bring towels) at the adjacent Diamond Waterfall and mineral baths located on the Soufrière Estate.

Drop-offs, caves, wrecks, and coral reefs make diving here exciting. Many reefs are accessible from shore and shallow enough to be enjoyed by snorkelers. One of the best areas is just off Anse Chastanet. Golfers can tee off at two nine-hole golf courses: at Cap Estate and at La Toc.

Especially for Lovers

- On Friday night, don't miss the "Jump Up," a lively street festival held every week in Gros Islet, a village north of Castries. Here, locals and visitors dance in the streets and munch on spicy local foods.
- Bring your passport for duty-free shopping at the Pointe Seraphine Shopping Center at Castries Harbor. You'll find a wide selection of imported goods and local crafts. More local crafts await in town. In the hills around Castries, you'll

find three wonderful shops: the Caribelle Batik Factory, which creates fashionable batik clothing; Bagshaw's, which offers silk-screened fashions; and Eudovic's on Morne Fortune, which sells carvings from local woods.

ST. MARTIN/SINT MAARTEN

Cosmopolitan and chic, this island is shared by two countries. A small monument marks the border. St. Martin is part of France, and its capital, Marigot, is a great place to shop for French imports. Sint Maarten, which pledges allegiance to Queen Beatrice of the Netherlands, is a bit more developed. Philipsburg, the capital of Sint Maarten, has two main streets—Front Street, which is lined with duty-free shops, and Back Street, where you'll find more shops and budget restaurants. It's fun to travel around the island, stopping for lunch in a French restaurant, finding a pretty strand for water sports or tanning, or trying your luck at a casino on the Dutch side of the island.

It's also easy to connect to neighboring islands including Anguilla, St. Barts, St. Kitts, and Nevis (covered earlier) as well as tiny mountainous Saba, where the mountain continues underwater to the delight of divers, and tranquil St. Eustatius, where you can hike up the Quill (a volcano) or dive and explore the remains of two hundred or so sunken ships.

Divers have several wrecks to explore around St. Martin/Sint Maarten as well. There's also yachting, sailing, water skiing, jet skiing, windsurfing, parasailing, pedal boating, and a host of other water excitement. Accommodations range from exclusive, intimate hideaways to grand casino-resort complexes. Other options include rental apartments, villas, houses, and inexpensive guesthouses.

Among the liveliest Dutch-side beaches is Mullet Bay. Dawn Beach, guarded by two offshore reefs, is a good bet for snorkelers; Guana Beach, just down the road, attracts bodysurfers. Cupecoy, backed by rugged cliffs, is one of the prettiest, while Maho Beach, by the airport, has Sunday beach parties with live music. On the French side, the Ranch Bar on Grand Case beach hosts live music every Sunday. You can also tee off at Mullet Bay Resort's eighteen-hole golf course and play tennis at most of the major resorts.

Nearly everyone in Sint Maarten speaks English, although Dutch is the official language. In St. Martin, outside of the hotels, most people speak only French.

Especially for Lovers

- For fun à la française, settle in at a bistro at the Marina Port La Royale and watch the grand yachts pull in. Later, head for the bars along Grand Case Beach, which host live music every weekend.
- Nude sunbathing is acceptable at many beaches; topless, almost everywhere. Sunbathe au naturel at Baie Orientale, a beguiling beach, but save your swimming for elsewhere; there's a strong undertow. Plum Beach and Cupecoy also have areas where you'll want to apply allover sunscreen.

- Have an evening on the town. Start with a romantic dinner and catch a Caribbean revue. Then try your luck at one of the casinos. Still have some energy? At about 2 A.M., L'Horoscope at Simpson Bay is the place to be.

ST. VINCENT AND THE GRENADINES

Sailing; scuba diving; and secluded, unspoiled settings—that's what these islands have to offer. Forget schedules. Forget television. You'll probably fly into St. Vincent, the largest island, where you might decide to hike into a rain forest or up a recently active (1979), still-sulphurous volcano, but most honeymooners head right out to one of the smaller isles or charter a yacht to sail through the hundred-plus isles and uninhabited islets of the Grenadines. Several are single-resort isles that seem right out of a celebrity magazine. On Bequia, a favorite harbor with charming boutiques and cafés, the Frangipanai Hotel terrace is the gathering place for yachters and locals as well as hotel guests. Isolationists especially like Mustique, a favorite of royalty and rock stars, and Petite St. Vincent, with its surprising attention to luxurious details. Young Island, just a few minutes by boat from St. Vincent, and Palm Island are for those with a more sociable bent.

TRINIDAD AND TOBAGO

Tranquil Tobago is a true getaway island, where diving, snorkeling, and bird-watching are the main pursuits, although if you're interested, many locals are quite willing to share tidbits of their West African roots, which are quite strong here. Its sister island, Trinidad, bustles with the sounds of calypso and the multi-cultural city life of capital Port-of-Spain, while bird watchers flock to the Asa Wright Nature Center to see rare flora and fauna and the Caroni Bird Sanctuary, where a sunset boat trip will take you to watch hundreds of scarlet ibis return to roost in the mangrove trees.

TURKS AND CAICOS

The main excitement in these islands is found amid underwater reefs, walls, and pirate shipwrecks and the quiet joys of sailing off to a private isle and basking on a pristine white-sand beach shared only with some seabirds. Many of the best diving and snorkeling spots are within swimming distance of shore. Providenciales is the main island for visitors. With few exceptions, accommodations are in small guest houses, hotels, and villas.

U.S. VIRGIN ISLANDS

Its license plates proclaim it "An American Paradise," and the island trio that makes up this U.S. territory is truly both American and a paradise. English is the language, with an island lilt; dollars are the currency, and you'll find McDonald's and mainland efficiency along with dreamy beaches and crystalline waters. Steady, predictable sea breezes make these islands a haven for sailors as well as beach lovers. It's easy to charter a crewed yacht, complete with gourmet chef, and go exploring, and it costs less than you'd think.

Each island has its own personality. Lively St. Thomas is best known for the shopping in its bustling waterfront capital, Charlotte Amalie. On Lush St. Croix, the largest island, old sugar mills and plantation houses dot bucolic hillsides. And just a twenty-minute ferry ride from St. Thomas, the pristine island of St. John has set aside two-thirds of its land as a national park. Frequent scheduled flights connect St. Thomas and St. Croix, too. Car and jeep rentals, taxis (with set, posted rates that vary with the number of people), and organized tours are readily available on all three islands. If you rent a car or bicycle, remember to drive British-style—on the left side of the road.

Especially for Lovers

St. Thomas

- Buy fancy his-and-her watches and congratulate yourselves on all the money you've saved.
- Walk through a dazzling coral reef—and stay dry—at Coral World's bubble tank, which sits right in the reef.

St. John

- Rent a jeep and follow the winding roads through lush mountains to tranquil beaches. Later, drive to Bordeaux Mountain, the island's highest peak, for breathtaking views of St. John and the neighboring British Virgin Islands.
- Snorkel at Trunk Bay's marked underwater snorkeling trail, or better still, at quiet Cinnamon Bay.

St. Croix

- Shop along the narrow, winding streets of historic Christiansted, the island's capital. Stop by the former Scalehouse—now home to the Visitor's Bureau—for a free walking-tour map.
- Get a taste of the wealth of the sugar era at the Whim Plantation Museum and dine at Sprat Hall Plantation, a greathouse that dates to 1650, now a family-run guesthouse.
- Cruise to Buck Island Reef National Monument, an untouched isle with a marked underwater trail just offshore.

CHAPTER 24

Mexico

Dining in a courtyard garden restaurant, listening to the heartfelt songs of a mariachi band singing about *amor;* dancing under the stars with the sea breeze caressing your faces; strolling down the cobblestoned streets of a centuries-old Spanish colonial town; sitting atop an ancient pyramid and hearing tales of the people who built it; bargaining for colorful Mexican crafts such as blankets, pottery, serving trays, and jewelry—all of these can be part of a honeymoon in Mexico. Mexico also can mean hiking through verdant jungle and stopping to refresh yourselves at the base of a sparkling waterfall and snorkeling through coral gardens as well as dancing the night away as you watch for celebrities at a sleek disco. Most couples head directly for Mexico's coasts, but each region has its unique allure.

If you can tear yourselves away from Mexico's glorious shores, the cobblestoned streets, courtyard gardens, and magnificent sixteenth- and seventeenth-century buildings of Mexico's Spanish-colonial cities such as Mérida, Guanajuato, and Morelia beckon with art galleries, boutiques, cafés, and hotels housed in former mansions and townhomes.

Sports: Waterskiing got its start in Acapulco, and imaginative Mexicans have been offering a creative array of water sports ever since. In addition to the usual windsurfing, sailing, jetskiing, watercycling, parasailing, and banana boat rides, the Pacific resorts of Mazatlán, Manzanillo, and Los Cabos draw big-game fishermen from around the world, while the colorful coral reefs and clear Caribbean waters off Cancún and Cozumel are prime snorkeling and diving spots. Yachters find haven at Puerto Vallarta's Nuevo Vallarta marina. Tennis is available at all the resort areas. Golfers have their choice of courses at most of the major resort areas. You can also go horseback riding, on the beach or in the mountains.

Memories to Go: Mexico has few rivals when it comes to locally made—and mined—shopping opportunities. You'll find finely crafted Mexican silver jewelry (look for the .925 stamp) as well as $2 silver-plate necklaces; colorful hand-embroidered blouses and shirts, hand-loomed shawls and sashes, as well as Aca Joe and other Mexican-made resort wear; and traditional pottery, onyx chess sets, and pyramid-shaped ashtrays. In some shops, prices are set, but in the markets, expect to haggle before settling on a price. Often, the asking price is more than double what the merchant expects. It's a good idea to visit the fixed-price shops before hitting the markets to get a sense of the price/quality relationship.

Remember that bargaining is a way of life here, and if your offer is met, it's considered bad form not to make the purchase.

Cuisine: If you think Mexican food is just spicy enchiladas, rice, and beans, happy surprises are in store. Each region has its unique cuisine, and while Mexican food is generally spicy, meaning tasty, much of it is not hot. For example, a Yucatecan dish, pollo pebil, consists of chicken marinated in a mild tomato sauce and baked in banana leaves. Or try mole, a complex sauce made with up to ninety spices, often including unsweetened cocoa—which is amazingly tasty. And be sure to try the Mexican version of lobster, served with mojo de ajo, or garlic sauce.

Lodgings for Lovers: The Mexican tourist industry caters to honeymooners with a wide array of hideaway styles. You'll find hotels in every price range as well as villas and condominiums. Luxury chains offer deluxe, oceanside properties in the resort areas. There are also a number of intimate, upscale hotels, both in the resort areas and the inland colonial cities.

Climate and Clothing: Temperatures at Mexico's beach resorts average around 80 degrees throughout the year. Afternoon showers are fairly common between May and October along the coasts, except in Baja California, which receives very little rain year-round. Bring bathing suits and cover-ups for the beach and pool; shorts (not short-shorts), sundresses, or lightweight slacks for shopping and sight-seeing. You'll want dressier clothes for the discos at night, especially in Acapulco and Cancún. Pack good walking shoes for the cobblestoned streets of the colonial cities and the archaeological sites. For the colonial cities, bring comfortable dresses and pants for daywear and a dressy outfit or two as well as warm sweaters or light jackets for the evening.

Language: The official language is Spanish, although most staff at hotels, restaurants, and shops in popular tourist areas speak English. You'll also find your attempts to speak Spanish rewarded with friendly smiles and encouragement.

Getting Around: Most honeymooners pick one resort area and stay there, taking tours or hiring a taxi to visit nearby attractions. Taxi fares should be agreed upon before you enter the car.

Money: At press time, Mexico still had two currencies; the "new peso" will eventually replace the "old peso" (1 new peso = 1,000 old pesos). If you're in doubt about a price, ask. Most shopkeepers quote prices and accept payment in U.S. dollars as well. There's no need to change money before you arrive; exchange houses and banks are everywhere, from the airport and your hotel to shopping centers. Major credit cards are widely accepted, although you can negotiate better rates if you pay in cash.

Formalities: You'll need proof of citizenship, such as a passport. U.S. and Canadian citizens can use an original birth certificate accompanied by a photo ID. You'll receive a tourist card free from the airline or your travel agent; keep it during your stay in Mexico, because you'll need to turn it in when you leave. Also, be sure to reconfirm your return flights (ask your hotel concierge) after you arrive. Otherwise, most international airlines have the right to cancel your reservations.

Cancún/Cozumel: The Caribbean Coast

For superb diving and snorkeling through rainbow-hued coral reefs, choose Cancún or Cozumel, two islands off the Caribbean coast. Sophisticated Cancún, which connects to the mainland by two bridges, offers white-sand beaches that go on forever and ever; a seemingly endless array of restaurants, discos, sparkling shopping centers, and water sports; and a string of luxury resorts—in the shape of pyramids and other fantastic forms—that have sprung up along its crescent of powdery sands. More laid-back and a long-time favorite with serious divers, Cozumel boasts a number of deluxe beachfront hotels while retaining its small-town feeling. Resorts are also springing up along Mexico's mainland Caribbean coast.

Especially for Lovers

- Climb the pyramid at the Maya ruins at Tulum and listen as your guide regales you with tales of the early Maya. Then see the smaller temples and swim with the dolphins at Xcaret, an ecological park.
- Go bargain hunting in the street markets and air-conditioned shops and pick up a Yucatecan hammock for your backyard.
- In Cozumel, rent a jeep or mopeds and drive to the windward side. The water is too rough for swimming, but the secluded beaches are idyllic.

Acapulco

Acapulco, the grand dame of Pacific Coast resorts, stays young with round-the-clock excitement, from volleyball and dancing on the beach to discos that stay lively through dawn. Dance between courses while lunching at one of Condesa Beach's seaside party restaurants, such as Paraíso or Beto's. Later, take a horse-and-buggy ride along the Costera Miguel Alemán, Acapulco's main boulevard, and then dine at one of the cliffside restaurants such as Casa Nova, Kookaburra, or Madeiras as the twinkle of starlight forms a natural dome over the shimmering lights of the city that frame Acapulco Bay. Toward midnight, it's time to hit the dance clubs. Warm up at News, a giant disco with a friendly bar and huge dance floor. Head up Las Brisas Hill to catch the 1:00 A.M. fireworks at Fantasy and then go down the road to Extravaganzza, where eighteen-foot-tall windows command spectacular views of the bay. Slip off for a stroll along the beach or cuddle in a chaise longue and then head to the Costera for more dancing at Baby 'O, which stays lively until sunrise.

Especially for Lovers

- Settle into a hammock at Pie de la Cuesta, a laid-back beach about forty-five minutes by car from Acapulco. On your way back, stop for drinks at Hotel Plaza Las Glorias's bar and watch the famous cliff divers at La Quebrada.

Ixtapa/Zihuatanejo

The resort hotels, shops, and restaurants of Ixtapa sit minutes away from the friendly fishing village-turned-tourist-town of Zihuatanejo. Spend at least one day in Zihuatanejo, shopping and sipping your way through its tangled web of cobblestoned streets, and then stroll along the waterfront, where fishermen still mend their nets and head out to sea in small brightly painted boats.

Especially for Lovers

- Take a boat to Ixtapa Island to snorkel or scuba dive or go board sailing and discover one of the small private coves, accessible only by water.
- Jet-skiing, waterskiing, parasailing, and banana boat rides are just a sampling of the water sports you can enjoy along Ixtapa's Palmar Beach, also known as "hotel row."

Manzanillo

Manzanillo beckons with luxurious self-contained resorts along endless stretches of beach. You may have seen Manzanillo before: Las Hadas was the setting for the sexy movie *10*.

Especially for Lovers

- Head for the seaside hamlet of Barra de Navidad and take a boat to one of the rustic thatched-roof seafood restaurants that beckon across the lagoon.

Puerto Vallarta

White-washed, red-tile-roofed houses climb up bougainvillea-adorned hillsides, offering a romantic combination of traditional Mexico and contemporary hideaways. Here you can shop for handicrafts and art as you stroll the cobblestoned streets and then return to your luxury resort for an elegant continental dinner.

Especially for Lovers

- Spend the afternoon at one of the jungle restaurants outside of town such as Chico's Paradise, where you can swim at the base of jungle waterfalls.

Mazatlán

This seaside city has long been a favorite with fishermen and fiesta lovers. Join a deep-sea fishing expedition and see why anglers come from around the world to stalk billfish, marlin, and other game fish. Catch a fringe-topped *pulmonía,* Mazatlán's unique brand of taxi, and head to tour the Golden Zone to browse the elegant shops and feast on shrimp, fresh off the boats of Mexico's biggest shrimp fleet. Later, go club-hopping and see why university students love to come here on their breaks.

Especially for Lovers

- Cruise over to Deer Island, Isla de Venados, to swim, snorkel, or simply relax on secluded shores. Or head for Isla de las Piedras and stroll off to find a private spot for a picnic for two.

Los Cabos

Across the Sea of Cortés on the Baja California peninsula, trendy Los Cabos charms couples with its easygoing twin towns and desert beauty. Shop your way along Boulevard Mijares, the main street of the eighteenth-century village of San José del Cabo, picking up stylish resort wear and handicrafts such as hand-blown glass and coral jewelry. Enjoy the tranquil waters of Cabo San Lucas, San José's sister town, located about twenty miles away. Go swimming or head out for the marina and angle for the 100-pound marlin that helped put Los Cabos on the map. And for a real adventure, join a desert safari and go exploring in an ATV (all-terrain vehicle). You'll visit secluded beaches and mountain villages and see towering saguaro cacti. In a social mood? Pancho and Lefty's showcases Baja's hottest live bands, the glamorous Cactus Video Disco goes strong every weekend, and Corona Beach Club and Lukas can keep you dancing until sunrise. And on Friday evenings, the Stouffer Presidente's Fiesta Mexicana offers al fresco partying starting at 6:30 P.M.

Especially for Lovers

- Rent a paddleboat in the late afternoon and gently glide past ducks, herons, and egrets as you listen to more than one hundred species of birds who sing their evensong in the freshwater lagoon beside the Stouffer Presidente Los Cabos. Or rent a dune buggy and head north to explore miles of deserted beaches, with a backdrop of steep mountains.
- Pack a picnic and hire a boat to take you to Playa del Amor (Lover's Beach). You'll have great views of the famous arches at Land's End, where the Pacific Ocean tumultuously meets the Sea of Cortés. You may see sea lions sunning on the rocks, and between late December and March, watch for the whales who often frolic quite close to shore.

CHAPTER 25

Florida

The "Sunshine State" is the number-one honeymoon destination in the world, thanks to Orlando's Walt Disney World and the beach resorts that line the state's 1,200 miles of Atlantic and Gulf Coast beaches. The quality and variety of its resorts and restaurants are rivaled only by its water sports, golf (more than one thousand and fifty courses), tennis, and other land sports, including some of the most important car-racing events in the world. Along with the many well-developed resort areas, there are still vast, unspoiled stretches where nature remains largely untouched.

Sports: You name a warm-weather sport and Florida is sure to offer it, world-class. Golf courses range from Scottish-style links to courses laid out by the top names in golf. The state hosts about twenty annual professional golf tournaments. Tennis buffs can play on clay, grass, or hard courts and watch the pros take center stage at one of the many professional tournaments. Or get back to nature at any of twelve state parks, which include seven of the top-ranked beaches in the country. Deep-sea fishing, island-hopping on a chartered yacht, scuba diving coral reefs and shipwrecks, canoeing, or kayaking—for active honeymooners, Florida has it all!

Memories to Go: To see the top of the line, with prices to match, Palm Beach's Worth Avenue is the shopping street. Souvenirs of an Orlando honeymoon might include talking Mickey Mouse watches and just about anything you can imagine with Disney characters emblazoned on them.

Lodgings for Lovers: Orlando, the world's theme park capital, has themed resorts to match, with ambiences ranging from Polynesian and the Wild West to turn-of-the-century elegance. The state also boasts world-renowned spas and a vast array of golf and tennis resorts. Your choices also include everything from laid-back cottage colonies to villa rentals, from Victorian-style inns to neon-bright Art Deco hotels. You can even stay right *on* or *under* the water—charter a yacht or a houseboat or hide away in an underwater lodge in the Keys.

Climate and Clothing: In southern Florida, a subtropical climate generally means swimming weather year-round. Summers bring high temperatures and humidity. From Orlando north, winter are generally mild, averaging in the low 50s, but can dip below freezing in the northern part of the state. Unless you're headed for one of the more formal resorts, restaurants, or night clubs, *casual* is the byword for clothes. You're likely to spend far more time in the sun than you're accustomed to, so protect yourselves with hats, sunscreen, and sunglasses.

Getting Around: Rental car rates in Florida are among the most competitive in the country, so it pays to shop around for the best rate. (See chapter 5 on car rentals.) In some areas, you'll even be able to get around by bicycle on designated trails or public transportation.

Orlando and the Central Atlantic Coast

Pose in front of Cinderella's Castle in the Magic Kingdom and then whip through Frontierland's Big Thunder Mountain Railroad, Splash Mountain, and Tomorrowland's Space Mountain for white-knuckle roller-coaster thrills. Take a screen test at MGM Studios. Travel around the world in a day at Epcot Center. And in the evening, you can club-hop and join the nightly New Year's Eve celebration at Pleasure Island. You could easily spend a week at Walt Disney World and not run out of new adventures—and just to make sure, new attractions are being added all the time. Walt Disney World is just the start of the theme park excitement in Orlando.

At Universal Studios Florida, the largest working film studio outside of Hollywood, you can view live shows in various stages of production and tour the back-lot sets. At Sea World, dolphins and killer whales are star performers, while at Cypress Gardens, stunt waterskiing and exotic gardens are the focus.

And there's more. Tee off on one of Walt Disney World's five championship courses, go horseback riding, play tennis, or take your choice of watercraft—from canoes to sailboats.

Want to spread your towel on a secluded Atlantic strand? Just over an hour's drive away is the Canaveral National Seashore along the "Space Coast." While there, visit NASA Kennedy Space Center's Spaceport USA, where you can see a piece of moon rock and view spacecraft.

Ready to party? Check out the pubs on Cocoa Beach Pier. Heading north, you can actually drive on the hard-packed sands of Daytona Beach. Best known for its International Speedway and Spring Break bashes, Daytona also attracts surfers, motorcycle enthusiasts, and sun-lovers to its broad shores.

Especially for Lovers

- Break away from theme park pleasures and head for Wekiva Springs State Park, where you can canoe through quiet channels, go horseback riding, or hike along more than thirteen miles of trails.
- Winter Park, a turn-of-the-century town just north of downtown, now delights visitors with small boutiques, courtyard gardens, art galleries, gourmet restaurants, and the Morse Museum, known for its fine Louis Comfort Tiffany art collection.

MIAMI AND THE GOLD COAST

Trend-setting nightlife; lively ethnic enclaves; and chic, intimate neighborhoods . . . Miami sparkles with city excitement, while across a causeway, legendary Miami Beach beckons with gorgeous Atlantic beaches and showy seaside hotels. The trendiest neighborhood is South Beach, where pastel-painted Art Deco buildings house hip cafes, bars, and restaurants and form the only twentieth-century historic district on the National Register of Historic Places. Walking tours of the district depart from the Art Deco Welcome Center. Miami also boasts the world's busiest cruise-ship port, the jumping-off point for cruises to the Bahamas, the Caribbean, and beyond. Stroll around Coconut Grove, an intimate village of cafés and boutiques, and amble through perfectly manicured Mediterranean-style Coral Gables.

Want to sample some Cuban coffee and visit with Miami's vibrant Cuban community? Head for Calle Ocho, the main street of Little Havana. Then walk by Máximo López Domino Park and watch men in guayabera shirts play dominoes. For a taste of Little Haiti, take your appetites to the Caribbean Marketplace, where you can try Haitian cuisine such as fried goat as well as an array of fresh tropical fruits.

Heading north from Miami, glittering hotels line the beaches and inland waterways. In Fort Lauderdale, which boasts 300 miles of manmade canals and waterways, even modest homes often come with yacht slips in their backyards. Miles of beaches, along with golf, tennis, parasailing, and diving, offer Fort Lauderdale visitors plenty of excitement. Shop the trendy galleries and boutiques of gas-lighted Las Olas Boulevard, and as the sun sets, take a leisurely horse-drawn carriage ride. Then hop a water taxi to Ocean Boulevard, where beachside bars and eateries beckon.

Up the coast, zoning codes compel tony Boca Raton to maintain its Mediterranean Revival look; arches, bell towers, and red-tiled roofs adorn even the new buildings. To see most opulent homes, head to the town of Palm Beach, where Worth Avenue boasts some of the ritziest shopping in the world. Visit Whitehall, the garish, white-marble wedding cake mansion. It was built by railroad mogul Henry Flagler as a wedding gift to his third wife.

Farther north are a series of tranquil resort communities, sometimes referred to as the "Treasure Coast" for the Spanish galleons laden with gold and jewels that sank offshore. Sport fishing and quiet beaches are the main attractions in towns along this shore such as Jupiter, Hutchinson Island, Port St. Lucie, Fort Pierce, Vero Beach, and Sebastian.

Especially for Lovers

- Stroll along woodland trails at Bill Baggs Cape Florida State Recreation Area on Key Biscayne, where you can also swim along a beautiful, unblemished strand of the Atlantic.

- Miami nightlife sizzles, especially in Coconut Grove and South Beach, where you can take your pick of intimate bars and clubs that invite you to dance to Latin and Caribbean music or the latest popular hits.
- Ogle the spectacular homes of some of the nation's wealthiest. Take a Rolls Royce tour of Palm Beach to see the stunning oceanfront estates or cruise along the Fort Lauderdale waterways past spectacular homes and yachts.

THE FLORIDA KEYS AND KEY WEST

South of Miami, Caribbean-class coral reefs and laid-back islands—called *keys*—beckon. You won't have to fly to get there (but you could); the "overseas highway" (U.S. 1) hopscotches from one islet to the next over turquoise waters. If Key Largo sounds familiar, it may be thanks to the Humphrey Bogart/Lauren Bacall movie of the same name. Fans can relive their favorite scenes at the Caribbean Club bar. Key Largo also attracts divers and snorkelers with a 78-mile living reef, home to forty types of coral and hundreds of species of fish, safeguarded in the John Pennekamp Coral Reef State Park and Key Largo National Marine Sanctuary.

Diving and snorkeling are favorite diversions along the one-hundred-plus mile stretch of the Keys, and so is world-class fishing. Join a fishing excursion from Islamorada or Marathon to angle for deep-water fish such as marlin, sailfish, and tuna or match wits with a bonefish in the shallows.

As you approach Key West, signs welcome you to the "Conch Republic," where conch fritters and key lime pie are among island specialties. Laid-back but certainly not lazy, this is a place where you'll feel far removed from the mainland yet never get bored.

Walk or cycle along tranquil, tree-shaded streets lined with gingerbread architecture and then head for lively Duval Street to stop in at fashionable boutiques. You can visit the house where Ernest Hemingway wrote several novels and raise a glass in his honor at his old hangout, Sloppy Joe's.

Especially for Lovers

- Don't miss the sunset celebration ritual at Mallory Square, where artisans, fire-eaters, and other street entertainers compete with the blazing orange orb as it casts its last fiery glow across the sea. The sunsets often receive—and deserve—standing ovations!

THE SOUTHWEST COAST

Championship golf courses and wildlife preserves compete with seductive beaches along this stretch of the Gulf of Mexico shoreline, which includes the towns of Naples and Fort Myers as well as the islands of Sanibel, Captiva, and Marco.

Tranquil and tony, Naples offers chic boutiques and upscale resorts. From here, it's a short drive to the Marco Island beachfront hotels or to the Everglades, where you can take a canoe or boat trip around mangrove islands and pick up souvenirs at the Miccosukee Indian Village.

In Fort Myers, you can visit Thomas Edison's home and laboratory. Fort Myers is also the gateway to the alluring resort islands of Sanibel and Captiva as well as smaller barrier islands, many of which are accessible only by boat. Excursions depart from South Seas Plantation on Captiva; or charter a boat to go island-hopping on your own and lay claim to a deserted isle for the day. Hunting for shells is a popular pastime on these islands, thanks to the copious starfish, conch, sand dollars, and other shells that pile up on the shores.

Especially for Lovers

* Roseate spoonbills, egrets, herons, ospreys, pelicans . . . these are just a few of the fascinating birds you can spot along the southwest cost. Some of the best viewing is often right outside your door, but nature preserves offer entry into more difficult terrain. The Corkscrew Swamp Sanctuary features a mile-long boardwalk. The J.N. "Ding" Darling National Wildlife Refuge offers a self-guided drive tour, or you can bike, canoe, sea-kayak or take a naturalist-guided tram tour.

THE CENTRAL WEST COAST

Its sunny climate, fine natural beaches, cultural events, sports resorts, and historic lodgings, including three that are on the National Register of Historic Places, make the Gulf Coast resort communities around Tampa, Clearwater, St. Petersburg, and Sarasota a favorite with newlyweds.

Tampa, the region's largest city, is home to Busch Gardens, a 300-acre African theme park. In town, stroll around Ybor City, a turn-of-the-century Cuban neighborhood whose claim to fame is its cigar-making heritage.

In nearby St. Petersburg, the Salvador Dalí Museum boasts the largest collection of the works of this surrealist artist. You'll also find a number of fine museums and historic homes. When you get hungry, head for The Pier, where you'll have your choice of eateries and shops.

Culture-rich Sarasota is filled with art galleries, fine restaurants, and showplaces where you can watch Broadway plays, concerts, and ballet. John Ringling, millionaire co-owner of the Ringling Brothers Barnum and Bailey Circus, gave the city its cultural cue when he built his Venetian-style mansion and fine-arts museum, known for its outstanding collection of Rubens paintings. These, along with a circus museum, are open to visitors.

Especially for Lovers

* Head north to Homosassa Springs State Wildlife Park for an up-close encounter with manatees, friendly sea mammals also known as sea cows.

- Pack a picnic and hop the shuttle-ferry to Honeymoon Island, where you can luxuriate on a beautiful white beach.

THE HISTORIC NORTHEAST

Along Florida's northeast coast, stunning beaches and championship golf courses are just a short drive from charming Spanish Colonial districts and Southern plantations. In much of this region, historic inns are more common than high-rise resorts. St. Augustine is Florida's—and the nation's—oldest city. The Old Town historic district has changed little over the centuries. Climb the ramparts at the seventeenth-century Castillo de San Marcos for a lovely view of the city. Don't miss the Spanish Quarter Living Museum, where "Spanish settlers" work at spinning wheels, anvils, and wood lathes.

On posh Amelia Island, the town of Fernandina Beach has been governed under eight different flags. Admire the town's gingerbread-trimmed Victorian houses as you follow the self-guided walking tour and then stop at the Palace Saloon, which claims to be Florida's oldest watering hole. Fort Clinch State Park features Civil War reenactments, while forty-foot sand dunes back the island's miles of tranquil beachfront. In addition to water sports, golf, and tennis, Amelia Island invites couples to go hiking and bicycling. Or saddle up for a sunset gallop through the surf.

Among the other seaside resort communities in this area are Ponte Vedra Beach, known for its professional golf and tennis tournaments.

Especially for Lovers

- Stroll through St. Augustine's eighteenth-century City Gate and hire a horse-drawn carriage for a tour of the historic city. While in St. Augustine, be sure to drink from the spring said to be the one Ponce de León discovered at Fountain of Youth Archaeological Park.
- Jungle cruises and glass-bottom boat tours are the way to explore Silver Springs, a multitheme nature park and national landmark, near Ocala, known for its clear artesian spring water.

THE PANHANDLE

Rolling dunes and sea oats fringe talcum-powder-fine, glistening, snow-white Panhandle beaches, praised as among the finest in world. Inland, magnolia trees and live oaks draped with Spanish moss form canopies over many streets. Although you'll find plenty of luxury villas, hotels, and inns as well as motel- and fast-food-lined strips, the area remains relatively undeveloped, thanks to the Gulf Islands National Seashore preserve and to its cool winters (temperatures hit average lows in the 40s, offset by prices that drop proportionately).

In this laid-back region, days are likely to be spent enjoying the beaches and sports, and nights, strolling under the stars. Eighteen beach communities, known as "the Beaches of South Walton," stretch between Panama City's "Miracle Strip" of hotels, amusement parks, miniature golf, and restaurants and Destin's 250-acre dune-lined Henderson Beach Park. Don't miss Seaside, a planned resort and residential community, known for its re-created pastel-colored Victorian architecture.

Architectural treasures include the North Hill Preservation District in Pensacola. Across town, you can climb into the cockpit of an F-8 Crusader at the National Museum of Naval Aviation.

Especially for Lovers

- Stroll along the one-and-a-half-mile nature trail at Grayton Beach State Recreation Area, near Seaside. You'll see forty-foot dunes and observe the wildlife that thrives in the salt marshes and natural scrub. Then, relax at the beach named "best in the United States" in a study by the University of Maryland Coastal Research department. Amazing sand dunes and beautiful blue-green waters also beckon at the beach in St. Joseph State Park in Port St. Joe, named number five in the survey.

CHAPTER 26

Hawaii

*W*aterfalls cascading through lush rain forests, rainbows reaching over emerald cliffs, and graceful hula dancers . . . this is Hawaii. Here, you can hike across a still steamy volcanic crater, watch some of the best surfers in the world, and bask on sands of white, red, black, and even green. If you ask for directions, don't be surprised if your "hosts" take the time to tell you about their favorite places. It's all part of the spirit of *aloha,* a word that means "love" and "welcome" as well as "hello" and "goodbye." It implies an almost mystical joy at meeting you and probably accounts for the strong affection most visitors have for Hawaii.

No matter which island you visit, you'll enjoy delectable beaches, a wide array of land and water sports, incredible waterfalls that cut through lush mountains, and plenty of opportunities to immerse yourselves in Hawaiian traditions. Attend a luau, where you'll dine on traditional specialties and learn the secrets of the hula dances. Your hardest decision may be choosing which island to make your honeymoon home.

Sports: Surfing was the sport of Hawaiian royalty; today, surfers come to the Hawaiian Islands from around the world. You can also water-ski, windsurf, sail and kayak, enjoy excellent snorkeling and scuba diving, and play golf on all the islands. For a unique experience, try (snow) skiing atop the Big Island's Mauna Kea—weather permitting.

Memories to Go: Wearable art ranges from aloha shirts to hand-painted tee shirts to exquisite original jewelry. Local artists show their works in galleries on all the islands.

Cuisine: Luaus, an important part of Hawaiian culture, are a great place to taste Hawaiian specialties such as kalua pig, cooked in an underground oven, and poi, a staple vegetable with a distinctive flavor (described by many visitors as wallpaper paste). You'll also enjoy experiencing the cuisines of Hawaii's more recent settlers: Chinese, Japanese, Portuguese, and others whose cooking styles often come together in unique blends.

Lodgings for Lovers: Resorts on a grand scale got their start here, and some of the world's best are on these islands, offering all the sports, dining, and entertainment you could want right at your doorstep. You'll also find hotels in every price range as well as quaint bed-and-breakfast inns and condominiums, where you can prepare your own meals while still enjoying the facilities of a full-service hotel.

Climate and Clothing: The islands are pleasantly warmed by almost eternal sunshine and cooled by trade winds. Generally, rain only hits one side of an island at a time, although occasionally storms blanket the islands. Year-round temperatures average between 70 and 80 degrees in the daytime and about 5 to 10 degrees cooler at night—except in the mountains, where it can get quite cold.

By day, you'll wear bathing suits, shorts, and tee shirts—with frequent applications of sunscreen, please (coconut and kukui oils are not enough protection). Evenings can be casual or dressy, but bring a sweater or light jacket because of air-conditioning as well as cooler evening and mountain temperatures. Few restaurants require men to wear jackets for dinner—ties, never!

Getting Around: Most flights from the mainland United States stop in Oahu; some continue to the other islands. Commuter flights make it easy to island-hop. Take the Waikiki Trolley around Honolulu and Waikiki. Free shuttles are available for transportation within a few resort areas, but to explore the islands, a rental car or organized tour is the best way to go. Reserve cars in advance. Fly/drive, hotel/car, and island-hopping packages can save you money.

Helpful Hints: Look for posted signs warning of dangerous surf conditions, and swim only in public parks with lifeguards.

OAHU

Oahu is home to Hawaii's capital, Honolulu; hip and happening Waikiki Beach; and the quieter north and west coast resorts. Framed by Diamond Head crater and Honolulu harbor, Waikiki's two and one-half miles of palm-lined beach host a round-the-clock party. Let a sun-bronzed surfer teach you to ride the waves and then sip mai tais as you watch hula dancers sway to hypnotic Hawaiian rhythms. Quality dining and nightlife abound around Honolulu and Waikiki, where shopping is also a chance to sightsee. Wander from a quiet Japanese setting to the bustle of Hong Kong Alley at the Rainbow Bazaar, next to the Hilton Hawaiian Village. Stop for free lessons in Hawaiian crafts at the Royal Hawaiian Shopping Center. Nearby, the cobblestoned streets of King's Alley transport you to the days of royal rule—complete with the changing of the guard.

The North Shore is touted by surfers around the world. Watch them ride the big ones along these famous beaches, where waves tower up to twenty-five feet in winter. Want to try? Hire a teacher and rent a surfboard at one of the shops in the New Age surfer town of Haleiwa. Then treat yourselves to a shave ice, a popular local specialty of ice shavings doused with your choice of flavorings.

At nearby Waimea Falls Park, more adventure awaits. Ride through rugged mountains in an all-terrain vehicle, kayak and join in traditional Hawaiian games, and then take a dip in a pool at the base of a waterfall. (Bring bathing suits and towels.)

Want to know more about Pacific Island life? Visit recreated South Seas villages at the Polynesian Culture Center, where natives from the islands of Hawaii, Fiji, Samoa, Tonga, Tahiti, and the Marquesas as well as members of the Maori tribe of New Zealand demonstrate traditional crafts. All are Brigham Young University students who work here to supplement their tuition. More recent history is the subject at Pearl Harbor, where you can watch a film and then board a ferry to the *Arizona* Memorial, built over the partially visible ship that sank here during World War II.

Especially for Lovers

- Check out the local nightlife. Extravaganza-style entertainment includes the long-playing Don Ho show performed at the Waikiki Beachcomber Hotel. The dancing crowd flocks to Studebaker's. Or take a moonlight dinner cruise into Honolulu Bay, where the starlight is as luminous as the city lights.
- Set out early one morning for Hanauma Bay with snorkels and masks. You'll swim through crowds of wildly colored fish, later joined by an equal number of people.

MAUI

Maui is an active island, with organized adventures such as mountain biking and horseback riding as well as snorkel, sunset, dining, and whale-watching cruises. Kaanapali, Wailea, Kapalua, and Makena—planned resort communities—combine diverse dining, sports, and shopping options with a hideaway feeling.

Strolling along Front Street in Lahaina, it's fun to imagine life in the early 1800s when the town was a rough-and-tumble whaling port. Restaurants, boutiques, and art galleries have now replaced the rowdy seamen's bars. If you're visiting between late November and early May, join a whale-watching expedition. These friendly giants can often be glimpsed from the shore, but these special cruises usually bring you even closer. Nearby Kaanapali is rimmed with uncrowded, sugary-white sand beaches and a wide range of accommodations. The more intimate resort area of Kapalua, with villas and two luxury hotels, lies a bit further north.

As you drive south, you'll come upon Kihei, a jumbled cluster of condominiums, hotels, and restaurants that attract couples looking for a young, casual ambience and lower prices, although accommodations here may not have air-conditioning or accept credit cards. Further south, Wailea and Makena are Hawaii's newest resort areas. Wailea boasts championship golf courses and a tennis center, nicknamed "Wimbledon West," where you can play on clay courts.

With a four-wheel drive vehicle, you can continue past Makena to La Perouse Bay, where you can snorkel—while being mindful of sea urchins. Then put on good walking shoes and continue on to the island's most recent lava flow—don't worry, it's had two centuries to cool! Climbing around this flow, you'll get a sense of the powerful forces that created the island.

The source of the lava, Haleakala Crater, is the world's largest dormant volcano and the single most visited site on Maui. Watching the sunrise from the rim of the crater is a Maui tradition. Guided cycling trips pick you up at your hotel to get you to the summit at sunrise and then outfit you and guide you down.

Drive through Upcountry, Maui's cowboy country, and stop at Makawao, a tiny New Age cowboy town. Then detour to Kula's Botanical Gardens to see the many varieties of oddly shaped protea flowers and continue on to Tedeschi Vineyards, a producer of pineapple- and grape-based wines.

More than six hundred hairpin twists and fifty-four one-lane bridges mean you'll need to allow at least three hours each way to take the fifty-mile drive to Hana. Plus, you'll want to stop. Often. Giant ferns and broad-leafed vines announce your entry into a tropical jungle. Parked cars—not signs—mark scenic spots along the way. Walk in and you may find a pool at the base of a waterfall or a dramatic valley haloed by a rainbow. Just before Hana, stop to see the black-sand beach at Waianapanapa State Park. Then discover "Heavenly Hana." Isolated from the rest of Maui, this area still feels lost in time. Horseback ride through a working ranch, hike to a private red-sand beach (where the snorkeling is terrific), and make reservations for lunch at the casually elegant Hotel Hana. Some couples stay overnight in Hana and then fly or drive back the next day.

Especially for Lovers

- Hike into Iao Needle State Park, where steep mountain slopes, eroded to knifelike edges, frame the landmark Iao Needle, a cinder cone that rises twelve hundred feet above the valley floor.
- Take a guided hike or horseback ride into the Haleakala Crater. Among the unusual life forms you may see in this stark, lunarlike environment are the nene, a rare Hawaiian goose, and a strange-looking silver-haired plant called silversword.

LANAI AND MOLOKAI

These two unspoiled islands are each a short hop from Maui. Lanai, with two luxury hotels and red dirt roads, is fun to explore by jeep; folksy Molokai has a single resort area, Kaluakoi. On Lanai, stopping in town is a chance to talk with locals and visitors alike. Lanai City, with only a general store, a bakery, an art gallery, and a community center, is an intimate, friendly place. Ready to explore? Rent a jeep. Unpaved roads lead to wonderful spots around the island: the Garden of the Gods, a geological wonder composed of strange lava formations and rocks, and Shipwreck Beach, where you can follow a marked trail to a field of ancient Hawaiian petroglyphs. Back on paved roads, head for Hulopoe Bay, a marine conservation area, where you just may find yourselves swimming beside some curious dolphins. Larger and lusher yet equally low-key, Molokai offers bungalow-style condominiums, several inns, and a single resort-style hotel.

Especially for Lovers

- On Lanai you can drive, rent a boat, or take an ocean-rafting expedition to discover remote areas where it's easy to find a beach all your own. Or take a snorkel cruise to pristine sites such as Honopu, where a spouting blowhole guards an underwater cave.

- On Molokai, you can join a jeep safari through the Molokai Ranch Wildlife Conservation Park. You'll feel like you're in the Serengeti as you bump your way through the 1,000-acre park, spotting rare species from Africa and Asia.

KAUAI

On Kauai, geologically the oldest island, Nature has sculpted long, deep valleys with steep, jagged cliffs, carved to perfection over six million years by thunderous waterfalls and sinuous rivers. Many of the most visited areas of the island remain accessible only on foot, from the sea, or by helicopter. Hop a helicopter for one of the most thrilling rides in the world, swooping down into river-carved valleys and hovering beside awesome waterfalls.

Remember the words to the song "Puff the Magic Dragon"? Well there really is a "land called Hanalei," and it's just past the golf-happy resort town of Princeville, across a one-lane bridge. The dragon? Ask someone to point out its outline as you look north along the Na Pali coast. The road stops where Haena State Park begins, but this coast is far from inaccessible; it's one of the most visited stretches of the island coastline. The current footpath was a highway for early Hawaiians. Most couples follow the eleven-mile trail only as far as Hanakapiai Beach—about two miles. Undertows and surf make swimming here unsafe, but you can hike inland for a refreshing dip at the base of a waterfall.

After a feet-on view from on land, it's fun to take a zodiac raft, kayak, or catamaran and see it from the sea. You'll pull up alongside cliffs that soar to two thousand feet, see surf lines on the rocks that mark swells of thirty feet in height, and perhaps see a pod of dolphins—they enjoy playing in the raft's wake—or come eye to eye with a sea turtle. You'll also learn the lore of valleys that were once home to the first Hawaiians.

You'll also want to drive to Wailua Falls, used in the opening scene of the *Fantasy Island* television series. Then, kayak up the Wailua River or join the Smith family's amusingly hokey boat ride to the Fern Grotto, where you'll be serenaded with the "Hawaiian Wedding Song."

Most honeymooners stay in Poipu, along Kaui's sunny southern coast, where reef-protected beaches are lined with spacious resorts and condos. Another popular area to stay is the "coconut coast," named for the coconut groves and fishponds cultivated by Kaui's last reigning monarch.

Especially for Lovers

- Hike into Waimea Canyon, nicknamed the "Grand Canyon of the Pacific." You'll see plants that grow nowhere else in the world. Stop at the museum at Kokee State Park and ask the rangers to help you select the best hike for you.

- Pick up some stationery and surprise each other throughout the year with love notes on cards designed with scenes of Hawaii. The most unusual place to shop is the mansion at Kilohana, a 1930s sugar plantation estate. Its rooms have been converted into boutiques selling handicrafts, jewelry, and artwork. Kauai also has more than its share of homegrown artists, whose works can be found in art galleries around the island and on everything from postcards to tee shirts and wall hangings.

THE BIG ISLAND OF HAWAII

The Big Island invites you to experience nature at its wildest—an erupting volcano—and at its tamest and most cultivated—resorts that are recognized as among the most lavish in the world, with golf courses built right into lava flows as well as sculptures, paintings, and other works of art in open-air settings.

Watch the Big Island get bigger at Hawaii Volcanoes National Park. If you're lucky, you'll catch a major eruption, which sends fountains of lava roaring out of the earth. These occasionally occur within a short walk of the roads (geologists constantly monitor the volcano, and rangers tell you how close you can get). At other times, a helicopter or plane ride is the only way to get a good view. Stop by the visitors center for a map and suggestions. Even if you don't see an eruption, you'll see plenty of signs of the power of Pele, the legendary volcano goddess who resides here. Hike across a still-smoldering crater, stopping to warm your hands at a steam vent. Then walk through a tube that once carried molten lava and see where streams of liquid rock flowed over one another as they raced down the mountain to the sea.

Across the island, the Kohala Coast resorts invite you to play golf on championship courses carved into a lava field, where greens seem to pop out from the stark, black rock. Nearby Kailua-Kona is the island's action center. Here, you can board a submarine at the Kailua Pier and then shop and snack your way along Alii Drive, stopping to see Hulihee Palace, summer home of Hawaii's King Kalakaua in the nineteenth century.

Especially for Lovers

- View the vast and steamy Halemaumau Crater from Kilauea Lodge and get cozy by the fireplace. Then dine there or at the intimate Kilauea Inn, a few miles away.
- Across the island, join a horseback expedition into Waipio Valley. You'll be surrounded by 2,000-foot-high cliffs and get a glimpse of traditional taro patches.

CHAPTER 27

The South

*H*orse-drawn carriages clip-clopping along the cobblestoned streets of a genteel city, gracious antebellum mansions and plantations, magnolia trees forming sweet-scented passageways through a busy metropolis . . . and all within a flip of a hot cake from delightful seaside and mountain resorts . . . no wonder the South attracts so many honeymooners. From Alabama, Arkansas, Georgia, Kentucky, and Louisiana to Mississippi, North Carolina, South Carolina, and Tennessee, "Southern hospitality" is more than just a catchword. Food comes in generous servings, and even in the big cities, people usually take the time to smile and exchange pleasantries.

Beach lovers flock to the Atlantic beaches of the Carolinas and Georgia and the southern fringes of Alabama, Mississippi, and Louisiana. Inland, the Blue Ridge, Great Smoky, and Ozark Mountains form a scenic setting for hiking, biking, rafting, and horseback riding. Throughout the land, Civil War buffs will find forts and restorations with reenactments commemorating the drama of the "Recent Unpleasantness." And you'll be in the hometowns of some of the country's great music traditions in New Orleans, Nashville, Memphis, and Branson, the latest music city.

Sports: Water sports are the draw along the Atlantic and Gulf coasts, while the mountains beckon with land and lake sports. Golfers have their choice of highly rated championship courses, especially in the resort areas of Florida and South Carolina.

Memories to Go: The Ozark Mountains are known for their interesting crafts. For furniture, the nation's shopping capital is High Point, North Carolina. Boaz, Alabama, is ranked among the top five outlet centers in the country. In New Orleans, pick up some jazz recordings and Creole spices.

Lodgings for Lovers: Hotels in all price ranges as well as luxury resorts line the coasts and dot the mountainsides. You might also choose to settle in at a cozy mountain cabin or intimate inn. Or you could rent a houseboat or a yacht and sightsee as you sail.

Climate and Clothing: Beach enthusiasts can enjoy water sports year-round along the Atlantic and Gulf Coasts of southern Florida. Summers along the coasts tend to be hot and humid; winters are generally sunny and mild. Temperatures often hover in the 60s by the shore and about 20 degrees lower inland, but snow is quite possible, especially in the northern and more mountainous regions.

Getting Around: Cities generally have good public transportation, and in some, you can even walk to most of the major sites. You'll want a car to explore the countryside, however, unless you plan to spend most of your time at one of the larger resorts.

ALABAMA

Active honeymooners head for white-sand beaches along Mobile Bay and the Gulf of Mexico. Here, the 6,000-acre Gulf State Park and Gulf Shores resort community invite you to water-ski, surf, and go boating as well as play golf and tennis. In nearby Mobile, the state's oldest city, you can stroll through Spanish moss–draped streets to tour nineteenth-century, Federal-style town houses and plantation homes. Antebellum Montgomery, the state capital, was the site of many famous events. You can visit the Dexter Avenue King Memorial Baptist Church, where Dr. Martin Luther King started his ministry; the first White House of the Confederacy, home to Jefferson Davis; and several Italianate, Greek, and Gothic mansions that maintain their period decor.

Especially for Lovers

- Honeymooning in the spring? Catch a "pilgrimage" tour of historic mansions, plantations, and gardens. Hosts and hostesses dressed in period costume talk about the early days, and the dogwoods, azaleas, and magnolias are in full bloom.
- While in Mobile, don't miss Bellingrath Gardens, with its bird sanctuary, woods, and sixty-five acres of beautifully landscaped gardens as well as a mansion that boasts the world's largest collection of Boehm porcelain. The gardens are at their best in early spring, when 200 species of azaleas burst into color. Then head for Battleship Park to board a harbor tour or dinner cruise.
- For a unique experience, sign up for Space Camp at the U.S. Space and Rocket Center in Huntsville and take a simulated flight on the Space Shuttle. Huntsville is also in the heart of northern Alabama's unspoiled mountains, which are filled with lakes, nature trails, and small towns.

ARKANSAS

From the Ozark and Ouachita mountains to the southern forests and delta and prairie regions, Arkansas earns its billing as the "Natural State." Honeymooners love the Victorian-style Ozark Mountain town of Eureka Springs with its picturesque inns, hotels, and cozy cottages that welcome couples with fireplaces and heart-shaped Jacuzzis. Its steep, winding streets are lined with boutiques full of mountain crafts and Victoriana, and in summer, you can catch the Great Passion Play, the largest religious outdoor drama in the country. To the west of Little

Rock are the Ouachita Mountains and the historic spa town of Hot Springs. To the south is Hope, President Clinton's birthplace, which is just a short drive from Crater of Diamonds State Park.

Especially for Lovers

- Reserve an evening in Eureka Springs for a romantic dinner on the ES & NA train. You'll chug through wilderness, spotting deer and other forest denizens as you enjoy dinner, graciously served on fine china.
- Munch on funnel cakes and watch artisans making candles, oak baskets, wood carvings, and quilts—all for sale—at the Ozark Folk Center in Mountain View.
- Soak in the naturally warmed waters of Hot Springs, which has been attracting visitors for centuries. Stop by the Fordyce Bathhouse, now a museum.
- Try your luck at Crater of Diamonds State Park, the only diamond deposit in the country open to the public. Finders, keepers!

GEORGIA

Stretching from the Atlantic Ocean to the foot of the Appalachian Mountains, Georgia is the largest state east of the Mississippi. Atlanta, the South's booming showplace and host of the 1996 Olympic Games, maintains its gracious charm while bustling with nightlife, cultural offerings, and fantastic shopping. Historic Savannah (just a stone's throw from Hilton Head, South Carolina), boasts the country's largest restored landmark district, with more than eleven hundred homes dating back to antebellum and Victorian eras. Farther south, Georgia's Golden Isles, former haunt of the Vanderbilts, Rockefellers, and other elite, delight sailors, beach lovers, golfers, and tennis enthusiasts. For mountain hideaways, head for northern Georgia, where you can enjoy hiking, horseback riding, a soak in a private Jacuzzi, and dinners by candlelight.

Especially for Lovers

- Shady tree-filled squares make Savannah especially lovely. Pick up a map and make up your own leisurely walking tour, stopping in at historic homes along the way. In the evening, enjoy club-hopping at the cobblestoned River Front area or the restored City Market.
- Enjoy shopping for crafts and antiques in northeast mountain towns such as Clarkesville, Clayton, and Dahlonega and dine on fresh-caught rainbow trout before settling in at a cozy cottage.
- Ferry over to Cumberland Island National Seashore, the most remote of the Golden Isles, where you can join a guided nature walk or take off on your own (bring food and water—there are no shops on the island). Want to see where former president George Bush honeymooned? Head back to The Cloister on Sea Island.

KENTUCKY

It's hard to mention Kentucky without thinking of horses. Louisville's Kentucky Derby, held every spring since 1875, helps make Kentucky the horse capital of the world. A stroll around the city also reveals interesting architecture, especially in Old Louisville, an elegant neighborhood with fine examples of Victorian Gothic, Italianate, and Beaux Arts architectural styles. To see where some of the best horses are bred and trained, visit Lexington and scenic bluegrass country, where you'll see barns that are as elegant as mansions. Kentucky's lakes and forests also offer plenty of opportunities for outdoor recreation. The lakes of the Western Waterlands are ideal for fishing and boating, and Land Between the Lakes offers a variety of water and land sports. In eastern Kentucky, Daniel Boone National Forest offers challenging white-water rafting (try the Red River Gorge) and canoeing as well as stunning cliffs, natural arches, and rushing streams. In south-central Kentucky, Mammoth Cave National Park boasts more than three hundred and thirty miles of explored passageways with colorful mineral-formed walls.

Especially for Lovers

- Racing season or not, the equestrian draw is unmistakable in Louisville. Stop by the Kentucky Derby Museum, next to Churchill Downs, if you're not visiting in season. Although the Derby is the biggest event at the Downs, there are also spring and fall races.
- Get around Louisville in historic style: hire a horse-drawn carriage or travel along the Ohio River aboard the *Belle of Louisville,* one of the last authentic stern-wheelers in the country.
- Learn all about horses at Lexington's Kentucky Horse Park, which offers films, breeds shows, farm tours, and a museum. You can also schedule a visit to Spendthrift or one of the other horse farms that allow visitors.
- Become a connoisseur of another state product, bourbon whiskey. Heaven Hill Distillery in Bardstown, Maker's Mark Distillery in nearby Loretto, Jim Beam Distillery in Clermont, and Ancient Age Distillery in Frankfort offer tours and tastings.

LOUISIANA

Fans of *Gone with the Wind* will remember New Orleans—"the city that care forgot"—as the place Rhett and Scarlet went for their honeymoon. The city still gets high ratings for its party potential as well as spicy Cajun and French Creole cuisine, traditional jazz, and historic neighborhoods. The partying peaks during the famous annual Mardi Gras celebrations, but Bourbon Street is ready to party and provide live jazz at almost any hour of the day or night. Catch a traditional Dixieland concert at Preservation Hall or try your luck at a casino. Quieter attractions include the antique shops along Royal and Magazine Streets, the upscale homes and restaurants of the Garden District, and several large parks, including City Park, with four eighteen-hole golf courses. Nearby Cajun country is the place to feast on spicy specialties such as jambalaya and gumbo. Drive along the Great River Road between New Orleans and Baton Rouge to view graceful old plantations, many of which are now restaurants, shops, and inns. Baton Rouge, the state capital, is home to elegant plantations. Lake-dotted northern Louisiana appeals to anglers and boaters.

Especially for Lovers

- Take a horse-drawn carriage ride through the historic French Quarter, where fancy wrought-iron balconies lean over pastel-painted stucco buildings, and return on foot to browse the boutiques and antique shops. On another day, hop the St. Charles streetcar for a tour of the lovely homes in the Garden District.
- Before turning in for the night, or when you wake up in the morning, stop at Café du Monde, an aptly named twenty-four-hour social spot, near the river, for cafe au lait and beignets.

MISSISSIPPI

One of the richest cotton-growing states in pre–Civil War times, Mississippi is filled with impressive plantations and mansions as well as heavenly Gulf Coast beaches. Its praises and tribulations have been expressed by native writers including William Faulkner, Eudora Welty, and Tennessee Williams and Delta Blues musicians B. B. King and Robert Johnson as well as rock and roller Elvis Presley, whose first home is now a museum/park in Tupelo amid the scenic northern hill country.

The Mississippi Gulf Coast, which includes Gulf Islands National Seashore (several islands accessible only by boat) and a twenty-six-mile stretch of sugary white sands, offers couples a choice of moderately priced restaurants, dockside cafes, night spots, and hotels in Biloxi, Gulfport, and other coastal towns. Natchez, the oldest city on the Mississippi, boasts more than five hundred antebellum homes, many open to visitors. Impressive mansions also beckon in Vicksburg, a historic port that sits strategically atop a bluff overlooking the Mississippi River. Join a hydro-jet boat tour, stroll along the Victorian waterfront, and take the self-guided driving tour through the Vicksburg Military Park that retraces this famous Civil War battle site.

Especially for Lovers

- From Gulfport, ferry over to Ship Island for the day. There, a U.S. park ranger will guide you through Fort Massachusetts and tell you tales of the island's past, including the brides sent by the French government for the early colonists.

- Looking for middle-of-the-night excitement? Try your luck at one of the Las Vegas–style casinos, aboard permanently docked boats in Gulfport, Biloxi, Bay St. Louis, and Waveland. The casinos, bars, lounges, and restaurants are open around the clock.

NORTH CAROLINA

With the Great Smoky and Blue Ridge mountains to the west and the pristine barrier islands of the Outer Banks to the east, North Carolina offers some of the best beach and mountain scenery in the country. The mountain-surrounded resort town of Asheville is known for its crafts and summer art festivals. From there, you can drive along the Scenic Blue Ridge Parkway, winding through quaint towns with spectacular views of the mountains, to Cherokee, home of the Cherokee Indian Reservation, where you can immerse yourselves in Indian lore at its attractions and museums.

The Pinehurst region is a favorite with golfers, who rave about the famed Pinehurst Number 2 and can choose from more than thirty other courses and stay at fine inns, cozy lodges, or top-rated resorts.

A series of barrier islands, the Outer Banks, stretches along the coast, dotted with scenic lighthouses, including the landmark Hatteras Lighthouse. Cape Hatteras and Cape Lookout National Seashores offer a choice of pristine beaches, while hotels and restaurants beckon in Ocracoke and the Nags Head/Manteo area.

Especially for Lovers

- Furnishing your new home? You can sometimes save up to 50 percent by shopping at the furniture showrooms in Highpoint and Hickory. Some stores will also take out-of-state orders once you've been to their showrooms. Local outlet stores also offer excellent buys on sheets, towels, and clothing—all produced in this region.
- Follow one of the nation's most scenic drives—the Blue Ridge Parkway, which winds through the Blue Ridge and Great Smoky mountains. Scenic overlooks invite you to stop and snap photos.
- Visit Asheville's Biltmore Estate, a 250-room chateau built in the 1890s by financier George Vanderbilt with sculpted gardens and its own winery. Then treat yourselves to a meal at the famed Grove Park Inn, whose guests have included Henry Ford, Thomas Edison, and John D. Rockefeller.

SOUTH CAROLINA

Historic treasures team up with seaside and mountain resorts to create one of the South's most popular honeymoon states. The Grand Strand runs along the northern coast with more than sixty miles of cream-colored, dune-lined beaches, ideal for water sports. Myrtle Beach offers a choice of accommodations, fresh seafood eateries, and golf courses, while Georgetown, one of the first settlements in North America, offers guided tours on water as well as land. Midway down the coast sits Charleston, a historic port city where much of the cobblestoned downtown appears to have never left the eighteenth century. Pastel-painted houses with wide verandas and pretty courtyards peer out from behind lacy iron gates. You can stay at a historic inn or fine city hotel or hide away on one of the nearby resort islands such as Kiawah, Seabrook, Isle of Palms, and Wild Dunes. More beachfront resort activity beckons to the south on Hilton Head Island, best known for its championship golf and broad beaches. To the northwest, the mountains of up-country South Carolina beckon with hiking and white-water rafting.

Especially for Lovers

- Clip-clop through the cobblestoned streets of historic Charleston in a horse-drawn carriage to the Battery, a narrow peninsula where grand mansions surrounded by fragrant gardens line up along the harbor.
- Between mid-March and mid-April, many historic Charleston homes open their doors to the public with symphony galas in their drawing rooms and candlelight tours, while the Spoleto Festival brings internationally known artists and musicians to town in May and June.
- From Hilton Head, drive to the beautiful antebellum town of Beaufort, where many of its baronial plantation homes are open to the public during annual fall and spring events.

TENNESSEE

There's rhythm in them thar' hills—the superscenic mountains of Tennessee, that is. Dolly Parton grew up around Pigeon Forge, now home to Dollywood, a country music extravaganza (closed January through March); there's always a musical show going on as well as amusement park rides and Appalachian crafts demonstrations. Down the road is picturesque Gatlinburg, with crafts shops and art galleries galore. Surrounded on three sides by the Great Smoky Mountains Park, Gatlinburg is also a popular wedding and honeymoon site. You'll have your choice of accommodations, from cozy honeymoon cottages and rustic inns to sports-filled resorts.

Nashville, the capital of the state—and of country music—is home to the Grand Ole Opry, which is now the heart of Opryland USA, a 120-acre entertainment park with music shows and rides. Stars also perform in clubs and concert halls around town, and there are museums devoted to C & W greats including Hank Williams Jr., Minnie Pearl, Elvis Presley, and Barbara Mandrell as well as studios where you can make your own recordings. Outside the town are a number of grand mansions, including Belle Meade, with a Victorian carriage museum, and The Hermitage, built by Andrew Jackson.

Elvis Presley fans flock to Graceland, his Memphis estate and resting place. Memphis was also home to W. C. Handy, "Father of the Blues," who performed on Beale Street during the 1920s. Today, the area sings with blues clubs, dining spots, and shops.

Especially for Lovers

- Pick up a honeymoon keepsake at the Great Smoky Arts and Crafts Community in Gatlinburg, where weavers, blacksmiths, quilters, and others demonstrate and sell their crafts.
- In Lynchburg, not far from Nashville, you can take a free tour of the Jack Daniels Distillery. Reserve weeks in advance to have lunch at Miss Mary Bobo's Boarding House to feast family-style on fried chicken, catfish, roast beef, and a variety of fresh vegetables, biscuits, breads, and pies.
- Visit Memphis during the month-long Memphis in May International Festival, when the streets and riverbanks play host to a series of musical, dining, and sporting events.

❦ CHAPTER 28

California and the Pacific Northwest

From the dreamers and dream makers of Hollywood to the expansive wilderness of Alaska, this is a land of grand proportions. In California, freethinkers explore the inner frontiers while in pristine areas of Alaska, Washington, and Oregon, the frontier can feel like a physical reality.

Sports: Hiking, rafting, kayaking, fishing, and skiing are popular throughout the region. California boasts several tournament-class golf courses, and its warmer weather makes it a favorite for water sports. Some stretches of the Pacific have big swells to delight surfers. Salmon fishing is popular in Alaska and Washington.

Memories to Go: Native American crafts are sold throughout the region; totem carvings are especially fine in Alaska and Washington. In California, it's fun to shop for crafts and original jewelry and artwork, and wineries in California, Oregon, and Washington will happily ship your purchases home.

Lodgings for Lovers: Victorian homes turned into bed-and-breakfast inns, sophisticated city hotels, elegant turn-of-the-century hotels with fourteen-foot ceilings and modern amenities, and sports-filled resorts are among your romantic options in this region.

Climate and Clothing: Temperatures vary greatly as you move from south to north and from coastal to mountain elevations. Even between night and day, there can be variations of up to 40 degrees. The coastal areas generally have mild weather year-round, with rains more likely between October and March. This weather pattern holds true even as far north as southeastern Alaska (the most visited Alaskan region), where summer temperatures average between 45 and 65 degrees. Ski season in the High Sierras and Cascades runs from October through March. Deserts are at their coolest between October and May; wildflowers peak in April.

Getting Around: You'll probably want a rental car for at least part of your stay. In the more compact cities such as San Francisco, you won't want a car until you're ready to leave the city limits. Alaska is one of the few states you probably won't want to explore by car; the distances are too great, and even locals usually travel by boat, train, or airplane. Ferries (which can carry cars and bicycles) are also the way to hop around Washington's San Juan islands.

ALASKA

How would you like to be transported in luxury through a land where dogsleds are still an important form of transportation, glaciers are still at work carving valleys, traffic jams are as likely to be caused by a moose as by too many cars, and many people still live by hunting, fishing, and trapping? In Alaska, you can be pampered at a luxury resort or a rustic lodge on the edge of vast wilderness, where bears, caribou, Dall sheep, and wolves own the land. Or sip hot chocolate on the deck of an elegant cruise ship as you watch a glacier calving (breaking noisily into the sea) and whales breaching. Although you can drive, keep in mind that Alaska extends further north, west, and east than all the lower forty-eight states combined; daunting distances mean most people fly or sail to and around this state. In fact, many places aren't even connected by roads.

The most popular region with honeymooners is southeastern Alaska, where waters teem with Pacific salmon and sea mammals; mammoth glaciers scrape across the land; and deer, moose, and bears wander the shores. Coastal communities cling to mountainsides, and cruise ships and ferries call at fascinating cities and towns. Many also spend a day cruising in spectacular Glacier Bay. At Ketchikan, stroll along Creek Street, where shops sit on stilts over Ketchikan Creek. Nearby Totem Bight State Historical Park boasts the largest collection of totem poles in the world. To the north, Sitka was Alaska's capital before 1867, when Russia sold it to the United States. You can still see the Russian cannons on Castle Hill and St. Michael's Cathedral, a replica of the original 1848 edifice, as well as authentic religious icons.

Juneau, the hilly state capital, was born as a gold-rush town. Get in the frontier spirit at the Red Dog Saloon and admire the onion-domed St. Nicholas Russian Orthodox Church, the oldest Russian church in the state. A wonderland of colossal glaciers and virgin forests beckons along the Inside Passage, where you might spot frolicking whales and bears rambling along the shore. At the top of the waterway, Skagway looks much as it did during its wild gold-rush days.

Further north is the pretty, mountain-backed port city of Anchorage. Aleyeska resort area, about forty miles from Anchorage, offers winter skiing and summer mountain biking. About two hundred miles from Anchorage and one hundred and twenty miles from Fairbanks is Denali National Park, six million acres of wilderness topped by majestic Mt. McKinley, the highest peak in North America. Bears, wolves, moose, Dall sheep, and arctic foxes call the park home.

Especially for Lovers

- The most luxurious way to visit Alaska is aboard a luxury cruise ship, where after a day of nature watching or exploring Alaska's historic frontier towns, you can savor a formal dinner before going to a show, a piano bar, or a disco. Smaller expedition ships also ply these waters, taking you closer to shore— and the wildlife—but with fewer entertainment and recreational options.

- Reserve in advance for a trip to Wonder Lake at Denali National Park. It's a full-day trip that almost guarantees you'll spot wildlife such as bears and caribou. Also try to catch the sled dog demonstration held daily by rangers at the Visitor Access Center.

CALIFORNIA

Beaches, both secluded and sociable; scintillating cities; acclaimed wine country; snow-capped mountains; and stark deserts . . . whether you pick one or combine a few, California's honeymoon possibilities are mind-boggling.

One of the world's prettiest and hilliest cities, San Francisco is fun to explore on foot—and when your feet want a rest, just hop on a cable car, America's only moving national historical monuments. The Powell-Hyde Line runs from the Union Square over posh Nob Hill to the waterfront Ghiradelli Square, a shopping complex housed in a nineteenth-century chocolate factory. Nearby, Fisherman's Wharf beckons with more shopping and fresh seafood eateries. Other interesting spots include Chinatown and the museums and gardens at Golden Gate Park. For great views of the skyline, walk across the Golden Gate Bridge.

Want to sample some of the country's finest wines at their source? Head for nearby Napa Valley and Sonoma County. Less than an hour north of San Francisco are the giant, centuries-old redwood trees of Muir Woods. Making your way inland (184 miles from San Francisco), prepare to be awed by the waterfall-spiked jagged cliffs that tower over Yosemite National Park's narrow valley, where deer, black bears, and coyote roam.

To the north, straddling the Nevada border 6,000 feet above sea level, Lake Tahoe sparkles like a giant blue sapphire set in snow-capped or opalescent mountains, a year-round playground. Want some casino excitement? Just cross the border to the Nevada side. One of the hotels actually sits on the state line!

Going south along the Pacific coast from San Francisco, State Highway 1 winds past steep palisades pummelled and splashed by the surf. The cliff-edged Monterey Peninsula is home to the exclusive town of Carmel, which boasts a Spanish mission and an ex-mayor named Clint Eastwood. In Monterey, you can follow the self-guided "Path of History" past adobe buildings that date to the town's days as California's capital under the Spanish and Mexicans. Then head to the tin-roofed canneries made famous by John Steinbeck's book *Cannery Row*, which now house restaurants, art galleries, shops, and the Monterey Bay Aquarium. In quaint Pacific Grove, Victorian homes now serve as charming inns.

Farther south, along Big Sur, cliffs seem to rise right out of the ocean, while the 115-room Hearst Castle certainly ranks among the most opulent palaces in the world. Santa Barbara's red-tiled roofs and white stucco walls evince its origins as a Spanish mission town.

In Los Angeles, "City of Angels," the line between reality and fantasy blurs. The palm-tree-lined, white-beach playgrounds of Venice and Santa Monica are laid-back yet almost frenetic with roller skaters, cyclists, and jugglers. And in Hollywood and Disneyland, fairytales and the American Dream really do come true.

A 1,000-square-mile "city," Los Angeles is really a series of discrete neighborhoods, connected by freeways and squeezed into a strip between the Pacific Ocean and the mountains. Plan your neighborhood-hopping to minimize freeway time. Take a studio tour and then check out your favorite star's footprints in front of Mann's Chinese Theatre. In nearby Beverly Hills, you can drive past mansions, flamboyant and elegant, and then shop with the celebrities along Rodeo Drive. At night, rub elbows with stars and wanna-bes at bars and pubs around the city. Then it's off to the fantasies of childhood at Disneyland.

Farther south lies sunny San Diego, with forty-two miles of beaches, pretty parks, and one of the best zoos in the world. And for a taste of the exotic, shop and dine across the border in Tijuana, Mexico. Across the desert, Palm Springs is an oasis of elegant resorts, perfect golf courses, and millionaires' mansions.

Especially for Lovers

- Taste your way through Napa Valley and Sonoma County wine country, where wineries range from rustic to elegant and from primitive to high-tech. While there, sample two of its special modes of transportation, a hot-air balloon trip or a rolling brunch, lunch, or dinner ride aboard the Napa Valley Wine Train between Napa and St. Helena.
- Cross the Golden Gate Bridge and visit the hillside town of Sausalito, which has the ambience of a Mediterranean artists' village. Waterfront restaurants line the main street, Bridgeway, offering wonderful views of the bay and yacht harbor.
- Get into the act in Hollywood. Become members of a television audience at NBC, CBS, or ABC studios; take a behind-the-scenes studio tour at NBC in Burbank and Universal Studios Hollywood; and keep your eyes peeled for your favorite stars as you dine and shop in their hometown!
- Tear yourselves from your Palm Springs pool and golf course and head for the desert. Join a guided jeep adventure and explore Indian Canyons and the Santa Rosa mountains. You'll find alluring waterfalls and dramatic, rocky gorges.

OREGON

The Willamette Valley was the promised land to nineteenth-century pioneers trekking across the country in search of fertile lands to farm, and for many people today it still is. The Willamette River winds through mountain-backed Portland, where an active arts community and lively bars and coffeehouses make Oregon's largest city hospitable as well as beautiful. South of Portland, the fertile Willamette Valley is a great place to sample Oregon's fine homegrown wines. Stop along the way to buy fresh fruit and berries from roadside stands. Visit restored pioneer homes and relive the days of the valley's early settlers, who came to farm and pan for gold.

Dramatic scenery unfolds to the east of Portland, where the Columbia River Gorge undulates through steep, waterfall-striped cliffs and mountain-backed valleys filled with apple, pear, and cherry trees. Mount Hood stands proudly in the distance, and the area boasts skiing and hiking trails as well as the historic Timberline Lodge, a national historic monument. Skiers also praise Oregon's other ski mecca, Mt. Bachelor, located in the center of the state, where spring skiing often continues well into June.

Crater Lake, the deepest lake in the country, sits in the caldera of an extinct volcano. The twenty-five-mile Rim Drive circles the lake, passing through dramatic frozen lava flows and wildlife-filled forests where you're likely to see black bears, deer, foxes, and marmots. Hiking trails and side roads spur off the main drive, tempting you to climb to scenic vistas such as the Pinnacles, where you'll see pumice spires rising from a canyon floor.

U.S. Highway 101 follows the Oregon coast along 400 miles of varied beaches. To the north, between historic Astoria and lively Newport, vast stretches of sandy beach are popular with summer swimmers, windsurfers, and boating enthusiasts at bohemian towns such as Cannon Beach and Lincoln City. Around Florence, rocky headlands reach out into the Pacific. Approaching the California border, goliath monoliths of rock strewn across the sea and along the beaches spew surf into the air, and rainbows often stretch out along the horizon.

Especially for Lovers

- "Discover Oregon Wineries," a map and guide to the wine country, is available free at wine shops and wineries. Most of the area's wineries welcome visitors, and the Willamette wine region is dotted with cozy bed-and-breakfast inns.
- Gold Beach, which sits at the mouth of the Rogue River along the southern Pacific Coast, is a great jumping off point for jet boat trips into the wilderness and white waters of the upper Rogue River. Between February and October, nearby picturesque Ashland, ensconced between the Cascade and Siskiyou mountains, is home to a respected annual Shakespeare Festival as well as friendly cafés and a host of charming inns in town and the surroundings.

WASHINGTON

From the observation deck atop Seattle's Space Needle, you can see the reasons why newlyweds enjoy honeymooning in Washington; beyond the theaters and museums of Seattle Center, you'll see Puget Sound, Mt. Rainier, and the Olympic and Cascade Mountains. In Seattle, the restored, red-brick buildings of nineteenth-century Pioneer Square and Pike Place Market make a picturesque setting for café- and shop-hopping, while Capitol Hill and the University

District offer plenty of nightlife. Home of Sub Pop records, which propelled local punk-metal–style "grunge" bands Mudhoney, Soundgarden, and Nirvana to fame, Seattle has a lively club scene.

Seattle is also the starting point for those who want to hide away or jump into action in the state's scenic mountains and islands. Ferries ply the Puget Sound, stopping at island retreats such as Whidbey, where you'll see nineteenth-century sea captains' houses at Ebey's Landing and dramatic cliffs that drop to rocky beaches. Further north, the San Juan Islands, ideal for cycling and strolling, offer Victorian resorts and inns, lively waterfront dining and shopping areas, and frequent sightings of orcas and other marine mammals.

Across the Puget Sound from Seattle, the Olympic Mountains drift in and out of rainclouds, and quaint towns such as Victorian Port Townsend lure you to the shores of the Olympic Peninsula. To the east, the Cascade Mountains offer spectacularly scenic hikes that lead to alpine meadows, waterfalls, lakes, and glaciers. The 14,410-foot-high, ice-capped Mount Rainier is the tallest of the region's dormant volcanoes; Mount St. Helens still wears a mantle of ash from its 1980 explosion.

Especially for Lovers

- Ferries connect Seattle and the major San Juan Islands, but there are many more islands that can be reached only by sailing off on your own. Rent a sailboat or kayak and you're sure to discover secluded beaches and tiny fishing villages that seem forgotten by time. Along the way, you may be greeted by an orca or the sight of seals sunning on the rocks.

- After a few hours of hiking at Olympic National Park, stop by Sol Duc Hot Springs for a soothing soak in hot sulphur pools (open from mid-May to October). For your hike, choose among the lush Hoa Rain Forest, areas where you'll see active glaciers, the alpine terrain of Hurricane Ridge, and the wild, rocky coast. Keep your eyes peeled for the otters, beavers, elk, and flying squirrels that inhabit the preserve.

- The Yakima Valley, with a latitude and growing cycle similar to that of the French wine-producing regions of Bordeaux and Burgundy, is gaining a reputation for its fine wines. You can sample some of the best as you drive around this pretty (and sunny!) region.

CHAPTER 29

Mid-Atlantic States

*F*rom Victorian towns and timeless Colonial hamlets to action-filled resorts to skyscraping cities, the Mid-Atlantic region—Delaware, Maryland, New Jersey, New York, Pennsylvania, Virginia, West Virginia, and Washington, D.C.—packs in a variety of experiences. Although this is the most populated and industrialized region of the country, it also encompasses large expanses of rolling countryside and mountainous wilderness. It's easy to combine a stay in a big city with a stint at a nearby seaside or mountain resort.

Sports: Ski and go snowmobiling and ice-skating in winter; enjoy whitewater canoeing and inner-tubing along the Delaware and Hudson rivers when the snows melt; go swimming, sailing, and yachting along the shore in summer; and try hiking into the mountains to admire the foliage in fall. Tennis and golf are also available at many resorts.

Memories to Go: As you might expect in this history-filled region, hunting for antiques is still a favorite sport. Flea markets and country fairs abound in the warm weather. Discount malls are opening everywhere; those in Secaucus, New Jersey, are the best known. New York City is a shopper's paradise, with some of the most elegant shops in the world as well as some of the best discount emporiums.

Lodgings for Lovers: You might stay in a colonial inn that dates back to the eighteenth or nineteenth century, an elegant resort that was the summer playground of the wealthy at the turn of the century, a rambling dude ranch, or a chic city hotel. In Pennsylvania's Pocono Mountains, you'll find couples-only resorts with honeymoon-oriented accommodations that feature in-room swimming pools, Jacuzzis, saunas, mirrored walls and ceilings, and more.

Climate and Clothing: Four definite seasons bring temperatures that range from the 80s and above in summer to below freezing in winter.

Getting Around: The major cities have well-developed mass transit systems and expensive parking, making cars a disadvantage once you arrive. However, outside of the cities, you'll want a car to get around. Amtrak runs frequent service and is a good way to connect between many of the region's bigger cities.

DELAWARE

Brandywine Valley is du Pont country. The family that created the state's major industries also chose this pretty region for their grand mansions.

Get a taste of American history at the Winterthur Museum Garden and Library, a 175-room mansion filled with Henry Francis du Pont's collection of early American furniture and decorative arts. Marvel at the automobiles, antiques, and formal French gardens at another former du Pont home, the Nemours Mansion and Gardens. To learn about the industries that made the family rich, visit the Hagley Museum.

For a seaside resort near miles of unspoiled Atlantic beaches, consider Rehoboth Beach, one of the more developed of the small resort towns along this wide, sand dune–lined stretch of sea.

Especially for Lovers

- Find yourselves a secluded stretch of beach—it's easy to do at Delaware Seashore State Park, which spans six miles of Atlantic coastline south of Rehoboth Beach.

MARYLAND

Most honeymooners head for Maryland's eastern shore, a broad peninsula shielding the Chesapeake Bay from the Atlantic. Quiet fishing villages and corn-fields cover much of the area, but there's plenty of action when you want it at nearby Ocean City.

You'll find shopping, dining, and entertainment day and night at Baltimore's modern Harborplace and The Gallery. Don't leave town without visiting the National Aquarium, acclaimed as the country's best. History buffs love Annapolis, Maryland's capital since colonial times. Stroll down its narrow streets and admire the colonial architecture. If you're lucky, you may catch a dress parade at the U.S. Naval Academy.

Especially for Lovers

- Sail around the Chesapeake Bay on a chartered boat, stopping to explore eastern shore towns such as St. Michaels and Rock Hall.
- Rent bicycles and explore the eastern shore—the traffic is light, and the road has wide shoulders. You'll pass through small Colonial villages where you can savor fresh crabs at waterfront restaurants. Free maps are available from the state tourist office (see Appendix B).
- For a day at a truly pristine beach, drive to the Assateague State Park and National Seashore, twenty miles of protected beach and marshland. Camp-ing is the only way to stay, but Ocean City, the state's most popular and jumping summer beach resort, beckons just five miles to the north.

NEW JERSEY

The New Jersey shoreline stretches for 127 miles along the Atlantic Coast, with resort towns almost shoulder to shoulder. Historic Cape May is filled with exquisite Victorian homes; many now serve as bed-and-breakfast inns. Towns such as Wildwood and Seaside Heights are known for their active beaches and lively nightlife. Atlantic City, with its casinos and fancy high-rise hotels, offers round-the-clock activity. Further north is Asbury Park, the place where rock star Bruce Springsteen got his start. Or shift gears and go inland to go antiquing and explore the historic towns of the state's northwest region.

Especially for Lovers

- Stroll along the lively boardwalks in towns such as Point Pleasant, Wildwood, Seaside Heights, and Atlantic City, stopping to try your skill at arcade games and ride the roller coasters and ferris wheels.
- Want to feel like you're on a deserted isle? Try Island Beach State Park, a twelve-mile stretch with both ocean and bayside beaches on Barnegat Peninsula.

NEW YORK

Say "New York," and most people think of skyscrapers and the intense energy of New York City, where Broadway, Wall Street, Fifth Avenue, and Greenwich Village are real places as well as activities. Catch a play, see the stock market in action, shop along one of the most chic avenues in the world, and listen to folk music at dozens of clubs in the center of bohemia. Here, you can dance all night, dine on some of the best food in the world, and sample a world of cultural attractions, from museums to ethnic neighborhoods.

Although New York City can easily be a honeymoon in itself, it's also romantic in combination with some of the attractions of New York State. Just east are the resort communities of Long Island, including Montauk and Fire Island, where much of city escapes in the summer. For a short jaunt by car, drive north along the Hudson River Valley, with its dramatic cliffs, orchards, vineyards, farms, and history-rich villages, stopping at colonial inns along the way. About two and a half hours north of the city, the Catskill Mountains earned their moniker "the borscht belt" by catering to city folk year-round with mountains of food and entertainment. These days, skiing, hiking, and country fairs attract most vacationers. Further on are the Adirondacks Mountains, a six-million-acre wilderness preserve with a 125-mile canoe "trail," and the Finger Lakes region, where you can sample fine local wines and hike to dramatic waterfalls and glacier-cut gorges, as well as the justly famous Niagara Falls.

Especially for Lovers

- Wear comfortable walking shoes and become intimate with New York City as the natives do—on foot. Much of the city is neatly laid out in a grid, so it's easy to find your way around, and the distances are short. If you'd like to start with an organized orientation, double-decker tour buses, which stop at major points of interest all around the city, can be boarded as often as you like for the price of a single one- or multi-day ticket.

- Slip away to an exclusive, rustic Adirondack resort, built to cater to turn-of-the-century millionaires. When you're ready to rough it, your resort or the visitors bureau can help you arrange a two- or three-day escorted canoe trip through the wilderness. Your guide will cook, set up camp, and regale you with Indian lore and wildlife information.
- After viewing Niagara Falls from above, take a ride on *Maid of the Mist*. You'll be given rain gear to shield you from the spray as you pass along the base of the falls.

PENNSYLVANIA

Amazing accommodation options such as in-room Jacuzzis, saunas, and swimming pools; mirrored walls; and round and king-size beds. Glorious mountains dotted with sparkling lakes and flower-filled meadows. Resorts that cater to newlyweds with four seasons of activities—indoors and out—for one all-inclusive price. This has helped earn the Pocono Mountains the title of "Honeymoon Capital of the World." Also nestled in these pine-covered mountains are quaint Victorian and Colonial towns, charming inns, and tempting name-brand outlet shops. Nearby Bucks County is also known for its antique shops, while Lancaster County is home to many Amish people, whose religion shuns the use of colorful clothing, electricity, cars, and other modern accoutrements. The nation's first capital, Philadelphia, proudly displays its history. Independence Hall, where the Declaration of Independence was adopted, and the Liberty Bell are among the sites in the four-square-block Independence National Park, nicknamed "America's most historic square mile."

Especially for Lovers

- Pocono couples-only resorts cater to honeymooners with unique suites and a fantastic array of activities. Entertainment, breakfast and dinner, and sports—including equipment and lessons—are generally included in the room rates, making this the perfect place to learn new sports. Interested? Write to the Pennsylvania Department of Commerce for brochures on all of the honeymoon possibilities and check out the multi-featured rooms. (See Appendix B.)
- The Pocono Mountains are crisscrossed with forested trails that are perfect for hiking, mountain biking, and horseback rides. In winter, snow sets the scene for skiing, toboggan rides, and snowmobile trips, while in summer, mountain lakes are ideal for boating and swimming.

VIRGINIA

Beachfront hotels and a lively boardwalk strip of eateries and clubs team up with long stretches of unpopulated golden sands in Virginia Beach for summer honeymoon fun. Bike or stroll along miles of beachside walkways, stopping to shop or have your photos taken in antique garb. Just an hour's drive away is Colonial Williamsburg, a reconstructed eighteenth-century city where costumed interpreters make candles, brooms, and other items as they did centuries ago. Colonial music, plays, militia exhibitions, and workshops here and at neighboring Yorktown and Jamestown also bring the past to life.

For stunning views of the mountains and the Shenandoah Valley, follow the Blue Ridge Parkway and Skyline Drive. The area is filled with opportunities for horseback riding, canoeing, and fishing as well as historic sights. Don't miss beautiful Charlottesville, home to a growing number of writers including Anne Beattie, Alexandra Ripley, and Phyliss Whitney. Just outside town is Monticello, lovingly designed by Thomas Jefferson and filled with his inventions.

Especially for Lovers

- Ride a horse-drawn carriage through the gas-lighted village of Colonial Williamsburg and then dine at one of the numerous Colonial taverns or at the formal Regency Room at the Williamsburg Inn.
- Spend a day plantation-hopping along the James River on Virginia Route 5 between Williamsburg and Richmond. You can also visit Belle Grove, where James and Dolley Madison spent their honeymoon, and the homes of six other U.S. presidents.

WASHINGTON, D.C.

Washington is one of the few cities in the world that was custom-built as a seat of government. The Capitol Building, home to Congress and the Supreme Court, sits on "The Hill," the city's highest ground; city law ordains that no building shall be higher. Radiating out from the Capitol, four wide, tree-lined avenues divide the city into neat geographical quadrants: northeast, northwest, southeast, and southwest. Most of the famous sights are clustered in the northwest quarter. At the foot of the Capitol Building, the Washington and Lincoln Memorials, as well as most of the museums of the Smithsonian Institution, line up along the Mall. Here, you can see the Hope Diamond, a living coral reef, and art collections from around the world. Washington is truly a cultural capital: Kennedy Center, the historic Ford's Theatre, and the National Theatre are just a few of the famous venues. Check the local papers for current listings. Washington, D.C., can easily be part of your itinerary during visits to neighboring Virginia and Maryland.

Especially for Lovers

- Stop for lunch and shopping at Union Station. This pretty Beaux Arts train station is often the setting for the presidents' inaugural balls. For some of the trendiest shopping and nightlife, head for Georgetown. The fashionable Du Pont Circle neighborhood also has good restaurants and clubs.

- For unique souvenirs, check out the gift shops at the Smithsonian museums. You'll find a wide selection of famous paintings reproduced on postcards and note paper as well as fine jewelry.
- The city is at its most romantic in April when the Japanese cherry trees blossom. One of the prettiest sights: the reflections of the pink and white blossoms in the Tidal Basin, which runs between the Lincoln and Jefferson memorials.

WEST VIRGINIA

"Mountaineers Are Always Free" is the state motto, and it is an obvious fit for this rugged, mountainous state. Small towns nestle in the hollows, while rustic lodges and resorts sporting world-class golf courses sprawl across the hilltops. Here, you can ski in winter and enjoy some of the most challenging white-water rafting in the country when the snows thaw.

Especially for Lovers

- After a morning of hiking, pamper yourselves with massages and a soak in the Roman baths at Berkeley Springs, the country's first spa and a favorite summer retreat for George Washington and the Colonial elite. In nearby Harper's Ferry, you can stroll down cobblestoned, streets lined with eighteenth-century brick and stone buildings, now part of a national historic park where blacksmiths, cobblers, and other tradespeople carry on their traditional livelihoods.
- Spectacular views of the Allegheny Mountain wilderness beckon in the Monongahela National Forest. Highlights include Blackwater Falls and the 1,000-foot limestone cliffs of Seneca Rocks, acclaimed as the East Coast's most challenging rock climb. The area is laced with trails for hiking, cycling, and skiing.
- New River Gorge, a 1,000-foot-deep canyon, towers over the brave travelers who go rafting along the rough-and-tumble New River. Quieter stretches invite more sedentary types to enjoy rafting as well. After a splashy day on the river, treat yourselves to dinner by candlelight at the historic and plush Greenbrier Hotel in White Sulphur Springs, where you can also go horseback riding, choose from three golf courses, and swim indoors or out.
- Experience the arts, crafts, and music of the Appalachians at the summer-long Augusta Festival, held in July and August in Elkins.

CHAPTER 30

The Rockies

Gold, silver, and precious furs drew the first adventurers into these mountains. Frontier settlements developed into ornate Victorian towns. These days, those quaint towns combine with spectacular scenery and a more pampered style of outdoor expeditions than the early explorers enjoyed, making the mountains of Colorado, Idaho, Montana, and Wyoming a romantic choice for a honeymoon. Couples can choose from a diverse array of plush yet rustic accommodations, and local tour operators can provide the expertise for casual as well as competitive athletes to participate in unique backcountry adventures. In winter, you might try dogsledding, cross-country skiing across untracked wilderness, a snowmobile safari, or perhaps taking a sleigh ride to a gourmet feast in the wilderness. Active days can be followed by a soothing massage and a soak in a hot tub, probably under the stars, before dressing for an elegant dinner and a night on the town. In summer, the mountains become playgrounds for mountain biking, hiking, and white-water rafting. How about floating over a herd of bison or elk in a hot-air balloon and then celebrating with a champagne brunch? Or hiking to an alpine meadow for a picnic amid thousands of wildflowers and then continuing on for a dip in a natural hot spring?

Sports: Outdoor sports are why most people go to the Rocky Mountains. Skiers rave about the feather-light powder snow, long runs, and great facilities. Of course, there's not just skiing. There are sleigh and toboggan rides as well as dogsled and snowmobile tours. And come summer, hiking, trail biking through the mountains, and horseback riding are just some of the options. Rental equipment, lessons, and experienced guides and tour operators (who will supply you with needed equipment) make it easy for novices to get started—just pick a trip geared to your fitness and experience level. You can also take guided horseback or dogsledding trips and participate in a cattle roundup. In spring and early summer, (from April to June in the southern rivers, June through August to the north) melting snows make for excellent—though icy—rafting, canoeing, and kayaking. The roughest waters are encountered early in the season. Mountainside resorts also offer golf, tennis, and swimming.

Memories to Go: Native American jewelry, pottery, and fine Navajo rugs make great honeymoon keepsakes. You'll also find a wide selection of Western wear, including cowboy boots, fringed jackets, and fine leather belts, as well as skis, hiking boots, thermal clothing, and other outdoor clothing and gear. The awesome landscapes, wildlife, and Western traditions have inspired artists and sculptors, whose works are sold in art galleries throughout the region.

Lodgings for Lovers: Victorian inns, dude ranches where you actually help herd the cattle, and guest ranches where you can go on horseback rides as well as enjoy a variety of recreational facilities are among the romantic options. Rustic cabins, historic lodges, ultramodern resorts, and rental condos and villas . . . they're all here.

Climate and Clothing: Mountain weather is unpredictable. All year round, storms can roll in and out quickly—raising and lowering temperatures precipitously—so never go off without warm and waterproof layers to peel off or add. The first snows can fall by October and often linger on mountain passes into July. By April, temperatures often are in the 50s by day. In July and August, temperatures usually hover between the high 60s to the low 80s by day but can drop into the 40s at night. Generally, the higher you go, the lower the temperatures get. Unless you'd like to dress up for dinner, you'll probably never need anything fancier than jeans. If you plan to do much hiking, be sure to get supportive footwear and break it in long before your trip. Because the sun is stronger at higher altitudes, be sure to use plenty of sunscreen.

Getting Around: Unless you're going touring, this is one area where you can get around without a rental car, especially in winter. Ski resorts generally run shuttles to the slopes and into town. If you stay at a hotel in town or a full-service resort, you may find that you can walk to everything you want to do. If you're driving, gas up when you can, because gas stations are often few and far between. Also, be on the lookout for deer and other animals that don't have car sense. In winter, snow conditions actually close some roads, and snow tires or chains are necessities. If you get mired in a snowbank, your best bet is to bundle up and wait in your car until someone comes by—it usually doesn't take long.

Helpful Hints: Plan to take it easy and go easy on alcoholic drinks for the first few days; high altitudes hold less oxygen, making some people feel dizzy or weak until they adjust. If you get severe headaches and nausea, see a doctor.

COLORADO

The most mountainous state in the United States, Colorado is one of the skiing capitals of the world. It attracts lovers of the great outdoors with spectacular scenery, a growing array of winter and summer sports, and festivals that celebrate everything from ski films and wild mushrooms to classical music. Frontier settlements, rich from the gold and silver of their mines, grew into opulent Victorian towns that today accommodate movie stars and honeymooners with lavish hotels, gourmet dining, and a plethora of athletic options. The most star-studded example is the mountain-surrounded town of Aspen, known for its tony boutiques and lively après-ski scene. Every summer, from late June into August, the Aspen Music Festival fills the air with music—in formal concerts, in the streets, and in the town's restaurants. More laid-back and low-key, Crested Butte's ski slopes attract mountain bikers from around the world during Fat Tire Week in early July. Cyclists can take a shortcut from there to Aspen, 21 miles along Pearl Pass, versus 190 miles by road. Telluride, once infamous as a hideout for bandits such as the bank-robbing Butch Cassidy, now rivals Aspen as a hideaway for the stars. The nouveau-riche cousin to these mining towns–turned–tourist resorts, Vail lures skiers with its varied ski trails—1,220 acres on the front side of the mountain and double that on the secluded Back Bowls.

Each ski resort has its own unusual activities. At Winter Park, sixty-seven miles out of Denver and a popular ski area for locals, you can snowmobile across the Continental Divide in winter and catch a Saturday night rodeo in summer. At Steamboat Springs, you can follow a bobsled ride or sled-dog expedition with a soak at the nearby Strawberry Park Hot Springs. In summer, Brecken-ridge offers toboggan rides down an alpine slide, while in winter, a four-in-one Ski the Summit Pass lets you shuss down Keystone, Arapahoe Basin, and Copper Mountain as well.

Summer is the time to visit Rocky Mountain National Park, which straddles the Continental Divide with large expanses of above-the-treeline tundra. Stop by the visitors center at Estes Park for suggestions on hiking trails and drive along Trail Ridge Road, which runs forty-five miles to the town of Grand Lake and claims the title of highest highway in the world. Along the way, watch for moose, coyotes, mountain lions, and beavers.

Across the state, Grand Junction is the gateway to Colorado National Monument, where erosion has carved rock spires and other strange formations out of the red, purple, and orange-toned stone. And in southwestern Colorado, you can catch the Durango & Silverton Narrow Gauge Railroad through the Animas Valley to the gold-rush town of Silverton, where a daily shoot-out cele-brates the days when Bat Masterson was city marshal. More mining towns await along the pretty San Juan Skyway, and in Ouray, you can bathe in Nature's own versions of the Jacuzzi. Also in this area is Mesa Verde National Park, site of the impressive Anasazi cliff dwellings.

Especially for Lovers

- Catch a summer concert at Red Rocks Amphitheater, about twelve miles west of Denver. The outdoor theater is wedged into the surrounding red rocks for which it is named.
- After a day on the slopes, relax in an outdoor hot tub—most resorts and condos have them. Or better still, head for the nearest natural hot springs such as Ouray or Glenwood Springs. Then, settle back in front of the fire-place—you might even have one in your room—with some warm cider or wine and decide what kind of gourmet food you'll have that night!

IDAHO

Say "Idaho," and most people think potatoes. They're not wrong; agriculture is the number-one industry. But upscale resort areas and wilderness that covers

more than one-third of the state make this an ideal destination for honeymooners seeking a stunningly scenic hideaway and outdoor adventures. The Salmon
River offers some of the most challenging and scenic river rafting in the world,
and grizzly and black bears, moose, antelope, mountain goats, and bighorn sheep
still run wild. Idaho also boasts Hells Canyon, the deepest river gorge on the
continent; superlative fly fishing for trout and thirty-nine other species of game
fish; and the Idaho Panhandle National Forests, with the world's largest stand of
white pine. Silver as well as gems, including garnets, opals, onyx, sapphires, and
rubies, are still mined here.

The northern part of the state is dotted with beautiful mountain lakes. The
forest-embraced Lake Coeur d'Alene sets the scene for water sports, dinner
cruises, and luxurious accommodations, while Lake Pend Oreille is home to the
resort town of Sandpoint. In central Idaho, Sun Valley, America's first ski resort, is
a world-renowned sports center. Skiers praise its powder snow, while summer
visitors can enjoy boating, kayaking, horseback riding and white-water river raft
trips as well as hay rides, tennis, and golf on an eighteen-hole Robert Trent Jones
Jr. course. The nearby Sawtooth Mountains offer some of the country's most
pristine wilderness. And for scenery that is truly otherworldly, visit Craters of
the Moon National Monument, where the lava landscape is so lunarlike that
NASA has brought astronauts here for training.

Especially for Lovers

- At pretty Lake Coeur d'Alene, you can play golf on the world's only floating
  green and stroll along the world's largest floating boardwalk. Ready for soli-
  tude? Rent a boat and sail off to claim your own private beach.
- Take a dip in one of the natural outdoor mineral pools at Lava Hot Springs,
  a resort area that claims to have the most highly mineralized water in the
  world.
- Take a rafting or jet boat trip along the Snake River into Hells Canyon, a
  5,500-foot-deep river gorge that is deeper than the Grand Canyon. Giant
  rock formations rise like black towers over the river.

MONTANA

Vast open spaces that stretch for miles and miles earn America's fourth-largest
state its nickname: Big Sky Country. Like a big circus tent, the sky stretches
across dazzling displays of nature. Bald eagles soar over craggy mountain ridges,
and cougars and bears share the land with wild horses and elk. When night
comes to turn down the lights, twinkling stars blaze against a black sky, and when
conditions are right, the northern lights offer laser shows in red and green.

Eastern Montana's plains and rolling hills are home to sprawling ranches and
farms as well as the Little Bighorn Battlefield National Monument, where a self-
guided drive tour recreates the famous Native American victory over George
Armstrong Custer—better known as "Custer's Last Stand." The monument is

located on the Crow Indian Reservation, where you can buy Indian crafts and sometimes catch a powwow that includes traditional dancing, parades, dinner dances, and a rodeo. About one hundred miles west is the historic resort town of Red Lodge. From here, you can follow scenic, steep, and twisting U.S. 212 across Beartooth Pass to the northeastern entrance of Yellowstone National Park, which sprawls across the border into Wyoming.

The Rocky Mountains loom large in western Montana, attracting honeymooners with dramatic scenery, outdoor adventures, and laid-back yet lively nightlife. Here, river rapids offer exciting rafting opportunities, and mountain biking is a way of life. Skiers are drawn to Big Sky and Big Mountain, while anglers and water sports enthusiasts head for Flathead Lake, the largest freshwater lake west of the Mississippi River. Glacier National Park's Going to the Sun Road, open June through late October, climbs its tortuous way through thick forests interspersed with splendid meadows and overpowering peaks; hiking trails lead to wildflower-filled meadows, waterfalls, and glacier-fed lakes. Western Montana is also dotted with mining-spurred towns such as Butte, Helena, Anaconda, and Missoula that proudly preserve grand, turn-of-the century mansions, while the rip-roaring frontier mining days are preserved at ghost towns such as Virginia City, Bannack, Garnet, and Nevada City.

Especially for Lovers

- Try to catch a Native American powwow, where traditional songs, dances, foods, and crafts are shared. Among the largest: the Crow Fair, held every August, and Custer's Last Stand Reenactment in June—both held at the Crow reservation.
- Watch for the highway signs that look like a pair of binoculars. These indicate the best places to see wildlife. Pull over and you may see moose, elk, bighorn sheep, bears, and more. Pick up a copy of the Montana Department of Fish, Wildlife and Parks's "Montana Wildlife Viewing Guide," which is keyed to the marked sites and sold in bookstores.

WYOMING

Looking for true cowboy country and flamboyant scenery? In Wyoming, rodeos, country & western dance halls, and working ranches are still a way of life, while posh dude ranches and lodges cater to those who prefer their Western excitement with a coddling touch. And for nature at its most imaginative best, you can't beat the Yellowstone National Park, where the earth's interior seeps to the surface in spouting geysers, bubbling mud pots, and soothing hot springs. Its recovery from the 1988 fires makes for an interesting ecology lesson; the waterfall-laced peaks are a photographer's dream.

Just south, the Grand Tetons tower over the Jackson Hole ski resorts, whose steep bowls and chutes have earned a reputation with expert skiers, while Grand Teton National Park invites summer visitors to hike to its summits and take to its streams and lakes in all sorts of watercraft. The Old West lives on in the town of Jackson, where art galleries, craft shops, and Western-wear boutiques line its boardwalk-lined main street and shoot-outs are staged in the town square on summer evenings. East of Yellowstone, more Wild West lore awaits in Cody, named for Pony Express rider and entertainer William F. "Buffalo Bill" Cody. Follow the self-guided walking tour brochure and don't miss the Buffalo Bill Historical Center, often called the "Smithsonian of the West," where collections include Western and Plains Indian art, Buffalo Bill memorabilia, and the world's largest variety of American firearms; and Trail Town, where buildings date from frontier days. Summer brings nightly rodeos and the annual July 4th Cody Stampede, with parades and rodeos.

Across the state, Cheyenne, the state capital, still feels like a frontier town, especially when it hosts the annual Cheyenne Frontier Days festival in late July, the world's largest outdoor rodeo. Top country stars perform, and there are chuckwagon races, air shows, and nonstop festivities.

Especially for Lovers

- Sightsee the natural wonders of Yellowstone National Park, keeping your eyes peeled for bison, grizzly bears, and other wildlife along the way. Stop by one of the visitors centers for suggestions on hikes, which can be topped off with a dip in a naturally heated swimming hole, such as the one at Firehole River canyon. Cruise across Yellowstone Lake. Drive to the Grand Canyon of Yellowstone, and don't miss the dramatic Lower Falls. Catch a performance by Old Faithful and feel the heat at bubbling mud pots, hot springs, and steam vents warmed by underground magma.
- Honeymooning in winter? Ride a horse-drawn sleigh among a thousand-strong herd of elk at the National Elk Refuge, just north of Jackson.

CHAPTER 31

New England

*F*resh-caught lobsters served to the sound of waves crashing on the rocky promontory below . . . leaves crunching underfoot as you walk through a forest canopied in the brilliant russet and gold tones of autumn . . . a white-steepled church and stately town hall set around a village green, watching over a town of whitewashed, clapboard homes . . . following the trail of Paul Revere through Boston's historic streets . . . these are some of the pleasures of New England.

The six New England states, Connecticut, Maine, Massachusetts, New Hampshire, Rhode Island, and Vermont, were among the first areas settled by Europeans in the New World. Quaint villages and port towns throughout the region proudly maintain much of their storied heritage, while historic recreations and restorations such as Connecticut's Mystic Seaport and Massachusetts's Sturbridge Village replicate early Colonial life. Small wonder that antiquing is such a popular pastime.

Each season paints the countryside in a new set of colors and activities. Fall is the most famous and visually flamboyant season. Leaves burst out in a blaze of color, inviting lovers to traipse through a forest for a private picnic. Stop at a farm to pick your own berries or apples while enjoying a leisurely drive through this picturesque region.

Winter snows cast a peaceful hush over the land. It's a time to cuddle by a crackling fire and sip hot mulled wine. If quiet isn't your thing, head over to the ski resort areas of the White and Green mountains where you can rev up for days of downhill and cross-country skiing balanced by nights of pubbing and dancing. Spring moves slowly northward, with melting snows surmounted by waves of wildflowers. By early May, ski resorts have switched gears and are swinging into action with golf and tennis. It's a great time to join a bicycling expedition. Summer cloaks the land in rich shades of green, and water sports are added to the roster of activities. Sail off on a tall ship to explore coastal towns and secluded offshore islands. Whiz across a lake on water skis. Or head for the cooler hills for some hiking or perhaps to catch a music festival. Any time is the right time to hide away in a charming Colonial inn, go antiquing, and explore historic New England towns and quaint villages.

Sports: Hiking is best in summer and fall. In winter, skiing is the main sport at legendary areas such as Vermont's Stowe, Killington, Mount Snow, Stratton, and Sugarbush; New Hampshire's Waterville Valley, Bretton Woods, Cannon, and Loon; and Maine's Sugarloaf. Swimming is most comfortable in the lakes and Atlantic in late summer, when the water has had a few months to warm up.

Memories to Go: Antiques, handmade quilts, and all kinds of handicrafts are sold throughout New England. Picturesque barns, clapboard houses, and converted mansions all serve as antique shops in this history-rich region. For the bargain-hunter in you, there are discounts on clothing, housewares, and other items in the outlets of Manchester, Vermont; Kittery, Maine; and North Conway, New Hampshire; as well as Filene's Basement in Boston and the L.L. Bean clothing outlet in Freeport, Maine.

Cuisine: Seafood is the true regional specialty here, from Maine lobster to New England clam chowder. Try a traditional clambake, which may start with digging the clams and includes steamed clams and corn on the cob.

Lodgings for Lovers: New England is famous for its charming country inns; many are known for their gourmet cuisine as well as their antique-filled decor. Some are quite elegant and formal, with prices to match (see chapter 3 on country inns for tips on what to look for). There are also less expensive bed-and-breakfast guest houses as well as resorts that buzz with sports, restaurants, and entertainment facilities.

Climate and Clothing: Winters can be positively frigid, especially when the winds kick in, but that's what makes New England so cozy. Dress for warmth. Spring and fall temperatures can drop below freezing but can also reach the 50s and 60s. Summer temperatures range from the 80s in the south to the 60s and low 70s in the northern regions. Year-round, it's cooler in the higher elevations. Plan to dress in layers and be prepared for swiftly changing mountain temperatures. Even in summer, you'll want sweaters for the cooler evenings and higher elevations. And be sure to bring a raincoat for sudden squalls.

Getting Around: Outside of the cities, the most convenient way to get around is by car. Rental cars are readily available at the major airports. Buses also crisscross the region, and bicycling is a popular mode of transportation, with rentals available from some of the inns and in most resort towns.

CONNECTICUT

Although this state makes its living from industry, insurance, and its status as a bedroom community for New York City, almost 75 percent of the state is still forested and dotted with small villages built around traditional village greens. Three main areas vie for honeymooners' attention in New England's southern-most state: the Connecticut River Valley, Mystic Seaport, and Litchfield Hills. Feeling lucky? Near to Mystic is one of the state's newest attractions, the Native American–owned Foxwoods Resort Casino, one of the highest-grossing casinos in the country.

Especially for Lovers

- Take a leisurely drive through the Connecticut River Valley. The twenty-two-mile stretch from Westbrook to East Haddam is lined with picturesque towns such as Old Lyme and Essex. The region is studded with delightful inns and historic sites such as the restored nineteenth-century mansion of Captain Stannard in Westbrook, now a hostelry and antique shop. Many unusual museums dot the area, such as the Florence Griswold Museum in Old Lyme, where turn-of-the-century "Lyme School" American Impressionist artists often paid for their rooms with the works now on display.

- Litchfield County beckons with bucolic charm and lots of history. Rolling hills covered with forests and farmland are ribboned with sparkling rivers and lakes. White Christopher Wren church steeples peer over the trees, and gracious mansions fill charming eighteenth-century villages. You can go rowing, canoeing, or sailing on nearby lakes, and if you want a change of pace, you're just a short drive from Massachusetts's Berkshire Mountains.

- Stroll through the open-air museum of Mystic Seaport, a nineteenth-century maritime town where you can attend a sea chantey songfest, see demonstrations of traditional crafts, and step aboard a historic Yankee whaling ship.

MAINE

The largest New England state, Maine is also the most sparsely populated and remote. There's something of a frontier spirit to this rugged state, where many people still make their living from the land, cutting timber, growing potatoes, and fishing. But the biggest industry is tourism. Visit lovely coastal towns such as Kennebunkport, Ogunquit, and Bar Harbor; enjoy the rugged beauty of Acadia National Park; or shop for discounted clothing and housewares at the outlet stores in Kittery.

Especially for Lovers

- Relax at one of the three town beaches of Ogunquit, which aptly means "beautiful place by the sea," and then stroll along "Marginal Way," a path overlooking the rocky coast that leads to the shops and galleries at Perkins Cove.

- After browsing Kennebunkport's galleries around Dock Square, drive along Ocean Avenue to see the resort's finest mansions; among them is the summer retreat for former president George Bush.

- Sail along Maine's rugged and rocky coastline on a graceful, historic tall ship, stopping to stroll around quaint fishing villages, enjoy a beachside lobsterbake, and spot seals, porpoises, eagles, and maybe even a whale or puffin.

MASSACHUSETTS

The Pilgrims landed near Boston at Plymouth Rock in 1620, and this state has been flaunting its history ever since. Boston's fun-to-follow Freedom Trail winds past sixteen historic sites. When the sun sets, you'll discover that Boston is also a rollicking college town filled with nightclubs and pubs.

The delightful Berkshires welcome visitors year-round to centuries-old towns and inns, especially in summer, when the region becomes a center for the arts, attracting world-class musicians. To the east, Cape Cod's colonial towns are just steps away from long stretches of golden sands and pounding surf. Even more laid-back are Nantucket and Martha's Vineyard, two islands off the Cape Cod coast, where lighthouses, unspoiled beaches, and historic monuments provide plenty to explore—by bicycle or on foot.

Especially for Lovers

- Follow the Freedom Trail, a double row of red bricks or red painted lines that leads to Boston's historic sites, such as Paul Revere's House and the Old North Church. Hungry? Stop by the restored red-brick eighteenth century warehouse–turned–shopping and dining mall, Quincy Market/Faneuil Hall Marketplace, located on the historic, cobblestoned waterfront. Or pick up some picnic fixings and then head over to the Public Garden for a ride on one of the famous pedal-powered Swan Boats. Then stroll through the elegant Back Bay area and Beacon Hill, where gaslights still illuminate streets lined with brick houses.
- After a day on one of Cape Cod's secluded beaches, drive to the artsy town of Provincetown to dine and browse through its galleries and boutiques.
- Pack a picnic, spread your blanket, and catch a concert on the lawn at Tanglewood, summer home to the Boston Symphony Orchestra. In Lenox and surrounding towns, you can also shop for heirlooms. Or catch a performance of the Jacobs Pillow Dance Festival or the Berkshire Theatre Festival.

NEW HAMPSHIRE

Beaches, mountains, and lakes: three good reasons to visit New Hampshire. The Atlantic coast is bordered by wide beaches. Inland, in the Lakes Region, you can rent a lakeside cottage, dine, dance, club-hop, and ride through the countryside on the Winnipesaukee Scenic Railroad. Skiers and hikers, as well as couples looking for a scenic drive, head for the White Mountains, capped by 6,288-foot Mt. Washington, the highest peak in New England.

Especially for Lovers

- Party and play at Hampton Beach, New Hampshire's Atlantic Coast resort center. Head north to bask on more secluded sands and reserve time for a stroll through historic Portsmouth.
- Dine and dance on a moonlight cruise across Lake Winnipesaukee. Cruises depart from Weirs Beach and other lakeside harbors.
- Pack a picnic into your backpacks, drive to Crawford Notch State Park in the White Mountains, and hike to a waterfall. Feeling more philosophical?

Drive to Franconia and visit poet Robert Frost's home. Then see if you can spot the profile of the "Old Man of the Mountains" at Franconia Notch.

RHODE ISLAND

Although it's the smallest state in the nation, Rhode Island has 400 miles of beautiful coastline where you can swim, sail, fish, or simply relax at seaside hideaways, such as Block Island, accessible only by ferry and air. The state's most famous tourist area is Newport, a yachting capital filled with opulent mansions built by the Vanderbilts, Astors, and other turn-of-the-century elite.

Especially for Lovers

- Follow Newport's Cliff Walk, which overlooks the Atlantic Ocean and passes many "cottages," the word that socialites once used for their palatial summer abodes.
- Visit some of the grand homes such as the Breakers, an Italian palace; Rosecliff, with a heart-shaped staircase; and Astors' Beechwood, where actors provide a theatrical tour.

VERMONT

Tall steepled churches. White clapboard houses. Red barns. Covered bridges. Fresh maple syrup. Rows of forested mountains that seem to extend to infinity. This is Vermont—*Verd Mont,* or "green mountain," as the French named it for the mountains that cover most of the state. The Long Trail, which runs 264 miles from north to south, is a well-maintained hiking route. One of the country's most rural states, Vermont is known for its ski resorts, which convert to warm-weather activities in summer. The largest city, Burlington, with only about 50,000 inhabitants, is a culture-rich college town with pretty cafés fronting Lake Champlain.

Especially for Lovers

- Join an organized bicycle-touring excursion. (The Vermont Department of Travel and Tourism can provide a list. See Appendix B.) You'll cycle from inn to inn, enjoy gourmet meals and, when you tire of cycling, be whisked—bicycles and all—by van to your next stop.
- Ride the Alpine Slide at Stowe. You'll take a scenic ride up in a chair lift and then race down, bobsled-style, on a twisting run.
- Hike up Mt. Mansfield, the state's highest peak, located near Stowe.

CHAPTER 32

The Southwest

R ide horseback through scenes that seem right out of an old-style Western
movie: rose-colored deserts, red sandstone mesas, ponderosa pine forests,
and high plateaus cut by wide river canyons. The dramatic terrain of the southwestern states—Arizona, Nevada, New Mexico, Texas, and Utah—offers a stunning backdrop for hot-air ballooning, hiking, and other active pursuits as well as
browsing for Native American crafts or trying your luck in the glittering casinos
of Las Vegas, Lake Tahoe, and Reno.

Sports: Horseback riding is a great way to get into the spirit of the region.
You'll also find some of the world's poshest golf and tennis resorts here. Water
sports abound along Texas's Gulf Coast and on expansive lakes such as Lake
Powell and Lake Mead. There's also white-water rafting, mountain biking, hot-
air ballooning, and backcountry all-terrain vehicle tours.

Memories to Go: Native American crafts are sold throughout the region
and have influenced more recent artisans in the area as well. Painters are also drawn
to towns like Santa Fe, where you can find wonderful works at prefame rates.

Lodgings for Lovers: A plush golf-and-sports resort. A cozy log cabin
with a fireplace beside a mountain lake. A dude ranch that pampers guests with
hot tubs and massages. An intimate bed-and-breakfast inn. These are just some
of the accommodations awaiting in this romantic region. You can also rent a
houseboat on a lake or choose from an array of themed fantasy suites at flashy
hotels or quiet mountain hideaways.

Climate and Clothing: Because of the variety of terrains, temperatures vary
greatly across the region. In spring, deserts bloom with wildflowers, and temperatures average in the 70s in many areas. Summers can mean extremely high temperatures and frequent thunderstorms in the deserts and plains, while the mountains can be quite pleasant. Autumn brings temperatures back to comfortable
levels in the 70s and 80s, with beautiful foliage in many of the forested regions.

Getting Around: Some couples pick one resort area and stay there.
However, in this region, most also want to get out and explore. For that, you'll
need a car, unless you join a tour or plan to hike or cycle.

ARIZONA

The Grand Canyon, located in this state, is one of the seven wonders of the
world. Hike or ride a surefooted mule into the canyon, drive or cycle along its

rim, soar over it on a flight-seeing trip, or raft between its towering walls. However you go, you'll be awed by the changing vistas of this 277-mile-long chasm. To the north is Lake Powell, where you can water-ski or go boating and find yourselves a secluded cove. Northeastern Arizona is also home to the Navajo Indian Reservation, the largest stretch of Native American–owned land in the country, where you can witness traditional dances as well as shop for Navajo rugs and other crafts and take guided hikes and horseback rides into the deep gorges of Canyon de Chelly.

The "Valley of the Sun," as the region around Phoenix and Scottsdale is known, lives up to its name with an average of 330 days of sunshine a year and temperatures that can soar well above 100 degrees in summer. Honeymooners find happy refuge in the sprawling swimming pools of the area's posh resorts, where world-class golf, tennis, and spa facilities await. To the north, Sedona is an artists' colony where you can buy Western art, Native American crafts, and Western fashions and take jeep excursions or llama treks into the surrounding red-rock mountains.

Especially for Lovers

- After exploring the much-visited south rim of the Grand Canyon, take the stunning 215-mile drive to the secluded north rim, stopping to admire the Painted Desert en route. (The road is closed in winter.) The 26-mile Cape Royal Drive takes you to the highest point in the park, with views of the Colorado River, Marble Canyon, and the Painted Desert.
- Visit Old Tucson, a Wild West amusement park built around movie sets, where you can ride a stagecoach, watch a bawdy saloon show, or witness a gunfight on Main Street. Nearby guest ranches and the preserved town of Tombstone invite you to live out your Wild West fantasies.

NEVADA

Glittering fantasylands where fortunes are won and lost in the roll of the dice or the spin of a roulette wheel, spectacular shows with international superstars, round-the-clock excitement—these are the attractions of a honeymoon in the dazzling gambling capitals of Nevada. Las Vegas sets the standard for the world when it comes to showy extravaganzas. The floor shows are just the start of outrageous entertainment options. A rash of wildly imaginative hotels, each larger and more spectacular than the next, are theme parks in their own right. At night, downtown Fremont Street is so bathed in neon that it may just be visible from the moon.

For a natural getaway, head to Lake Mead, the largest man-made lake in the hemisphere and a delightful place for swimming and boating. Also nearby is Valley of Fire State Park, with its colorful rock formations, Red Rock Canyon, and the forested Mt. Charleston area, where you can hike in summer and ski in winter.

Across the state, Lake Tahoe honeymooners are usually captivated more by the stunning scenery than the clanging of the casino action. Stretching across Nevada and California, Lake Tahoe's clear waters are ideal for summer sailing and water sports, while the surrounding mountains tantalize hikers in summer and skiers in winter. Nearby Reno uses a giant neon sign to welcome you to "The Biggest Little City in the World," and its showy casinos do come with a small-town friendliness.

Especially for Lovers

- While in Las Vegas, check out its outlandish hotels. A "Journey to the Center of the Earth" is just one of the rides at MGM Grand Hotel's theme park. Catch a jousting tournament in Excalibur's showroom, take a "Nile River cruise" at the Luxor Hotel, and watch pirate ships do battle outside the Treasure Island Hotel.
- If you're honeymooning in Las Vegas, don't miss the opportunity to go flight-seeing over the Grand Canyon. Organized tours will pick you up and return you to your hotel.
- Step back into the heady days of gold and silver prospecting in Virginia City, an authentically restored gold rush town, once again lively with the sounds of honky-tonk music. Just twenty-five miles from Reno, the city served the miners of the Comstock Lode, one of the largest ever found.

NEW MEXICO

Its license plates proclaim it the "Land of Enchantment," and those who honeymoon in New Mexico are sure to agree. The jagged peaks of the Sangre de Cristo Mountains and vivid desertscapes of the state's northern territory have been immortalized by Georgia O'Keeffe and other artists. The area is also rich in Native American tradition and memorabilia from the era of the Wild West. The chic state capital, Santa Fe, and nearby town of Taos are still magnets for artists. Santa Fe's historic Plaza is lined with art galleries and restaurants, and Native Americans sell jewelry and crafts in front of the Governor's Palace. Taos is also a popular ski resort in winter, and the Taos Pueblo is one of the oldest continuously inhabited communities in the country.

Especially for Lovers

- Try to visit one of the Native American pueblos on a feast day, when the public is often invited to attend ceremonial dances. Some pueblos require that you pay admission or request permission in advance.
- Hike to Spence's Hot Spring and bring your towels (according to local custom, bathing suits are optional except on weekend nights). Located about seventy miles west of Santa Fe near the town of Jemez Springs, it includes a series of waterfall-fed pools, ranging from warm to hot.

- Take the scenic High Route between Santa Fe and Taos. It winds through the Sangre de Cristo Mountains and passes through pine and aspen tree forests as well as a number of Native American pueblos.

TEXAS

"The Lone Star State," an apt name considering its independently minded people, is big—almost eight hundred miles from east to west and almost one thousand miles from north to south. It's also a state with heart; the state motto, "Friendship," describes the warm welcome that visitors receive. The terrain ranges from the spectacular canyons, deserts, and woodlands of Big Bend National Park, where roadrunners, coyotes, and mountain lions roam free, to the inviting beaches of the Gulf Coast, which stretch from pristine Padre Island National Seashore and the resort town of Corpus Cristi to historic Galveston. You can play out your cowhand fantasies throughout the western and Panhandle regions as well as in the Hill Country, where guest ranches and inns invite you to go horseback riding, hop on a hayride, and swing to the Texas two-step. Rodeos, cattle drives, and Wild West shows are part of the pageantry around Bandera, "Cowboy Capital of the World." And the LBJ Ranch House, in the Lyndon Baines Johnson Historical Park, brims with memorabilia of the thirty-sixth president of the United States. Not far off are two of the state's prettiest cities, San Antonio, where you can visit the Alamo, and Austin, which is a convenient gateway to the Hill Country. For true big-city excitement, Dallas is the place. Explore the Arts District; take a horse-drawn carriage through the West End Historic District to the Marketplace, a restored brick warehouse with restaurants and clubs; and visit Old City Park, a recreation of an 1800s Texas town. Fans of the television series *Dallas* can swing through J. R. Ewing's Southfork Ranch in nearby Plano. And just outside Dallas are two theme parks: Six Flags Over Texas and Wet & Wild.

Especially for Lovers

- In San Antonio, stroll along the twenty-one-block River Walk, a cobble-stoned, landscaped path along the banks of the San Antonio River, lined with restaurants, shops, and nightclubs. From here, you can take a dinner cruise or catch a river taxi. Don't miss La Villita, settled by Mexican squatters in the eighteenth century and now a National Historic District where artisans demonstrate and sell weaving, pottery, and other crafts.
- Sample the music scene for which Austin is renowned; the clubs of Austin launched the careers of Lyle Lovett and Steve Earle. Pick up one of the local newspapers for listings or simply head over to Sixth Street, which is virtually lined with bars.

UTAH

Southern Utah is rugged wilderness—striated sandstone canyons cut into red deserts, dense forests topping towering peaks, and mighty rivers carving steep canyons. Moab is the jumping-off point for adventures into the backcountry, much of which has been preserved in its natural state as national parks. Canyonlands' red rock chasms bear descriptive names such as Island-in-the-Sky, the Needles, and the Maze. Arches National Park takes its name from the red and golden sandstone arches and ridges that rise over its desert plain, and Capitol Reef National Park is also known as "land of the sleeping rainbow" for its colorfully striped canyon walls. In Bryce Canyon National Park, millions of years of geological sculpting have carved out colossal amphitheaters, with huge domes and pinnacles, while the multihued cliffs of Zion Canyon stand just to the west.

In the northeastern part of the state, the Great Salt Lake is dotted with sailboats in the summer. Resort areas in the nearby Wasatch Mountains such as Park City, Deer Valley, Snowbird, and Alta are well known to skiers for their fluffy powder snow. In summer, these mountains host arts festivals and concerts as well as golf, tennis, and other recreation.

Especially for Lovers

- For feet-on experience of the otherworldly scenery, you can't beat hiking, but hot-air ballooning, jeep and horseback trips, mountain biking, and river rafting also are wonderful ways to traverse Utah's backcountry.
- If you're honeymooning in January, you can combine skiing with a cultural experience at the annual Sundance Film Institute, a showcase for independent films, held at Sundance, a ski resort owned by actor Robert Redford.
- Visit Park City's restored Main Street and step back into the exciting days when Wasatch Mountain silver mines gave George Hearst the money to start his media empire. Stop by the visitors center's museum to learn all about the town's history and then meander through its trendy shops, art galleries, and restaurants.

CHAPTER 33

The Great Lakes Region

Deserted sandy beaches backed by massive dunes, tiny fishing villages and skyscrapers, craggy cliffs and wooded islands—all are mirrored in the Great Lakes. Interconnected, the lakes form the largest body of fresh water in the world and border six states: Illinois, Indiana, Michigan, Minnesota, Ohio, and Wisconsin. Inland, smaller lakes and sleepy villages spackle a patchwork of rolling woodland preserves and vast expanses of farm fields and pastures, while high bluffs line the Mississippi and Ohio river valleys. In the land where the car was born, you can also explore by steam-powered paddle wheelers and horse-drawn carriage. Here, modern cities are never far from lake resorts and are often graced with pretty riverfront areas.

Sports: Summer is the time for water sports on the lakes. Off-road trails traverse the region, ideal for bicycling when spring flowers and autumn foliage cast their colors across the hillsides and for cross-country skiing and snowmobiling when winter snows come.

Memories to Go: The most upscale boutiques and shops line the Magnificent Mile in Chicago. The country's largest shopping emporium, Mall of America, beckons in Bloomington, Minnesota (near Minneapolis/St. Paul), with more than four hundred stores and a seven-acre theme park.

Lodgings for Lovers: A cozy inn in a small village, a grand turn-of-the-century resort, a rustic cottage, or a houseboat on a lake . . . these are among your choices in the Great Lakes region.

Climate and Clothing: The Great Lakes has a four-season climate. Summer temperatures average in the 80s, comfortably moderated by lake breezes; winter temperatures often drop below freezing and can feel even colder when the winds whip off the lake. Fall and spring temperatures can range between the 30s and 60s.

Getting Around: Amtrak traverses much of the region, and cycling is pleasant in many of the lake areas. Having a car provides maximum flexibility outside of the cities.

ILLINOIS

Looking for a sunny summer honeymoon spot where you can enjoy beaches, sailing, bicycling, and the cultural attractions of one of the country's most vibrant cities? Consider Chicago, where beaches, marinas, and parks as well as elegant neighborhoods and soaring skyscrapers are strung along twenty-nine miles of Lake Michigan. Peruse the designer fashions along Michigan Avenue's elegant "Magnificent Mile." Take a crash course in American architecture as you stroll through Chicago's historic business district, The Loop, a virtual museum of architectural styles. Browse in the antique and art galleries of the River North area, also known for its jazz clubs. And for more nightlife, try the North Pier, Rush Street, and Old Town districts.

In the wooded hills northwest of Chicago, historic Galena and many of the tiny surrounding towns seem to have remained in the 1850s. Visit the home of Ulysses S. Grant, now a state historic site; hunt for antiques; and go biking or cross-country skiing.

Especially for Lovers

- Speculate on the past—during a riverboat gambling cruise. Replicas of nineteenth-century riverboats docked along the Mississippi River from Galena to East Saint Louis offer day and evening sailings. Cruises also depart from Joliet, about fifty miles from Chicago, and other inland river ports.
- In warm weather, Chicago's Lincoln Park is a wonderful place to enjoy nature in the middle of a big city. Rent bicycles for a spin along the lakefront, suit up for the beach, or pack a picnic for a paddleboat trip around the lagoon.
- Catch a free lunchtime concert. There's usually one in the Chicago Cultural Center. During the summer, there are also free concerts at the bandstand in Grant Park, at the Daley Plaza, and at the first National Bank Plaza at Madison and Clark.

INDIANA

Indiana's motto is "Crossroads of America," and nine different interstates traverse the state. Its most renowned route is the Indianapolis Speedway, site of the world-famous Indianapolis 500 car races, held every May. The state's largest and liveliest city, Indianapolis, is also an amateur sports center, hosting events such as the Pan-American Games and national Olympic trials. Don't miss the renovated brick and granite Union Station, with its spirited bars, cafés, shops, and impressive stained-glass ceiling. Stroll through the Lockerbie Square Historic District, where brightly colored, wood-frame homes line cobblestoned streets. Historic attractions beckon to the south, including Indiana's oldest community, 300-year-old Vincennes, the first capital, and New Harmony, site of two early-nineteenth-century utopian communes. Summer performances in Lincoln State Park and a museum and working farmstead at the Lincoln Boyhood National Memorial celebrate Abraham Lincoln's childhood home. To the north, enjoy water sports along the dune-lined beaches of Michigan City and the Indiana Dunes National Lakeshore.

Especially for Lovers

- Stroll along the charming Canal Walk in Indianapolis, a city park that runs for ten blocks along the canal system that was once an important shipping link between the Great Lakes and the Ohio River.
- Break away from the beaches of the Indiana Dunes National Lakeshore and discover the fairs, festivals, and tranquil backroads of Crystal Valley's Amish country.

MICHIGAN

"If you seek a great peninsula, look about you." That is Michigan's motto, and the state sports not one but two great peninsulas, surrounded by four of the five Great Lakes. Although best known for its cars and Motown music, the state is a four-season vacationland. The Upper Peninsula, bordered by Lake Superior and Lake Michigan, is a land of rugged, unspoiled nature, with giant boulders, impressive waterfalls, and 200-foot sandstone cliffs carved by pounding surf. In the "U.P.," as locals call it, a bed-and-breakfast inn will probably be your home base. In summer, you can fish, windsurf, and try sea kayaking. Fall and spring are hiking and mountain biking season, while winter invites you to try snowmobiling or skiing—cross-country or downhill.

In the straits separating the Upper Peninsula from the Lower Peninsula is Mackinac Island, a Victorian resort town accessible by ferry, where cars are banned and bicycles and horse-drawn carriages are the best way to get around. At Sleeping Bear Dunes National Lakeshore, dunes rise more than 400 feet high. Traverse City, in the heart of cherry orchard country and the resort center, invites you to play golf, go boating and fish in summer, and ski in winter. Across the peninsula, Detroit is the capital of the car industry, subject of the Henry Ford Museum and Greenfield Village in nearby Dearborn. In addition to museums and sports events, the city's cultural diversity enables you to enjoy traditional Greek music and belly dancing in Greektown, listen to the blues in the clubs of Rivertown, and taste Polish, Bulgarian, and other authentic ethnic cuisines and entertainment.

Especially for Lovers

- From Traverse City, drive to Petoskey, a Victorian resort town on Little Traverse Bay, known for its restored Gaslight District and its good shopping.
- From downtown Detroit, it's a short drive to Windsor, Canada (bring identification for customs and immigration). Enjoy a free tour and tasting at the Hiram Walker plant where Canadian Club is distilled and then sit at a riverside café and look back at the Detroit skyline.
- For a true wilderness experience, visit Isle Royale National Park, which lies fifty miles off the Upper Peninsula and is accessible only by seaplane or by ferry from Houghton or Copper Harbor.

MINNESOTA

Minnesota, a Sioux word that means "land of sky-tinted water," is a good description—more than twelve thousand lakes and grand rivers speckle the state, ideal for water sports–filled summers and winters of snowmobiling, dogsledding, and skiing. In southeastern Minnesota, drive along U.S. 61 to visit pretty Mississippi River towns such as Winona, where Garvin Heights Scenic Lookout offers panoramic views of the Mississippi River from a 575-foot bluff.

To the north, the Lake Superior city of Duluth is the jumping-off point for boat tours and forays into northern wilderness areas. Voyageurs National Park, which borders Canada (bring proof of citizenship), is best explored in summer on boat trips that take you into a true wilderness. Another protected region is the Boundary Waters Canoe Area Wilderness, where portages (overland trails) link more than one thousand lakes for canoeing. In winter, cross-country skiing and dogsledding are the ways to go.

Modern Minneapolis and historic St. Paul, known as the Twin Cities, face each other across the Mississippi River. Combined, they boast more theaters per capita than any city except New York and offer a rich variety of cultural attractions. And the nearby Mall of America, the largest shopping center in the world, draws consumers from every continent.

Especially for Lovers

- In Minneapolis, sample the nightlife in the clubs and cafés of the Warehouse District and along the "Mississippi Mile" and hop aboard a narrated paddleboat cruise.
- Take a guided boat trip into Voyageurs National Park. There are no paved roads; you'll be traveling through a pristine wilderness where you're likely to see more moose, bears, ospreys, and eagles than people.

OHIO

Although most people live in its trio of cities—Cleveland, Columbus, and Cincinnati—most summer honeymooners head for Lake Erie, where 288 miles of sandy beaches beckon along with timeless lakeside towns where seafood restaurants sit side-by-side with small boutiques and art galleries. The most popular town is Sandusky; from there you can board a ferry to camp on your own private island or be pampered at one of the grand hotels on the Lake Erie Islands. Put-in-Bay on South Bass Island, the most popular destination, offers hiking, parasailing, and swimming as well as tours of the Heineman Winery and adjacent Crystal Cave. Kelley's Island, the largest, where few buildings are less than one hundred years old, is a National Historic District. About sixty miles to the east, Cleveland has undergone a remarkable restoration. Near the stately nineteenth-century Beaux Arts Public Square are the shops and eateries of the waterfront and Historic Warehouse District. Cleveland is also home to the Rock and Roll Hall of Fame.

Cincinnati, a European-toned city on the Ohio River, features pretty parks and plazas and a cobblestoned riverside wharf, the departure point for sightseeing and dinner cruises. Nearby is picturesque horse country and pretty Clifton Gorge. In central Ohio sits Columbus, the state capital and headquarters for The Limited, Express, and Structure, among other shops in the Columbus City Center mall downtown. Stroll through the brick streets of nineteenth-century German Village and stop in at the cafés and shops of the nearby Brewery District.

Especially for Lovers

- Dine and stay in Victorian splendor at the grand hotels and inns of Lake Erie's islands, where dinners are often served by candlelight and canopy beds, stained-glass windows, and turrets grace many of the inns.
- You're sure to hold each other tightly as you whip around on the rides at the Cedar Point Amusement Park, home of some of the tallest and fastest roller coasters in the country.
- For nightlife, head for The Flats in Cleveland, made up of industrial buildings converted into an exciting nightlife area. In Cincinnati, trendy bars and boutiques occupy historic townhouses in the Mount Adams neighborhood, while Covington Landing, just across the river in Kentucky, is home to cafés, clubs, and riverboat cruises. In Columbus, the Short North is the liveliest district for nightlife.

WISCONSIN

Although best known for its dairy products and breweries, Wisconsin's fifteen thousand lakes and scenic river valleys with their dramatic bluffs are the draw for honeymooners. More than four hundred and sixty-six miles of off-road bicycle paths wind through pristine woodlands and along scenic lake- and riverfronts, and waterside resorts dot the state. The most famous region is the Wisconsin Dells, a fifteen-mile stretch of soaring rock formations carved into the soft limestone banks of the Wisconsin River. Sightseers also will find amusement parks and an array of eateries and hotels. Nearby Baraboo, original home of the Ringling Brothers circus, offers live acts and a daily parade at the Circus World Museum, while hikers head for Devil's Lake State Park, with sheer quartzite cliffs that rise to five hundred feet over the lake.

The Door County peninsula delights couples with quaint fishing villages and picturesque lighthouses. Summer is the most popular season for boating, sunbathing at the beach, bicycling, and browsing the galleries and festivals for the works of local artists and artisans who call this region home. Scuba divers can see where Door County got its name at the peninsula's tip, where the Portes des Mortes (Doors of Death) straits have sunk many ships. Spring hikers and bicyclists find hills quilted with apple and cherry blossoms, autumn brings brightly colored foliage, and winter snows carpet trails for cross-country skiers.

Seeking seclusion? Ferry over to Washington Island and then catch a ferry to Rock Island State Park, a wilderness preserve accessible only by hiking and backpack camping.

Sailors and hikers love Bayfield and the Apostle Islands National Lakeshore, with eleven miles of mainland shoreline and twenty-one islands. Charter a sailboat—crewed or bareboat—from one of the Bayfield outfitters, or join a sightseeing cruise, and you're off. Or combine city and lake pleasures in Milwaukee, where you can enjoy free tours and tastings at the Miller and Pabst Breweries, take a boat tour of the lakefront, tee off at one of the city parks, and catch one of the festivals for which the city is known, such as the Great Circus Parade and Summerfest in July.

Especially for Lovers

- See the Wisconsin Dells from the Wisconsin River. Sight-seeing tours on boats or World War II amphibious vehicles, nicknamed "Dells Ducks," explain the formation of the sandstone cliffs, narrow canyons, and unusual rock formations. For a unique souvenir, stop by the H. H. Bennett Studio Museum, commemorating the photographer who helped make the Dells area famous, and buy an enlargement from one of his original glass negatives.
- Don't leave Door County without attending a traditional fish boil: trout or whitefish, potatoes, and onions, cooked in a cauldron over an open fire. When the fish is almost cooked, kerosene fuels the fire, boiling out the fish oils and fat. Melted butter, coleslaw, and cherry pie round out the meal.
- Visit some of Wisconsin's architectural treasures, which include the Swiss-toned town of New Glarus and Taliesin, Frank Lloyd Wright's home and workshop. An hour north of Milwaukee, tour a reproduction of John M. Kohler's Austrian home along with the Kohler Design Center and the turn-of-the century American Club resort, originally created for Kohler employees.

CHAPTER 34

The Plains States

M ention the plains, and most people think of endless stretches of prairie grass and cornfields and sleepy towns. But the Great Plains region of the United States, which encompasses Iowa, Kansas, Missouri, Nebraska, Oklahoma, and North and South Dakota, is also the land of the legendary Wild West and wagon trains, peopled by the likes of Calamity Jane, Wild Bill Hickok, Billy the Kid, and Annie Oakley; a land where towns mushroomed around railroad stops and Native Americans clashed with pioneers until they—and the land—were subdued into the patchwork of farms that is now America's breadbasket. The legends live on in historical theme parks, reenactments, and cultural festivals such as Kansas's Dodge City Roundup Rodeo, the Oklahoma Cattlemen's Association Range Round-up, and the Black Hills and Northern Plains Indian Powwow and Exposition in South Dakota. The region is dotted with preserved forts, Old West towns, and museums that tell the stories of Native Americans and pioneers. Museums and monuments here also tell more offbeat stories: in Alliance, Nebraska, wrecked cars have been piled into a "carhenge." In Iowa, Dundee's Red Barn Model Railroad Museum is filled with whizzing Lionel, American Flyer, and other miniature trains.

Sports: Traffic-free trails around the region make bicycle touring popular from spring through autumn. Year-round resorts feature water sports, golf and tennis in warm weather, and cross-country skiing in winter.

Memories to Go: Quilts, woolen goods, furniture, and other crafts are featured in Iowa's Amana Colonies shops. Recordings of your favorite country & western music artists make good souvenirs of Branson, Missouri, while Western wear can remind you of fun times at Old West cow towns such as Dodge City, Kansas, and Deadwood, South Dakota. At Native American shops in Oklahoma and throughout the region, you'll find fine crafts and artwork.

Lodgings for Lovers: Bed-and-breakfast inns and small hotels dot the countryside and small towns. Many are in historic Victorian or turn-of-the-century homes. Lakeside resorts come in plain and fancy versions; many provide a full array of sports facilities, from golf, tennis, and boating to cross-country skiing and snowmobiling. You can also rent a cabin in the woods or beside a lake or stay in historic Old West–style hotels or upscale big-city luxury hotels.

Climate and Clothing: Most honeymooners come to the Plains states in the summer, despite the high temperatures and humidity and many attractions and hotels are open only from June through August, especially in the Dakotas.

Winters often bring temperatures well below zero, while spring and fall generally bring comfortable temperatures, ranging from 40 to 70 degrees.

Getting Around: A car is almost a necessity, although in many areas, dedicated trails make it easy to explore by bicycle.

IOWA

Bordered by the Missouri and Mississippi rivers and dotted with lakes and parks, Iowa provides plenty of opportunities for water sports in summer. More than one hundred miles of bicycling trails ramble through the gently rolling terrain, converting to cross-country ski runs in winter.

Iowa City, with its university and lively nightlife, is in the heart of farm country, where wooded river valleys wind past historic towns such as the Amana Colonies, seven villages settled 150 years ago as a utopian religious commune and known today for their crafts and folk art.

Along the Mississippi River, Victorian-style paddle wheelers offer riverboat gambling cruises from Dubuque, Clinton, Burlington, Fort Madison, Marquette, Bettendorf, and Davenport. The Great River Road, which winds along the Mississippi River, is prettiest in the northeast part of the state around Dubuque, where limestone bluffs and rolling green hills share the riverside with harbor towns and hiking trails. Nearby Dyersville, where *Field of Dreams* was filmed, is also home to several unusual museums, including the national Farm Toy Museum. Old West lore lives at Fort Dodge and the childhood home of William "Buffalo Bill" Cody in Scott County and at Winterset, near Des Moines, birthplace of John Wayne. This area was also the setting for the best-seller *The Bridges of Madison County;* that county actually does have six nineteenth-century covered bridges. In Des Moines, Living History Farms, a 600-acre open-air museum, recreates working farms from the 1850s and 1900s.

Especially for Lovers

- Shop for a finely crafted quilt in the Amana Colonies shops and then stop for a typical meal, perhaps wiener schnitzel mit spatzle (breaded veal with noodles), and try the unique, locally made rhubarb wine.
- Cruise across West Okoboji Lake, one of the only blue-water lakes and part of Iowa's "Great Lakes" region in the northwest corner of the state.

KANSAS

The endless prairie that Dorothy was whisked from in *The Wizard of Oz*—which also served as the inspiration for the *Little House on the Prairie* series—is only a small part of this surprising state. Think Old West and Old World cafés, rodeos, and pioneer towns. The Santa Fe, Oregon, and Chisholm trails all came through Kansas, and historic restorations across the state bring the days of pioneers and cowboys to life. In Kansas City, which spreads across the border into Missouri, the Mahaffie Farmstead & Stagecoach Stop commemorates the city's role as a stopping point along the Santa Fe Trail. The university town of Lawrence, with its cafés and turn-of-the-century architecture, hosts the annual Lawrence Indian Arts Show every fall, while Topeka's Historic Ward-Meade Park includes a restored cabin, one-room schoolhouse, and botanical gardens. Abilene, famous as a cattle-trail cow town, recreates the days when lawman Wild Bill Hickok was marshal at Old Abilene Town, where you can ride in a stagecoach and see staged gun fights. Wichita's Old Cowtown captures the town's nineteenth-century ambience, while two museums, the Mid-America All-Indian Museum and the First National Black Historical Society, bring less mainstream histories to light. More pioneer history awaits at Ft. Larned National Historic Site, a restored prairie fort, and the Santa Fe Trail center, which tells the history of the trail. To the west, amid the tumbleweeds and treeless terrain, lies the cow town popularized by silver-screen westerns, Dodge City, once known as the "Wickedest City in America." Here, you can stroll along the wooden sidewalks of Front Street, once walked by lawmen Bat Masterson and Wyatt Earp, and stop in at the old jail and schoolhouse, dance at the Long Branch Saloon, and hop aboard a stagecoach for a ride. And what of the Wizard of Oz? Follow the yellow brick road in Sedan to Munchkin Mall and have your names inscribed on a golden brick!

Especially for Lovers

- If you're honeymooning in September, check out the Kansas State Fair, when roller coasters and ferris wheel rides, quilting and livestock contests, and country music concerts come to Hutchinson.
- For Old World charm, stop at a cafe in Swedish-settled Lindsborg and then dip into the shops, where craftspeople dressed in traditional attire create wooden figurines and other souvenirs.

MISSOURI

In Missouri, history and the present are happily intertwined. The Gateway Arch of St. Louis, the symbolic portal to the West, soars proudly over the Mississippi River. Below it, the Museum of Westward Expansion celebrates the city's role as a provisioning point for westbound pioneers. Nearby, steamboats offer sightseeing trips, and the cobblestoned streets of Laclede's Landing buzz with restaurants, shops, and nightspots housed in restored nineteenth-century cast-iron warehouses. Downtown, elegant Union Station, a turn-of-the-century train depot, now glitters with shops and eateries. Head north along the bluff-lined Mississippi to Hannibal, the boyhood home of Samuel Langhorne Clemens, alias Mark Twain. The town celebrates his lore with museums and memorabilia.

For outdoor recreation amid beautiful lakes and forests, head for the Ozark Mountains. Waterside resorts at Lake of the Ozarks and Table Rock Lake make a good base for swimming, sailing, and fishing, while the country and pop music showrooms of Branson are attracting growing numbers of visitors—and stars.

Across the state lies Kansas City, Missouri's western metropolis. The city is dotted with lakes and parks where you can play golf, swim, or go cycling. For shopping and nightlife, visit the restored nineteenth-century Westport area. And don't leave without tasting some of the city's famed barbecue.

Especially for Lovers

- Browse the antique shops and cafés of the pretty Missouri River town of St. Charles, twenty-five miles northwest of St. Louis, and then go cycling or hiking in Katy Trail State Park, a rails-to-trails traffic-free route with sections stretching nearly two hundred miles west along the Missouri River.
- Drive south from St. Louis to Sainte Genevieve, where French and German architecture, cafés, and festivals celebrate the town's European roots. Farther downriver, the Victorian and antebellum homes of Cape Giradeau perch on a rocky ledge overlooking the Mississippi.

NEBRASKA

Stagecoach rides, Conestoga wagon tours that invite you to follow in the footsteps of the mid-nineteenth-century pioneers, horseback trips through steep canyons dotted with ponderosa pine trees, a stay at a working cattle ranch . . . these are just some of Nebraska's attractions. Omaha, which sits along the Missouri River, is the region's commercial center and easternmost city. It was the last outpost of civilization before early pioneers set out to cross the three hundred miles of prairie to the west. Most of central Nebraska's prairie is now devoted to livestock and agriculture. To experience the Old West pictured in the movies, head to northwest Nebraska—a land where outcroppings of pine trees stand along riverbeds and canyons and where strangely shaped bluffs rise abruptly over flat valleys. These bluffs were used as landmarks by the pioneers as they headed west. Among the more famous are Chimney Rock, now a national historic site, and Scotts Bluff, a national monument where you can still see the Oregon Trail wagon ruts. Throughout the state, the trials and excitement of pioneer days are recreated at museums and sites such as the Stuhr Museum of the Prairie Pioneer in Grand Island, Fort Kearny State Historical Park, Harold Warp's Pioneer Village near Minden, and the Buffalo Bill Ranch State Historical Park at North Platte.

Especially for Lovers

- Experience the Great Plains as the pioneers found them. Set out from Valentine to visit the Fort Niobrara National Wildlife Refuge where you'll see bison, elk, and Longhorn cattle; take a canoe trip on the Niobrara River; and hike or drive through the Valentine National Wildlife Refuge, where hawks, eagles, coyotes, and beavers are among the species you may spot.

- Follow U.S. 26 from Ogallala to Scotts Bluff, which traces 128 miles of the Oregon Trail, passing natural landmarks such as Courthouse, Jail and Chimney rocks, and the Scotts Bluff National Monument.

NORTH DAKOTA

Herds of elk, antelope, bison, mule deer, and bighorn sheep graze their ways through burgundy- and beige-striped canyons. Hawks and eagles circle over a landscape of solitary spires and steep ravines. The sounds of coyotes and prairie dogs echo in the stillness. Nature is both grand and stark in the Badlands at Theodore Roosevelt National Park—actually two parks connected by the Little Missouri National Grasslands. Stop by the Painted Canyon Overlook and Visitors Center for panoramic views and information on guided walks and campfire programs. For a sense of the awesome splendor of this rugged land, follow some of the foot and horseback riding trails. Near the north unit, Fort Buford State Historic Site and the Fort Union Trading Post National Historic Site are reminders of the Native Americans and fur traders who once lived here.

Across the state to the east, the fertile Red River Valley is a land of endless golden fields dotted with haystacks and grain silos. The state's largest city, Fargo, the region's shopping hub, is also home to Bonanzaville USA, a pioneer village and museum portraying life as it was here in the late nineteenth-century. To the north, Grand Forks was once a fur-trading center. Here you can tour the Center for Aerospace Science, a pilot training school, and view contemporary works at the North Dakota Museum of Art.

Northwest of Fargo, Devils Lake is the center of the Lakes Region, staging grounds for migratory waterfowl, a favorite area for duck and goose hunting, and lakeside recreation. Fort Totten Historic Site, built in 1867, is located on the Devils Lake Sioux Indian Reservation. If you're honeymooning the last weekend in July, catch the Fort Totten Days Powwow and Rodeo, where dancers from many tribes compete for prizes.

You can follow in the footsteps of Lewis and Clark by canoe or bicycle along the Missouri River, which runs down the center of the state. In Bismarck, the state capital, visit the landmark art deco capitol building, view Native American and pioneer artifacts at the North Dakota Heritage Center, and then hop a riverboat. Across the river in Mandan, Fort Abraham Lincoln State Park's reconstructed buildings include General George Armstrong Custer's house. Nearby is a reconstruction of the On-A-Slant Indian Village, former home of the Mandan tribe. Ready for some great fishing? Head north to Lake Sakakawea, whose shores are dotted with friendly resort communities.

Especially for Lovers

- Take a riverboat cruise on the Missouri River from Bismarck and you'll be following the route used by nineteenth century traders, trappers, and settlers.

- The small town of Medora, southern gateway to Theodore Roosevelt National Park, has interesting museums that tell the story of the region's frontier days and wildlife and rustic Western-style restaurants and pitchfork fondues feature generous servings of barbecued buffalo ribs and beef.
- Visit the International Peace Garden, which straddles the border with Canada and was planted as symbol of peace between the two nations. The 2,300-acre garden features a floral clock and a peace chapel.

OKLAHOMA

Here's a land where bison still roam the great plains and you can gallop on horseback through multicolored canyons and stands of towering cedars, where oil wells dot the grounds of the state capitol and guest ranches around the state invite you to herd cattle. And in Oklahoma, which means "red man" in the Choctaw language, you can attend the largest Native American powwow in the country. Here, too, you can play golf and enjoy a host of water sports at several of Oklahoma's more than two hundred lakes, canoe the Illinois River, or cruise Grand Lake on a Mississippi riverboat.

In Oklahoma City, the state capital, you can visit a re-created frontier town at the National Cowboy Hall of Fame and Western Heritage Center and attend the Red Earth Native American Cultural Festival, held every June, which attracts hundreds of dancers from the United States and Canada. About two hours' drive northwest, the Salt Plains Wildlife Refuge attract whooping cranes, bald eagles, and terns. Nearby, the salt flats "grow" selenite crystals that are yours for the digging. To the northeast, in Tulsa, the Gilcrease Museum has an excellent collection of Western and Native American art as well as a renowned art deco district. The Woolaroc museum in Bartlesville includes a drive-through preserve where bison and other species roam free and exhibits Native American crafts and western memorabilia. The Will Rogers Memorial and Birthplace in Claremore are also in this region. When you're ready for some water recreation, head to Grand Lake O' the Cherokees. Also nearby is Tahlequah, home of the Cherokee Nation, where the Cherokee Heritage Center offers daily summer performances of the drama *The Trail of Tears,* the story of the forcible resettlement of the Cherokees and other Native American tribes to Oklahoma.

Especially for Lovers

- In Guthrie, the original state capital, take the First Capital Trolley for a tour of one of the country's largest national historic districts, where you can dine, sleep, and shop for antiques in Victorian splendor.
- If you're honeymooning in September, catch the State Fair in Oklahoma City, the third-largest fair in North America. For nightlife, head to the Bricktown District or catch a country & western show at the Oklahoma Opry.
- Make reservations for a guided tour through the Wichita Mountains Wildlife Refuge in southwestern Oklahoma, where bison and Longhorn cattle graze

and limpid lakes reflect pine-clad mountains and cliffs. Nearby, Quartz Mountain Resort Park offers golf, water sports, and a nature center.

SOUTH DAKOTA

Frontier towns and Native American communities are sprinkled throughout the state, and the fertile, lake-dotted eastern region is rich in water sports, but most honeymooners head straight for South Dakota's western part. And with good reason. The terrain in the Badlands is otherworldly, while the adjacent Black Hills are laced with hiking and biking trails, lakes, streams, and historic attractions, including the famous Mount Rushmore (with its larger-than-life busts of Presidents Washington, Jefferson, Lincoln, and Theodore Roosevelt). Another monument work-in-progress, the Crazy Horse Memorial, dedicated to the Lakota warrior who helped defeat General Custer at Little Bighorn, is planned to be the world's largest mountain carving. The Lakota, who consider these mountains sacred, named them for their blue spruce and ponderosa pine covering, which looks black from a distance. Kevin Costner's *Dances with Wolves* has brought new attention to the region, including organized tours of the movie locations. The nineteenth-century gold-mining boomtown of Deadwood, final resting place of Wild Bill Hickok and Calamity Jane, with its cobblestoned streets and restored Victorian buildings, is now a thriving casino town (Kevin Costner is part-owner of one of the casinos).

Gold is still mined and sold in the region, and the Homestake Mining Company offers tours of the country's oldest operating mine at Lead, located about forty-five miles north of Rapid City. In the southern Black Hills, one of the country's largest herds of bison roams free at Custer State Park. Toward the east, Badlands National Park, with its dramatically eroded pinnacles, buttes, and ridges colored in russet and gold tones, has been likened to a mini–Grand Canyon. Just south of the park are the Pine Ridge Indian Reservation and the Wounded Knee Massacre Monument.

Especially for Lovers

- Native American reservations throughout the state celebrate their traditions with summer powwows. Visitors are welcome to watch the dances and buy crafts and artwork. Contact the tourist office for a schedule.
- While in the Black Hills, take a candlelit tour of Wind Cave National Park, which includes more than seventy miles of underground passages. Then head to Hot Springs for a swim in the naturally heated pool at Evan's Plunge or drive seven miles south to Breakers Beach Club at the Angostura Dam State Recreation Area, where you can rent jet skis to go zipping across the lake.
- Black Hills gold makes a good souvenir. The grape-leaf design you'll see sold in the region features three colors: frosted yellow, green and pink. The green and pink are gold alloys, mixed with silver and copper or zinc.

✥ CHAPTER 35

Europe

S urprising glimpses of age-old traditions await around every bend. Stop for pastry in a Viennese coffeehouse, join in an animated discussion with some students in a café on Paris's Left Bank, glide along the canals of Venice in a sleek gondola, and harken back to the days when monarchs ruled the world as you witness the changing of the guard at Buckingham Palace.

Europe is probably far less expensive than you'd imagine: the average U.S. couple spends just $4,762 on a European honeymoon, according to the most recent *Modern Bride* survey. Cutting expenses doesn't need to mean cutting corners, either. Many of the romantic suggestions you'll find here cost little or nothing to enjoy.

The distances are often short, so you'll find it easy to combine several places in one trip—but that can be the problem with a European honeymoon. Especially if this is your first trip, you may have a tendency to try to see everything at once. Resist! Keep in mind that strolling around a neighborhood is often more rewarding and memorable than cramming in hours of rushed sight-seeing and museum-hopping. Any trip, and most of all a honeymoon, should consist of more than checking off a list of "must sees"; relax and slip into the rhythm of the place. Settle back in a café, pub, or *heuriger* (wine tavern) and make some new friends. Go to the corner *épicerie* or even a local supermarket and pick up some picnic fixings and a bottle of local wine, beer, or cider; then find a pretty spot and dig in. Ask your hotel concierge for suggestions of local romantic spots to visit.

Sports: Generally, you can enjoy your favorite sports in Europe—with some foreign flair as a bonus. For example, alpine, or downhill, skiing takes its name from the Alps, which spread from France across Italy and Switzerland to Germany and Austria, where you can stay in one alpine village and ski to another for lunch. In summer, the mountains are ideal for hiking and other warm-weather sports. Sailing enthusiasts can rent a yacht—crewed or bareboat—to sail around the Mediterranean and explore the cradle of civilization as they discover private beaches and fun-loving seaside towns.

Memories to Go: Each region of Europe seems to have its own local special arts, crafts, foods, and wines, all of which make great honeymoon souvenirs. You can pick up delft china from the Netherlands; loden cloth coats in Austria; champagne from its namesake French province, where it was invented; or even a Mercedes direct from the factory—probably the only way your car will be worth more when you return home than what you originally paid.

Cuisine: You'll have lots of choices when it comes time to eat. In fact, the food is sure to be a highlight of your honeymoon. Every region has wonderful local specialties; sausages in Munich, moussaka in Athens, pizza (like none you know) in Italy. Wines, liqueurs, and beers are also matters of national pride. You can dine at some of the most touted and expensive restaurants in the world or sample delicious cuisine at small neighborhood eateries.

Lodgings for Lovers: Throughout Europe, castles, palaces, chateaus, convents, and country manors have been converted into luxury hotels and inns. City lodging options also include grand hotels as well as less expensive pensiones and bed-and-breakfast inns. In many countries, you can also be a guest on a working farm or rent a small cottage, chalet, or villa for a taste of everyday life.

Climate and Clothing: The climate varies greatly across the continent. Most of Europe has snowy or chilly winters; temperatures are more spring-like in the southern parts of France, Portugal, and Spain, while parts of Greece and Turkey enjoy warm weather year-round. Check with the tourist offices of the countries you're interested in for typical conditions. Across Europe, July and August are peak travel seasons.

Europeans tend to dress more formally than Americans, although this is changing. However, you'll feel out of place, for example, if you wear jeans to the opera in Austria, and some churches shun shorts and skimpy attire.

Getting Around: You won't need a car to get around Europe unless you enjoy meandering along back roads or plan to stay outside of town. Trains connect most cities, and mass transit systems are generally excellent within the cities. However you decide to go, planning ahead can save you money. Car rental rates, train passes, and even intra-Europe fares are all less expensive if reserved in advance.

Money Matters: In most countries, service is included in your restaurant, bar, and hotel bills, although it is expected that you will round up your bill to leave some small change. In most countries, taxis are metered; however, in some, such as Italy, you are expected to bargain and agree on a price before getting in the cab. (See chapters 9 and 12 on traveling abroad for suggestions on changing money, getting tax refunds, and other tips.)

Language: If you don't speak the language of your destination, pick up a basic phrase book. Although luxury hotels usually have someone available who speaks English (and sign language works wonders), there will be times when you'll want to be able to make yourselves understood.

Formalities: Passports are required to enter any of the European countries. If you're planning on renting a car, check to see if you'll need an International Driving permit, available from any American Automobile Association office.

AUSTRIA

Beethoven, Brahms, Haydn, Mozart, Schubert, and Strauss . . . these are just a few of the great composers who called Vienna home during the eighteenth and nineteenth centuries when Austria was the cultural center of Europe. Vienna's rich arts and social whirl live on today, as you'll discover when you don your best to attend an opera or waltz around a fairy-tale room at a glamorous winter ball.

Or discover the heady intellectual side of the city that produced the father of psychoanalysis, Sigmund Freud, as you exchange ideas with students at a *heuriger* (wine tavern) or coffee bar. You'll also want to try some of the rich pastries for which Austria is known. Most of what you'll want to see is along the Ringstrasse, which follows the line of the old city wall. Although you could easily spend a whole honeymoon in Vienna, it's also tempting to see more. A scenic Danube cruise will take you past castles and fortresses perched high over the river that guard medieval towns and wine-growing villages. Some continue all the way to Budapest, Hungary's pretty capital.

Salzburg, home to Mozart and more recently immortalized in the musical *The Sound of Music,* is dominated by the Hohensalzburg Fortress and adorned with enough Baroque architecture to be fairly described as a museum city. Sports lovers will want to visit Innsbruck, ski capital of the Austrian Alps and site of the 1964 and 1976 Winter Olympics. Many buildings in Innsbruck date to the fourteenth century.

Especially for Lovers

- Hire a horse-drawn *fiaker* (carriage) at St. Stephen's Cathedral for a stylish tour of Vienna's historic Inner City.
- Vienna is a classical music capital, and with street musicians and free summer concerts by city hall, its hard not to catch some. Dress in your best for an evening at the Staatsoper (opera); the gilded setting is as impressive as the music. The Vienna Boys' Choir performs every Sunday, except during July and August, at 9:15 A.M. in the Royal Chapel in the Hofburg. Tickets are expensive, but standing room is free.

FRANCE

Haute couture. Nouvelle cuisine. Ballet. Etiquette. Savoir faire. The words we use to describe the height of elegance and good taste in fashion, wines, culinary skills, and manners are French. For more than five hundred years, Paris has been the heart of chic and culture, and its legendary beauty and sense of style are not overrated. The Seine River divides Paris into the Rive Droite (Right Bank), where the finest hotels, shops, and business are located, and the Rive Gauche (Left Bank), home to Sorbonne University and known for its lively, student-filled cafés. You can explore it all on foot.

Many honeymooners combine Paris with a few days exploring—and often staying in—the chateaus of the Loire Valley. More chateaus and tastings beckon in the Champagne, Burgundy, and Bordeaux regions. The chic beaches of Côte d'Azur, better known as the French Riviera, are the most popular honeymoon spots in summer, when it's warm enough to swim; but springlike winters are a relaxed time to explore seaside cities such as Nice and Cannes and the historic walled towns that perch in the nearby mountains.

Especially for Lovers

- Take a romantic dinner cruise on one of the *bateaux mouches* (pleasure boats) that ply the Seine. As the sun sets, bright lights illuminate the landmarks that line the river.
- The French Riviera has inspired artists including Renoir and Matisse, and as you explore this region, you can see their works in the dreamy settings that inspired them.

GERMANY

For organization, you can't beat Germany. Major attractions are arranged neatly into routes, ready to be enjoyed with maps and information provided by the tourist office. The most popular is the Romantic Road, which begins in Wurzburg, east of Frankfurt, and runs to the alpine town of Fussen. Following this route, you'll pass through perfectly preserved medieval villages such as Rothenburg and two-thousand-year-old towns such as Augsburg, founded under the Roman emperor Augustus in 15 B.C. The Fairy Tale Road winds through the countryside where the Brothers Grimm lived and collected their tales, starting in the ancient port city of Bremen. Other routes take you to the wine-growing Rhine region between Mainz and Karlsruhe (the Wine Road), through the Baroque monasteries and churches of Swabia (the Baroque Road), and through the Black Forest between Stuttgart and Lake Constance. Also popular are Munich, with its lively beer halls and the nearby Bavarian Alps, and Garmisch-Partenkirchen, where the ski season runs from early December into April.

Especially for Lovers

- Take a cruise along the Moselle or Rhine River. You can cruise for several days or a week, watching the scenery as you refresh yourselves in the ship's pool and docking in historic towns, where half-timbered homes line cobble-stoned streets and castles and fortresses stand guard over terraced vineyards.

GREAT BRITAIN

Pomp and ceremony, pubs and punk—England is both formal and friendly. Watch the changing of the guard at Buckingham Palace and then attend a traditional afternoon tea. Later, dip in and out of late-night wine bars. And any time is a fun time to pop into the local pub. London is the focus of most honeymooners in the British Isles, and with good reason. The Tower of London, Buckingham Palace, Big Ben, boat trips along the Thames . . . you could easily spend weeks just visiting all the places you've always wanted to see. Your best bet: take a half-day double-decker bus tour of the city. You'll get a sense of where things are and an overview of the sights; then you can return to areas you want to explore in more depth.

Of course, there's far more to Great Britain than London. Small historic cities such as Oxford and Bath make history delightfully accessible. And anyone who has read *Jane Eyre* will probably enjoy visiting its setting in Cowan Bridge between the Lake District and the Yorkshire Dales. Scotland's highlands beckon with ancient castles, lakes, rolling moors, and Edinburgh, the capital. Less visited, Wales offers the visitor spectacular scenery and some of the finest castles in Europe. You might attend a festival of song, dance, and poetry known as an *eisteddfod* and taste traditional dishes using local game, fish, and meats.

Especially for Lovers

- Stroll around Westminster to admire the imposing Houses of Parliament, Big Ben, and Westminster Abbey; then pick up half-price tickets to a play from the West End Theater Society in Leicester Square.
- Edinburgh's Old Town dates to the sixteenth century, and its winding, narrow streets and arched stone walkways are a delight to explore. Stroll the Royal Mile and the cobblestoned streets that lead up to Edinburgh Castle, stopping at pubs and shops along the way.

GREECE

"Old" takes on new meaning when you're strolling down a street that dates back thousands of years. Of course, the marble sidewalks have crumbled in places, and the ceilings supported by exquisitely sculpted pillars are often imaginary. But thanks to archaeologists, you can "visit" many of the ancient Greek cities. And you can bask on beaches in sight of harbors where Cleopatra and Mark Antony once called.

Athens is the first stop for most couples, where many stay just long enough to visit the Acropolis and its imposing Parthenon, built in the fifth century B.C. Don't miss the historic Plaka area, alive day and night with the sounds of shopkeepers peddling jewelry, rugs, leather goods, and souvenirs and the clatter and chatter of sidewalk *tavernas* and cafés where Athenians go to socialize as well as dine.

Romance lures you to the islands, where pure white towns and dreamy beaches are lapped by the deep blue Aegean Sea. Lively nightlife, chic boutiques, and friendly beaches earn Mykonos its nickname as the "St. Tropez of Greece." For scenic splendor, arrive by sea at Skala Fira Harbor on Thira, better known as Santorini. The whitewashed town seems precariously balanced atop sheer cliffs. If you enjoy sightseeing with your beaches, Rhodes and Crete are good choices.

Especially for Lovers

- Can't decide which island to visit? Consider taking a cruise. You'll visit many of the most interesting and beautiful islands and be pampered and entertained as you go.

IRELAND

Natural beauty and friendly people are the main attractions here. This is one of the least-industrialized countries in Western Europe, where people take the time to produce fine crafts such as Aran sweaters, Irish lace, and handwoven tweed. Waterford crystal and Irish whiskey also make good mementos. The Irish also take the time to chat, as you'll see if you spend some time in the friendly pubs that exist in ample supply across the country. Often, you'll hear a folksinger or traditional pipe and fiddle music as well as interesting stories. Beautiful scenery is matched by equally lyrical names. Southwest of Dublin, thirteenth-century cathedrals and castles are set amid County Tipperary's green pastureland. Further on, the Blarney Castle in Cork promises eloquence. Killarney sits in the heart of a beautiful lake district, and dramatic cliffs border the Dingle Peninsula. Nearby, the Ring of Kerry offers a stunning drive through a land of spectacular mountain and coastal scenery. And to the north along the west coast of Ireland, you can visit Galway and the Cliffs of Moher, where the Atlantic crashes into seven-hundred-foot rock bluffs. These are just a few of the scenic highlights of a land where castles still stand guard over ancient cities and a bucolic countryside.

Especially for Lovers

- A great way to see Ireland is to take leisurely driving tours, staying at castle-hotels and friendly bed-and-breakfast accommodations along the way.

ITALY

Italy has been at the heart of Western civilization ever since ancient times, when it spread the ideas of codified laws and Christianity to a vast empire. Michelangelo, Botticelli, and even the musical form of opera come from Italy. Its splendid past lives on, entwined with everyday life in modern Italy. Sit in a café surrounded by centuries-old buildings and listen to the sounds of everyday life—modified by cars, but in many ways little changed since the days of the Roman Empire. The Vatican, Forum, and Coliseum are the most obvious sites to visit in Rome, but delightful bits of history await around every corner. In Florence, the green, white, and pink Duomo will serve as your orientation point as you make your way to treasure-filled museums and shop—as people have done since the bridge was created in 1345—along the Ponte Vecchio. In Venice, pleasures include being serenaded on a gondola ride along the canals and sipping aperitifs in the Piazza San Marco. Most honeymooners will also want to experience some of Italy's seaside pleasures. The dramatic cliffs and bays along Italy's Riviera are home to historic Genoa and the stylish resorts of Portofino and San Remo. Further south, the Amalfi Coast includes Positano, Sorrento, and the Isle of Capri. Ski enthusiasts may want to consider Cortina d'Ampezzo in the Dolomite Alps, one of Europe's top ski resorts.

Especially for Lovers

- Although most first-time visitors tend to stay in the cities and resorts, small cities throughout the country beckon like intimate islands from the past. A drive through the Tuscany region north of Florence will bring you to some of the most inviting of these, such as medieval Siena and Lucca.

PORTUGAL

Although the Algarve Coast runs along the Atlantic Ocean, its ports and beaches will have you thinking of the Mediterranean. Olive groves and vineyards, medieval and Moorish architecture, rocky coves and sandy beaches, golf courses and casinos, lively nightlife and grand resorts . . . you'll find them all along this sunny coastline. Thanks to the many English who vacation here, English is widely spoken. The same is true of Madeira, a lush, semitropical island where verdant peaks rise two thousand feet over hills and plains blanketed with flowers, sugarcane, bananas, and tropical fruits. In Funchal, the capital, vividly colored homes and shops climb the steep mountainsides that encircle its magnificent bay. Lisbon and the nearby fashionable resorts of the Estoril Coast are ideal for honeymooners who want to combine city sight-seeing with beach time.

Especially for Lovers

- To experience the quieter and more traditional side of Portugal, head for the "Silver Coast," where ancient castles and fortresses tower over vineyards and small historic burghs such as the twelfth-century university town of Coimbra, the religious pilgrimage destination of Fátima, and Nazaré, a fishing village with fine beaches and seafood.

SPAIN

In Spain, your jet lag will have you right on schedule with the locals. Just when you'd expect to be going to bed, the Spanish are heading out for dinner, which often stretches into an evening of drinking, dancing, and socializing. During the day, Spain's cultural achievements will capture your attention. In Madrid, visit the Prado museum and the Royal Palace and take a day trip to Toledo, home of El Greco, or the medieval walled city of Ávila. Many couples head for Spain's beaches. The Costa del Sol, with its year-round warm Mediterranean climate, golf, and varied accommodations, is popular with Americans and Europeans. The scintillating city of Barcelona combines the sociable cafés of Las Ramblas with a lovely Gothic quarter and the fanciful architecture of Antonio Gaudí, including the famed La Sagrada Familia church. Nearby, the spectacular cliff-lined beaches of the Costa Brava sport exclusive resorts.

Especially for Lovers

- Stay in a historic *parador.* Many of these government-run hotels and inns are refurbished palaces and castles. Some are rustic; others are quite luxurious.

SWITZERLAND

For a place with alpine scenery that's easily accessible and filled with opportunities for fine meals and picturesque accommodations, you can't beat Switzerland. Many of the world's best hoteliers and chefs come to this country for training, and the Alps are literally dotted with centuries-old villages containing fine restaurants and hotels. Rail service is frequent, far-reaching, and on time, so you can hike or ski from one village to the next and then hop a train back at the end of the day. Often, you can set out on skis right from the front door of your hotel. Making it even easier to get around this four-language nation, you'll find that English is widely spoken. As for the scenery, many of the highest peaks of the Alps are here, including the rightly acclaimed Matterhorn. The Jungfrau is but one of the immense glaciers still at work carving out gorges and valleys. Among the better-known resort towns are Zermatt, Saas Fee, St. Moritz, and Davos.

Many honeymooners also enjoy the mountain-backed lakeside resort towns of Locarno and Lugano and the Lake Geneva region, which includes cosmopolitan Geneva and Montreux, home of the annual summer jazz festival.

Especially for Lovers

- Switzerland's world-famous chocolates, watches, and precision pocket knives make wonderful souvenirs. Also consider music boxes, wood carvings, woolen sportswear, and linens.

TURKEY

Bazaars where you can bargain for rugs, jewels, and other treasures; lively beach resorts; cities with thousands of years of history; surprisingly low prices; and a genuinely warm welcome for visitors make Turkey's Aegean coast a happy choice for honeymooners. Most people's first trip to Turkey is on a cruise ship. Ports of call usually include Kusadasi, near the ruins of the Aegean city of Ephesus with its marble-paved Arcadian Way, and the ancient city of Pergamum, which reached its height around 197 B.C. Almost all itineraries to Turkey include Istanbul, formerly Byzantium, ancient capital of the Eastern Roman Empire and later of the Turkish Ottoman Empire; the city is rich in relics from all eras of its storied history. Istanbul is also the only city in the world to straddle two continents—Europe and Asia. Pulling in by sea, you're surrounded by minarets and domes. Topkapi Palace, home to the Ottoman sultans from the fifteenth to the nineteenth centuries, displays a wealth of crystal, silver, and Chinese porcelain as well as the famous jewels of the Imperial Treasury. Nearby is the Blue Mosque, with its elegant blue-tile interior, and Hagia Sophia, a cathedral-turned-mosque-turned-museum.

Especially for Lovers

- After looking at Turkey's ancient treasures, it's time to hunt down some of your own. In Istanbul, the Grand Bazaar is a grand place to get started. With more than four thousand shops, it's the world's largest covered marketplace.

HONEYMOON SNAPSHOTS

Europe's attractions don't stop here. In Belgium, Bruges is one of Europe's most charming medieval cities. The city's architecture stopped changing in the thirteenth century, when its trading access, the River Zwin, silted. Growth stopped, and centuries later, strict regulations maintain the city as a "living museum."

The Mediterranean island of Cyprus, mythological home of Aphrodite, goddess of love and beauty, has a history that can be traced back at least eight thousand years. Here, you can socialize in a friendly *taverna* surrounded by a pretty harbor, stroll through walled cities, and bask at a modern beach resort.

A hiker's dream, Luxembourg has more miles of walking trails than roads, a system of buses and trains (*trains pedestres*) to link them, and a countryside dotted with cozy mountain inns. The gentle Ardennes Mountains are coated in deep forests and watched over by medieval castles and towns. If you'd like to hike from town to town, some inns will even transport your luggage for you.

A scenic drive over the mountains from the French Riviera city of Nice, Monaco has been ruled by the Grimaldi family since the late thirteenth century. Stroll through narrow pedestrian streets of its capital, Monte Carlo, to the Place du Palais and visit the storybook Pink Palace, much of which is open to the public. The Belle Epoque buildings of the newer Monte Carlo area sprang up in the last century around the palatial Casino de Monte Carlo. Join residents and visiting royalty for a *jeu* (game) of roulette in this opulent casino.

Known for its open-minded tolerance, Amsterdam is a vital cultural capital, and many honeymooners remain right here, entranced by its friendly, multilingual people and accessible sights. The Netherlands is also a haven for cyclists, who will find bike paths even in the heart of Amsterdam. In nearby Delft, you can watch artists paint the city's renowned blue porcelain; Haarlem has a nine-hundred-year history; and if you visit in summer, Scheveningen becomes a lively seaside resort, just minutes from nation's political capital, The Hague.

Want a honeymoon where the sun never sets? Head north toward the Arctic Circle in Scandinavia and savor the long days of summer in "The Land of the Midnight Sun." Cruises through the fjords of Norway take you into a world of towering cliffs, mighty glaciers, waterfalls, and medieval towns. Reindeer and dogsled safaris and snowmobile excursions are among the ways to explore Lapland, which stretches across Norway, Sweden, and Finland. And for a fairy-tale honeymoon, visit Denmark, home to Hans Christian Andersen. You'll love romantic Copenhagen, its capital, where gabled houses line cobblestoned squares and a statue of the Little Mermaid guards the harbor.

CHAPTER 36

Canada

You'll feel like you're in France as you stroll along the cobblestoned streets of Quebec City. Afternoon tea in Victoria can feel downright British. The majestic Rocky Mountains are sure to bring out the nature lover in you. For cosmopolitan friendliness, Toronto is hard to beat. Stretching for nearly four million square miles across the North American continent, Canada offers a diverse array of attractions. And although Canadians share much in common with their neighbors south of the forty-ninth parallel, the differences are delightful and fascinating . . . from the "eh?" that sits like a "you know?" at the end of sentences to the unpretentious, easy-going attitude that seems just right for a honeymoon.

Sports: Quebec, Alberta, and British Columbia have the best-known ski areas. Snowmobiling and ice-skating also head the list of winter sports available across the country. Dogsledding, ice-fishing, bobsledding and inner-tubing down the slopes are also popular. In summer, mountain resorts convert to centers for hiking, canoeing, golf, tennis, and white-water rafting.

Memories to Go: Each region has its own special crafts. In Alberta and British Columbia, you'll find quality cowboy boots and other Western wear and Native American crafts such as carvings and jewelry. You'll also see soapstone sculptures by Inuit artisans. Alberta is also home to the Edmonton Mall, the world's largest. In eastern Canada, handknit Newfoundland sweaters, Quebec maple syrup candies, and Ontario Indian basketwork are among the good buys.

Lodgings for Lovers: Accommodations range from elegant hotels and intimate inns to rustic wilderness lodges and full-service resorts. The truly adventurous can stay in a fly-in lodge, only accessible by bush plane. Most lodges offer full room and board and guided excursions. Bed-and-breakfast inns are available across the country, and in the western provinces, would-be wranglers can stay at guest ranches and rustic farms.

Climate and Clothing: Temperatures vary across the country. Most honeymooners plan their trips to Canada for the warmer months, but many come for the skiing and other winter sports—and cozy après ski parties. Winter temperatures in Montreal often drop to about 15 degrees, and summers generally hover comfortably in the 70s. Coastal areas such as Vancouver and Halifax have slightly more moderate temperatures, ranging from an average low in the 20s in winter to the high 70s in summer. In Alberta and the Rockies, summer temperatures average 70° and June and July bring thirteen to fifteen hours of sunlight a day. Whenever you go, be sure to pack a pair of sturdy walking shoes, an umbrella, and some warm clothes—even in summer, evenings can get nippy in most areas. Canadians tend to dress casually; you'll find only a few restaurants that require dressy attire.

Getting Around: Canada is the largest country in the world, and if you're visiting more than one region, you'll probably want to fly. The cities have good mass transit, but you'll probably want a car to explore the countryside; rentals are readily available, and U.S. driver's licenses are valid. Ferries are good options for some coastal routes, and scenic train rides are popular in the west. Cross-country trains take about five days between Toronto and Vancouver; white-glove dining service and private roomettes are available.

Formalities: U.S. citizens will need some proof of citizenship, such as a valid passport, birth certificate, or voter registration card, to cross the border.

THE ATLANTIC COAST

The Atlantic provinces of New Brunswick, Nova Scotia, Prince Edward Island, Newfoundland, and Labrador are ideal for a laid-back honeymoon spent exploring quaint fishing villages, hiking in lush forests, and strolling along tranquil white-sand beaches. Across the border from the state of Maine is New Brunswick. Like Maine, it was a favorite hideaway for wealthy New Englanders, who built grand mansions there. Its beautiful offshore islands and wide beaches still make it a favorite vacation area.

Prince Edward Island, Canada's smallest province, sits in the Gulf of St. Lawrence. You can reach "PEI," as the island is known to those who've been there, by ferry from New Brunswick or Nova Scotia. After a day at one of its cliff-backed beaches, you might have a lobster supper at one of the island's small fishing villages. Or rent a bicycle and follow the quiet country roads to historic lighthouses.

Nova Scotia still reflects the Scottish heritage of the immigrants who settled here, pleased by its resemblance to the rolling hills and rugged coasts of their homeland. As you enjoy the beaches, fresh seafood, and crafts shops, you're likely to hear bagpipes at one of the many festivals. From the United States, you can hop a ferry from Portland and Bar Harbor, Maine. Among the picturesque fishing villages you'll see here, the most famous is Peggy's Cove. Nearby is Halifax, the province's largest city, alive with harborfront concerts and street performers in summer and home to an international airport. Across the isthmus, the Bay of Fundy is one of the wonders of the world. Here, about 100 billion gallons of seawater rush into the estuary twice daily, and at Yarmouth, tides rise up to twelve feet, reaching as high as fifty-four feet on Minas Basin. To the north, Cape Breton Island truly feels like the Scottish Highlands. Some of the most spectacular scenery awaits along the Cabot Trail road, which hugs sheer ocean cliffs.

Especially for Lovers

- If you honeymoon between August and September, bring plenty of film. You're likely to catch the great humpback whales frolicking near shore.

- Want a fast food that's healthy to eat? Try some salty dulse, a dried, purple seaweed that is prepared as a crispy snack—and is easy to find in the maritime provinces. And if you honeymoon in spring, try fiddleheads, a curly fern boiled and served with butter and lemon.

QUEBEC

As you stroll past the cafés, bookstores, and jazz clubs of Montréal's Rue St. Denis or along the cobblestoned streets of Québec City, you'll find it hard to believe you haven't flown across the Atlantic and landed in France. Cosmopolitan Montréal, the province's capital, is a blend of old and new. The narrow, twisting streets of Vieux-Montréal are alive with shops, restaurants, businesses, and nightclubs. The modern Underground City offers ten miles of indoor excitement, from movie theaters and hotels to shops and bars—a big plus in the winter.

Only three hours north by train from Montréal, Québec City feels centuries away. Its ancient city walls and fortified citadel guard cobblestoned streets that still resound with the clip-clop of horse-drawn *caleches* (open carriages) winding their way past bistros, sidewalk cafés, and boutiques.

Skiers head for the Laurentian Mountains, which begin northwest of Montréal and stretch north past Québec City. Mont Tremblant, the highest peak, has a vertical drop of 2,300 feet, but there are many other major ski centers, including Mont Blanc, St. Sauveur, and Gray Rocks. The region is known for its friendly hospitality and joie de vivre. Here, you can enjoy a moonlit sleigh ride and then sip hot spiced wine while socializing around a blazing fire. And year-round, chalet- and Victorian-style shops and restaurants and postcard-perfect lakes and rivers make this region an excellent place to sport and shop. More dramatic scenery beckons north across the St. Lawrence River in the Gaspé Peninsula. Drive along the craggy, cliff-lined coast to discover secluded coves and quaint fishing villages ready to cook you up some sublime seafood.

Especially for Lovers

- About an hour's drive southeast of Montréal are the Eastern Townships, with charming country inns, forest-bordered fields, and glacial lakes as well as alpine ski centers and sports-filled lakeside resorts.
- Montréal's most romantic warm-weather adventure is a jet boat ride up the St. Lawrence River rapids. The trip leaves from Victoria Pier. Your guide will tell you tales of the early explorers who took this route as you enjoy a quiet ride upstream. Then, you'll suit up in slickers and sou'westers as you bounce along white-capped rapids. Looking for a less splashy view of the river? Take a sunset cruise through the harbor. Many sight-seeing boats offer dinner and dancing as you glide along.

ONTARIO

Toronto, with its many neighborhoods and active waterfront, stands ready to entertain day and night. Catch a free concert in the Harbourfront park as you shop in the renovated Queens Quay Terminal. Cruise the harbor in a gondola or a Chinese junk. Dine in a dockside restaurant watching colorful sailboats breeze by. A fifteen-minute walk from Harbourfront is Ontario Place, an entertainment complex with water slides, theaters, and restaurants, all on three man-made islands connected to the mainland by bridges. For the trendiest shops, head to the Yorkville area, in the center of town. For a refreshing swim, follow Queen Street East to beaches. Later, visit the clubs and cafés of Queen Street West, the artsy part of town.

Just a ninety-minute drive from Toronto is one of the natural wonders of the world, Niagara Falls. At Horseshoe Falls, on the Canadian side, you'll stand directly over the falls. Be sure to view the falls at night, when they are floodlit with colored lights. And don't miss the vista from under the falls on a *Maid of the Mist* cruise. Niagara-on-the-Lake, a preserved eighteenth-century village and home to the annual George Bernard Shaw Festival, awaits just twenty miles down the scenic Niagara Parkway.

Especially for Lovers

- While in Toronto, dine and dance atop the world's tallest freestanding structure, the CN Tower. The disco, Sparkles, claims the title of highest disco in the world, and from the 1,200-foot-high observation deck you can view Toronto's islands, parks, and Harbourfront and sometimes even see the mist rising from Niagara Falls, some seventy-five miles away.
- One of the best places to view the falls is from the dining room of the fifty-story Skylon Tower in Niagara Falls. As you dine on some of the best cuisine in the area, the room slowly revolves, offering a constantly changing vista.

BRITISH COLUMBIA

Its busy yacht-filled harbor, backed by skyscrapers and snow-capped mountains, makes Vancouver one of the prettiest port cities in the world. Cosmopolitan yet friendly, its attractions include Stanley Park, with twenty-two miles of forest-lined hiking and bicycling paths, and the Gastown district, where restored nineteenth-century red-brick buildings house restaurants and boutiques along a historic cobblestoned stretch of the harborfront. Don't miss the art studios and market on Granville Island or the shops of fashionable Robson Street. In winter, ski slopes beckon just twenty minutes from downtown.

Only two hours by car from Vancouver in the Coastal Mountain Range, the alpine village of Whistler is a favorite with romantics. Helicopters ferry expert skiers to more than one hundred trails, and both Whistler and Blackcomb mountains feature a variety of trails, some of which are more than seven miles long. Summer visitors find lakes and trails for hiking, horseback riding, and mountain biking.

The British-style city of Victoria sits on Vancouver Island, across the Strait of Georgia and south of Vancouver. (The city of Vancouver is on the mainland.) You can go from one to the other by bus, ferry, helicopter, or floatplane. The capital of British Columbia, Victoria's pubs, architecture, and gardens all harken back to England. Ride a horse-drawn carriage to tea at the Palm Court of the grand Empress Hotel and visit Butchart Gardens, a lovely thirty-five-acre botanical showcase. But be sure to reserve some time for the island's natural attractions as well: sandy beaches, stunning fjords, and deep forests of Douglas fir and red cedar. Head for Duncan and the Native Heritage Centre, where you can watch traditional dances and crafts and enjoy a Native American–style grilled salmon dinner.

From Victoria, you also can catch ferries to the Gulf Islands, where bicycling is the favorite way to get around. En route, you're likely to see sea lions and other marine life. You may also catch sight of gray whales, which migrate along the coast in spring and fall.

Especially for Lovers

- What could be a better souvenir of British-toned Victoria than English Harris tweed jackets, Irish linens, or Scottish woolen goods? You'll find them all in Victoria's shops.
- Vancouver's varied nightlife includes casino gambling—with a twist: a percentage of the money made by the casinos is donated to charity.

ALBERTA

The snowcapped peaks of the Rocky Mountains shelter rustic lodges and grand turn-of-the-century resorts. Winter brings skiers to these rugged peaks. Summers are generally sunny, and resorts become the jumping-off points for horseback riding, canoeing, golf, tennis, hiking, and driving through the dramatic scenery around Moraine Lake, Valley of the Ten Peaks, and Lake Louise.

You can drive or take a train from Vancouver, but for many couples, Calgary is the gateway to the Canadian Rockies. Within a two-hour drive, you can reach Banff and Kananaskis Country. Kananaskis Country, the least known, offers 140 miles of hiking and cross-country ski trails and two ski sites built for the 1988 Winter Olympics: Nakiska, the alpine mountain, and the Nordic site, Canmore.

An hour and a half west of Calgary, the small but lively town of Banff is encircled by the towering, white-topped peaks of Banff National Park. Banff Springs Hotel, the focus of activities, offers twenty-seven holes of golf, tennis, stables, and a variety of restaurants. In winter, skiers can test their skills on the "Big Three": Mystic Ridge/Mount Norquay, Lake Louise, and Sunshine Village, and then treat themselves to a dip in the Sulphur Mountain hot springs.

About a half hour's drive northwest of Banff, Lake Louise sparkles like a giant emerald in its mountain setting. Tobogganning, curling, ice-skating, horse-drawn sleigh rides, and dogsled treks are among the activities that you can arrange from the elegant Chateau Lake Louise.

One of the most beautiful drives through these rugged mountains is the 145-mile Icefields Parkway, which connects Lake Louise and Jasper. Pack a picnic and detour to the famous Columbia Icefield, where you can traverse the glacier on an all-terrain vehicle. For a great panorama, take the Jasper Tramway to the top of Whistlers Mountain. From here, you can drive to Maligne Lake for a cruise around the second largest glacial lake on earth—its mountain setting certainly makes it among the most beautiful.

Especially for Lovers

- Cowboy boots and Stetson hats let you know that Alberta is Canada's Wild West. Catch the West in action in July during the Calgary Stampede and Edmonton's Klondike days.
- From Lake Louise, you can hike, ski, or ride horseback to backcountry tea houses and lodges, where your tea or dinner will be made on a wood-burning stove. The Lake Agnes lodge was the setting for the winter scenes of the film *Dr. Zhivago.*

CHAPTER 37

The South Pacific

From the serene beauty of a starlit Tahitian or Fijian beach and the sheep-dotted countryside of New Zealand to Sydney, Australia's biggest city, the exotic South Pacific beckons. It once was a destination only for the very rich and adventurous. These days, luxury resorts, competitive airfares, and package deals make its pleasures more accessible than ever. According to *Modern Bride*'s most recent survey, the average honeymoon couple spends about $7,085 for a sixteen-day vacation in the South Pacific. Because the area's attractions are so diverse, many couples combine several destinations, for example, Australia and Tahiti or Fiji and New Zealand.

Sports: Some of the world's best scuba diving awaits along Australia's Great Barrier Reef and around the calm, clear, atoll-dotted waters of Fiji and Tahiti. Skiing and hiking are among the prime attractions in athletic New Zealand, where bungee jumping is just one of the innovative ways to test your fortitude! And Australian adventures include camel treks and bushwalk trips through the outback with naturalist guides.

Memories to Go: In Australia, opals, leather, woolen goods, and aboriginal art make quality souvenirs. You might also want to bring home some of your favorite Australian or New Zealand wines for your anniversary. New Zealand buys also include sheepskin goods and jewelry made of greenstone, a type of jade, as well as Maori crafts. Fiji purchases might include *sulus* (wrap-arounds) and *masi* (decorated paper cloth). Tahiti is a good place to buy pearls, including black pearls, and hand-dyed *pareus* (wrap-arounds).

Lodgings for Lovers: How about a private island resort, where you and a handful of other couples are pampered like royalty? Consider Fiji and Australia's barrier islands. How about a Tahitian bungalow that sits over the water on stilts so that you can feed fish from an opening in your floor? Or check out the cozy inns of Australia's outback and bucolic New Zealand.

Climate and Clothing: Practically speaking, Tahiti and Fiji have two seasons: the warm and rainy season runs from November to April, and the cooler, drier season runs from May to October. The average temperature is 76 to 80 degrees. Pack lightweight summer clothes, avoiding short shorts, especially in towns.

New Zealand and Australia are located in the Southern Hemisphere, so their seasons are the reverse of those of North America and Europe, making July and August the ski season. The weather varies greatly from region to region within these countries, but there, people head north for warmer weather!

Getting Around: Excellent rail, bus, and air connections make it easy to hop around Australia and New Zealand. In Fiji, many of the exclusive resort islands are accessible only by seaplane. Most of Tahiti's islands can be reached by plane or ferry.

Language: English is the official language in Australia, New Zealand, and Fiji (along with Fijian and Hindi in Fiji). In Tahiti, French is the official language, but English and Tahitian are also widely spoken.

Formalities: Valid passports are required for all four destinations. Fiji and New Zealand require them to be valid at least three months beyond your departure date. Australia requires visas, which can be obtained in advance free from any Australian consulate. Those staying in Tahiti more than a month can obtain visas upon arrival.

AUSTRALIA

Koala bears and kangaroos. A coral reef that extends 1,250 miles—the longest in the world. Animals and plants that exist nowhere else on earth. Friendly people with a relaxed attitude and a sociable spirit. These are just some of the reasons to honeymoon in Australia.

Most couples start out in Sydney, where most international flights land. Its pretty harbor and parks make it one of the world's most beautiful cities. Explore the trendy shops and pubs of its historic district, The Rocks, and then join Sydneysiders at Bondi or Manly Beach, each just a few minutes from town. Or head for the picturesque Hunter Valley vineyards.

The stately city of Melbourne pleases couples with Victorian architecture, tree-lined boulevards, and exciting arts, dining, and sports scenes. And just outside Melbourne on Phillip Island is one of Australia's most engaging spectacles, the nightly parade of the fairy penguins returning to their cliff-top homes. Another fun stop: Ballarat, site of Australia's 1850s gold rush, where you can pan for gold. Or take a day trip into the Dandenong Ranges.

Few honeymooners come to Australia without "going troppo," as Aussies call vacationing in the tropical islands of Queensland, Australia's sunshine state—and the jumping-off point for excursions to the Great Barrier Reef. Head for the lively Gold Coast or sequester yourselves on a private-isle resort in the Whitsunday Islands. Or stay in a cottage along the low-key Sunshine Coast.

Many couples fly to the outback town of Alice Springs, gateway to Uluru National Park and Ayers Rock. Looking at the 1,100-foot-tall mammoth rock, which towers dramatically above the surrounding flat red earth, you'll understand why it has so much spiritual significance to the Aboriginals who live here. While in the area, visit a traditional Aboriginal village, where you'll learn about the spiritual realm known as Dreamtime, which refers to an age when ancestral beings roamed the earth, forming the features of the landscape.

Other honeymoon options include a trip to the graceful Victorian city of Adelaide and the nearby Barossa Valley wine country; the southwestern sister cities of Perth and Fremantle, site of the famed America's Cup races in the 1980s; and Tasmania, an island off the southeastern coast, where you'll find English-style villages along with gentle mountains, rain forests, high moorlands, and placid lakes.

Australia is roughly the size of the continental United States. It's impossible to see it all in one trip. But "no worries, mate," as the Aussies say; by the time you leave, you're sure to have a host of new friends who will want to see you when you return.

Especially for Lovers

- A dinner cruise around Sydney Harbour is a real treat. Choose a paddle wheeler, a replica of an eighteenth-century three-masted square rigger, or a ferry. Then, dance and dine as you admire the white, sail-style roof of the Sydney Opera House and the city lights twinkling in the background.
- From Brisbane you can take a cruise up the Brisbane River to Lone Pine Sanctuary, where you can feed kangaroos and pet koalas.

Fiji

Stay in a thatched-roof *bure* (bungalow) at an exclusive private-island hideaway, shared with just a few other couples, or at a grand resort complete with tennis and golf facilities. Snorkel or scuba dive through fascinating seascapes, which await right outside your room. Enjoy a champagne brunch on a beach that's yours for the day. Sail through clear, turquoise waters past coconut tree–fringed isles. Share a ceremonial drink with a village chief. Enjoy a *meke,* an evening of traditional dances that tell folk stories with their sensuous movements. Follow the directional arrows at your resort to tennis, golf, the beach—and fire-walking demonstrations! These are some of the extraordinary pleasures that await during a honeymoon in Fiji. Yet exotic as it is, you'll have no problem communicating; English is one of Fiji's official languages. And visitors receive a warm welcome in this corner of the world, where friendships form quickly and run deep.

Fiji consists of more than three hundred islands, of which about one hundred are inhabited. Its population, about seven hundred thousand, is almost evenly divided between East Indians and native Fijians whose communal village lifestyle has changed little over the centuries. Village girls still weave mats and make *masi* (bark) cloth for wall coverings, and bedrolls, floor mats, and roofs are still woven from palm fronds. Both Indians and Fijians practice ritual fire walking.

One tradition you're sure to encounter is a *yaqona* ceremony, where kava, the national beverage, is imbibed. The drink is made from pulverized pepper plant root and may make your tongue feel a bit numb. Some say kava causes mild euphoria, but more important, the act of sharing creates a bond of friendship. Feel free to decline, but if you do, show your respect for the ceremony and appreciation for being included by letting your hosts know that you can't partake because of health reasons. One Fijian tradition you certainly will want to experience is a *magiti* (banquet), at which meats and native crops are wrapped in huge leaves and slowly cooked underground.

Most visitors arrive at the international airport in Nadi on the largest Fijian island, Viti Levu. Many resort hotels are located around Nadi or along the island's southwestern Coral Coast.

Especially for Lovers

• Stay at one of the exclusive private-island resorts, where you can be served gourmet meals at a secluded beach or paddle off in a kayak on a voyage of discovery. Some of the resorts also offer golf, tennis, and horseback riding.

NEW ZEALAND

For unusual adventures in diverse and dazzling natural settings, you can't beat New Zealand. In an area about the size of the state of Colorado, New Zealand packs in geysers, snow-capped mountains, subtropical island beaches, and rain forests. The nation that brought bungee jumping and jet boats to the world has hundreds of exotic yet accessible ways of exploring it all.

The country is divided into two islands: North and South. On the warmer North Island, temperatures rarely drop below the mid-50s, and the landscape is dominated by sheep, cattle, and deer (for venison) grazing grounds. Auckland, home to the international airport, quickly gets visitors into an outdoors state of mind with its active sailing harbor and fine sandy beaches. Sailors and anglers for marlin, swordfish, and mako sharks head north to the Bay of Islands, also known for its secluded beaches and plentiful water sports. South of Auckland, trails at Rotorua's Whakarewarewa Thermal Reserve lead through a surreal landscape of steaming ponds, pools of boiling mud, and geysers. This is also a rich center for the Maori, the original inhabitants. Here, a traditional *hangi* feast of foods cooked in an underground oven and steamed in the boiling pools is often accompanied by song and dance. Feeling adventurous? Join a four-wheel-drive vehicle safari through rugged bush to mountaintops for panoramic views or hike into the crater of a dormant volcano and then be whisked back to town by helicopter.

Across the Cook Strait from the North Island, Nelson is a popular resort area, with lovely beaches, wineries, orchards, and New Zealand's sunniest weather. Further south, gracious Christchurch—with its double-decker buses, pubs, and gardens—has been described as "more English than England." Once outside its cities, you'll see that most of South Island is wilderness, with rugged glaciers, rain forests, endless fjords, and twelve-thousand-foot-high mountains. About five hours from Christchurch, Mount Cook National Park is the place for winter sports, including heli-skiing and glacier skiing. The park takes its name from the country's highest peak, which towers at 12,350 feet. The Tasman Glacier is one of the longest outside the Arctic. More skiing awaits in the Remarkables mountain range around Queenstown. And in the summer, you can take to Lake Wakatipu on jet boats and go white-water rafting through spectacular gorges. Golf, horseback riding, flight-seeing, and panning for gold are among the popular activities. Queenstown is also the gateway to the Milford Sound, with its spectacular cliff-lined fjords.

Especially for Lovers

- Take a cruise of Milford Sound. You'll glide past towering peaks and steep rock walls that lead into narrow valleys and tumbling waterfalls.
- While in Christchurch, take a gondola ride to the top of Mount Cavendish for panoramic views of the city, the Canterbury Plains, and the dramatic Southern Alps beyond.

TAHITI

Steep, jagged mountains cloaked in lush greenery. Pearly beaches lapped by turquoise seas. The sweet scent of frangipani and monoi, a floral-scented coconut oil. Tahiti embodies the idea of a South Seas paradise. Although Tahiti is actually the name of only one island, most people use it to refer to the hundred-plus islands that make up French Polynesia. As a French territory, Tahiti's connection to France is delightfully apparent in its cuisine and stylish charm. (French and Tahitian are the official languages, but many people at larger hotels and attractions speak English as well.)

The island of Tahiti is the first stop for most travelers. Its capital, Papeete, is like a cosmopolitan French town in the South Seas. Your fine French cuisine will probably be served by a waitress wearing a *pareu* (wrap-around sarong) and a tiare lei made with fragrant Tahitian gardenias. Shop for French perfumes, fashions, and Tahitian crafts and then relax at a waterfront café or snack at *les roulettes,* mobile food vans that are set up along the waterfront in the late afternoon as the fishermen bring home their catch. Out on the island, visit the Gauguin Museum in Papeari and the tiny village of Mataieo, island home to the artist whose paintings captured the romance of these islands.

Short flights or leisurely ferry rides connect to Tahiti's many sister islands, whose very names are romantic: Moorea, with its jagged, volcanic peaks and ancient stone temples, called *marae;* Bora Bora, encircled by a coral reef ideal for snorkeling; Raiatea, famous for its archaeological sites; traditional Tahaa, where fishing is still a way of life; Huahine, with ancient temples and an open-air museum of an ancient island village; and the pristine atolls of the Tuamoto island chain, including Rangiroa, the world's second-largest atoll, and Tikehau. And there are more. Pick one island or sail around the region on a chartered yacht.

Especially for Lovers

- Pick accommodations to suit your style of romance. Choices include a traditional thatched *fare* (Polynesian cottage), a bungalow that perches over the water on stilts with the floor cut out under a sliding coffee table so you can invite the fish to share your dinner, or a luxurious room with handcarved furnishings and a private balcony with a Jacuzzi overlooking the lagoon.
- Be sure to attend a *tamaraa* feast, a Tahitian luau with traditional Polynesian food, dance, and song. Many of the hotels and restaurants offer them.

APPENDIX A

Sources for More Information

PART ONE: HONEYMOON PLANNING

Chapter 1: Picking a Destination

Modern Bride Subscriptions
P.O. Box 51622
Boulder, Colorado 80321-1622
303-447-9330

Chapter 2: Free Expert Advice

For brochures on a variety of travel subjects, including safety, packing, and avoiding scams as well as a list of ASTA agencies in your region, contact

American Society of Travel Agents
Consumer Affairs Department
1101 King St., Suite 200
Alexandria, VA 22314
703-739-2782

For a list of destination specialists and certified travel agents in your region, send a self-addressed, stamped envelope to

Institute of Certified Travel Agents
148 Linden St., P.O. Box 56
Wellesley, MA 02181-0503
617-237-0280; 800-542-4282

Chapter 3: Checking into Accommodations

The following companies are among those offering discount hotel programs:

Entertainment Publications
2125 Butterfield Rd.
Troy, MI 48084
800-285-5525

International Travel Card
6001 N. Clark St.
Chicago, IL 60660
800-342-0558

Privilege Card
3473 Satellite Blvd., Suite 200
Duluth, GA 30136
404-623-0066

Quest International
402 East Yakima Ave., Suite 1200
Yakima, WA 98901
509-248-7512; 800-638-9819

Chapter 4: Getting There by Air

Here are toll-free numbers for many of the major airlines:

Aer Lingus	800-223-6537
Aeromexico	800-237-6639
Air Canada	800-776-3000
Air France	800-AF-PARIS
Air New Zealand	800-262-1234
Alaska Airlines	800-426-0333
Alitalia	800-6-ALITALIA
All Nippon Airways	800-2-FLY-ANA
ALM-Antillean Airlines	800-327-7230
Aloha Airlines	800-367-5250
Aloha Islandair	800-323-3345
American Airlines	800-433-7300
America West Airlines	800-247-5692
Austrian Airlines	800-843-0002
Avianca Airlines	800-AVIANCA
British Airways	800-AIRWAYS
BWIA International	800-327-7401
Cayman Airways	800-422-9626
Continental Airlines	800-525-0280
Delta Airlines	800-221-1212
El Al Israel	800-223-6700
Finnair	800-950-5000
Garuda Indonesia	800-3-GARUDA
Hawaiian Airlines	800-367-5320
Iberia Airlines of Spain	800-772-4642
Icelandair	800-223-5500
Japan Airlines	800-525-3663
KIWI Airlines	800-538-5494
KLM Royal Dutch Airlines	800-374-7747
Lacsa Airlines	800-225-2272
Lufthansa German Airlines	800-645-3880
Malaysia Airlines	800-421-8641

Mexicana Airlines	800-531-7923
Midway Airlines	800-446-4392
Midwest Express Airlines	800-452-2022
Northwest Airlines	800-223-2525
Olympic Airways	800-223-1226
	212-838-3600
Qantas Airways	800-227-4500
Sabena Belgian World Airlines	800-955-2000
Singapore Airlines	800-SIA-3333
South African Airways	800-SAA-WORLD
Swissair	800-221-4750
TAP Air Portugal	800-221-7370
Thai Airways International	800-426-5204
Tower Air	800-221-2500
Trans World Airlines	800-221-2000
United Airlines	800-241-6522
USAir	800-428-4322
Varig Brazilian Airlines	800-GO-VARIG
Virgin Atlantic Airways	800-862-8621

Chapter 5: Travel by Land

For information about international driver's licenses and other services, contact your AAA local office or AAA headquarters:

American Automobile Association
Travel Related Services Dept.
1000 AAA Dr.
Heathrow, FL 32746-5063
407-444-8000

For train information, contact

Amtrak National Railroad Passenger Corp.
60 Massachusetts Ave. NE
Washington, D.C. 20002
202-906-3000; 800-872-7245

Rail Europe
230 Westchester Ave.
White Plains, NY 10604
914-682-2999; 800-438-7245

Via Rail Canada
2 Place Ville-Marie, Suite 400
Montreal, PQ H3B 2C9 Canada
514-871-6000; 800-304-4842

For the free comparison shopping worksheet, *Car Rental Guide,* write to

Public Reference
Federal Trade Commission
Washington, D.C. 20580

For information about rental cars, contact

Alamo Rent A Car	From U.S.: 800-327-0400
	From Canada: 305-522-0000
Auto Europe	800-223-5555
Avis Rent A Car	800-331-1212
Budget Rent A Car	From U.S.: 800-527-0700
	From Canada: 416-622-3366
Dollar Rent A Car	800-800-1000
Enterprise Rent A Car	800-325-8007
Hertz Rent A Car	800-654-3131
The Kemwel Group	800-678-0678
National Car Rental/InterRent	800-328-4567
Snappy Car Rental	800-669-4802
Thrifty Car Rental	800-367-2277
Value Rent A Car	800-GO-VALUE

Chapter 6: Choosing to Cruise

For a free copy of the brochure *Answers to Your Most Asked Questions,* send a SASE to

Cruise Lines International Association
500 Fifth Ave., Suite 1407
New York, NY 10110
212-921-0066

Chapter 7: Package Pros and Cons

Three helpful brochures about package tours, *How to Select a Tour Vacation Package, Worldwide Tour and Vacation Package Finder,* and *The Standard for Confident Travel* are available free from

United States Tour Operators Association
211 East 51st Street, Suite 12B
New York, NY 10022
212-750-7371

Chapter 8: International Honeymoons

For the latest State Department Advisories, call 202-647-5225.

For up-to-date health information, call the Centers for Disease Control at 404-332-4555. Information is available by phone or fax.

A free brochure, *Your Trip Abroad,* is available for $1 from

Public Affairs Staff
Bureau of Consular Affairs, Room 5807
U.S. Department of State
Washington, D.C. 20620
202-783-3238

For details on customs regulations, write for the booklet *Know Before You Go,* available from

U.S. Customs Service
P.O. Box 7407
Washington, D.C. 20044

For Canadian passport information, call 800-567-6868.

For Canadian customs information, pick up the *I Declare* brochure at your nearest customs office or call 613-993-0534.

Chapter 9: Money Matters

For listings of cash machines in the place where you are going, call

Cirrus	800-424-7787
Plus	800-843-7587

For foreign currency exchange by mail, you can contact

Reusch International	800-424-2923

Here are some sources of travel insurance:

Access America, Inc.	800-424-3391
American Express Travel Protection Plan	800-234-0375
Carefree Travel Insurance	800-323-3149
Travel Assistance International	800-821-2828
Travel Assure, Tele-trip Division, Mutual of Omaha	800-228-9792
Travel Guard International/Gold	800-634-0644
Travelers Travel Insurance PAK	800-243-3174

PART TWO: PLANNING A DESTINATION WEDDING

Chapter 14: About Destination Weddings

Cele Goldsmith Lalli and Stephanie H. Dahl
Modern Bride Wedding Celebrations (John Wiley & Sons, 1992; $14.95)

Contains detailed wedding planning and etiquette information.

Judy Petsonk and Jim Remsen
The Intermarriage Handbook: A Guide for Jews and Christians (William Morrow/Quill Paperbacks, 1991; $12.45)
A guide for interfaith families.

Chapter 16: Picking a Place

For a list of members in the area where you plan to marry, write to

Association of Bridal Consultants
200 Chestnutland Road
New Milford, CT 06776

If you are marrying abroad, the local tourist office should be able to supply you with a list of local consultants. (See tourist office listings by destination in Appendix B.)

Chapter 17: Making Sure Your Marriage Is Legal

If you plan to marry abroad, the tourist office can usually provide you with the basic requirements. (See tourist office listings by destination in Appendix B.)

U.S. citizens planning to get married abroad can also obtain an information sheet by writing

Citizens Consular Services
U.S. Department of State
Room 4811
2201 C Street NW
Washington, D.C. 20520

Books with ideas for personalizing your vows include Barbara Elkof, *With These Words . . . I Thee Wed: Contemporary Wedding Vows for Today's Couples* (Holbrook, MA: Bob Adams, Inc., 1988; $7.95).

Chapter 19: Bringing the Children

For premarital preparation programs, contact

Prepare MC (married with children)
P.O. Box 190
Minneapolis, MN 55440
800-331-1661

For counseling, membership, newsletters, and resources in your area, contact

The Stepfamily Foundation, Inc.
National Headquarters
333 West End Ave.
New York, NY 10023
212-877-3244

For information on a Family Medallion and a special ceremony to recognize the new family, contact

The Coleman Collection
706 W. 42nd St.
Kansas City, MO 64111
800-237-1922

For information on weddings that include exchanging vows with children, contact

Disney's Fairy Tale Weddings
Walt Disney World
P.O. Box 10020
Lake Buena Vista, FL 32830
407-828-3400

Chapter 20: Photography and Videography

For the brochure *What Every Bride Should Know About Wedding Photography* and a list of professional photographers and videographers in your area, send a SASE to

Professional Photographers of America, Inc.
57 Forsyth St. NW, Suite 1600
Atlanta, GA 30303
404-522-8600; 800-786-6277

Tourist Offices

THE CARIBBEAN, THE BAHAMAS, AND BERMUDA

Caribbean Tourism Organization, 20 E. 46th St., New York, NY 10017; 212-682-0435. Or contact one of the tourist organizations listed below.

Anguilla Tourist Information, 775 Park Ave., Suite 105, Huntington, NY 11743; 516-271-2600

Antigua Tourist Office, 610 Fifth Ave., Suite 311, New York, NY 10020; 212-541-4117

Aruba Tourism Authority, 100 Harvard Blvd., Weehawken, NJ 07087; 201-330-0800

The Bahamas Tourist Office, 150 E. 52nd St., New York, NY 10022; 212-758-2777 or 800-422-4262

Barbados Board of Tourism, 800 Second Ave., 2nd Fl., New York, NY 10017; 212-986-6516

Bermuda Department of Tourism, 310 Madison Ave., Suite 201, New York, NY 10017; 212-818-9800 or 800-223-6106

Bonaire Tourist Information Office, 10 Rockefeller Plaza, New York, NY 10020; 212-956-5911

British Virgin Islands Tourism Board, 370 Lexington Ave., New York, NY 10017; 212-696-0400

Cayman Islands Department of Tourism, 420 Lexington Ave., Suite 2733, New York, NY 10170; 212-682-5582

Curaçao Tourist Board, 475 Park Ave. South, 20th Fl., New York, NY 10016; 212-683-7660

Dominica Division of Tourism, P.O. Box 73, Roseau, Commonwealth of Dominica, W.I.; 809-448-2351

Dominican Republic Tourist Information Center, 1501 Broadway, Suite 410, New York, NY 10036; 212-575-4966

French West Indies (Guadeloupe, St. Barthelemy, St. Martin, Martinique) Tourist Board, 610 Fifth Ave., New York, NY 10020-2452; 212-757-1125

Grenada Tourist Board, 820 Second Ave., Suite 900-D, New York, NY 10017; 212-687-9554

Jamaica Tourist Board, 801 Second Ave., New York, NY 10017; 212-688-7650

Puerto Rico Tourism Company, 575 Fifth Ave., New York, NY 10017; 212-599-6262

Saba Tourist Office, 271 Main St., Northport, NY 11768; 516-425-0900 or 800-SABA-DWI

St. Kitts and Nevis Tourist Board, 414 E. 75th St., New York, NY 10021; 212-535-1234

St. Lucia Tourist Board, 820 Second Ave., New York, NY 10017; 212-867-2950

Sint Maarten Tourist Office, 675 Third Ave., New York, NY 10017; 212-953-2084 or 800-786-2278

St. Vincent/Grenadines Tourist Office, 801 Second Ave., New York, NY 10017; 212-687-4981

Trinidad and Tobago Tourist Board, 25 W. 43rd St., New York, NY 10036; 212-719-0540

Turks and Caicos Islands Tourist Board, Department of Tourism, P.O. Box 128, Grand Turk, Turks and Caicos BWI; 800-241-0824.

U.S. Virgin Islands Division of Tourism, 1270 Avenue of the Americas, Suite 2108, New York, NY 10020; 212-332-2222

MEXICO

Call 800-44-MEXICO or contact one of the Mexican Government Tourism Offices listed below:

10100 Santa Monica Blvd., Suite 224, Los Angeles, CA 90067; 310-203-8191

1911 Pennsylvania Avenue NW, Washington, D.C. 20006; 202-728-1750

2333 Ponce de Leon, Suite 710, Coral Gables, FL 33134; 305-443-9160

70 East Lake St., Suite 1413, Chicago, IL 60601; 312-565-2778

405 Park Ave., Suite 1401, New York, NY 10022; 212-755-7261

2707 North Loop West, Suite 450, Houston, TX 77008; 713-880-5153

THE UNITED STATES

Alabama Bureau of Tourism & Travel, 401 Adams Ave., Suite 126, Montgomery, AL 36104; 334-242-4169 or 800-ALABAMA

Alaska Division of Tourism, P.O. Box 110801, Juneau, AK 99811-0801; 907-465-2010

Arizona Office of Tourism, 1100 W. Washington St., Phoenix, AZ 85007; 602-542-8687 or 800-842-8257

Arkansas Department of Parks & Tourism, One Capital Mall, Little Rock, AR 72201; 501-682-7777 or 800-NAT-URAL

California Division of Tourism, P.O. Box 1499, Sacramento, CA 95812-1499; 800-862-2543

Colorado Information Line: 800-COLORADO

Connecticut Department of Economic Development, 865 Brook St., Rocky Hill, CT 06067; 203-258-4355 or 800-CT-BOUND

Delaware Tourism Office, P.O. Box 1401, Dover, DE 19903; 302-739-4271 or 800-441-8846

Washington, D.C. Convention & Visitors Association, 1212 New York Ave. NW, Suite 600, Washington, DC 20005; 202-789-7000

Florida Department of Commerce, Division of Tourism, Visitor's Inquiry, 126 W. Van Buren St., Tallahassee, FL 32399-2000; 904-487-1462

Georgia Department of Industry, Trade & Tourism, P.O. Box 1776, Atlanta, GA 30301; 404-656-3590 or 800-VISIT-GA

Hawaii Visitors Bureau, 2270 Kalakaua Ave., Honolulu, HI 96815; 808-923-1811 or 800-257-2999

Idaho Travel Council, c/o Division of Travel Promotion, P.O. Box 83720, Boise, ID 83720-0093; 800-635-7820

Illinois Bureau of Tourism, 620 E. Adams St., Springfield, IL 62701; 800-223-0121

Indiana Department of Commerce, Tourism Division, One North Capitol, Suite 700, Indianapolis, IN 46204-2280; 800-759-9191

Iowa Department of Economic Development, Division of Tourism, 200 E. Grand Ave., Des Moines, IA 50309; 515-242-4705 or 800-345-4692

Kansas Department of Commerce & Housing, Travel & Tourism Division, 700 SW Harrison St., Suite 1300, Topeka, KS 66603-3712; 913-296-2009 or 800-2-KANSAS

Kentucky Travel Department, P.O. Box 2011, Frankfort, KY 40602; 800-225-TRIP, extension 67

Louisiana Office of Tourism, P.O. Box 94291, Baton Rouge, LA 70804; 504-342-8119 or 800-633-6970

Maine Publicity Bureau, P.O. Box 2300, Hallowell, ME 04347; 207-623-0363 or 800-782-6496

Maryland Office of Tourism Development, 217 E. Redwood St., 9th Fl., Baltimore, MD 21202; 410-333-6611 or 800-543-1036

Massachusetts Office of Travel & Tourism, 100 Cambridge St., Boston, MA 02202; 617-727-3201 or 800-447-MASS

Michigan Travel Bureau, P.O. Box 30226, Lansing, MI 48909; 517-373-0670 or 800-5432-YES

Minnesota Office of Tourism, 121 7th Place East, St. Paul, MN 55101; 612-296-5029 or 800-657-3900

Mississippi Division of Tourism Development, P.O. Box 1705, Ocean Springs, MS 39566; 800-WARMEST

Missouri Division of Tourism, P.O. Box 1055, Jefferson City, MO 65102; 314-751-4133 or 800-877-1234

Montana Department of Commerce, Travel Montana, 1424 9th Ave., Helena, MT 59620; 406-444-2654 or 800-VISIT-MT

Nebraska Division of Travel & Tourism, P.O. Box 94666, Lincoln, NE 68509-4666; 402-471-3796 or 800-228-4307

Nevada Commission on Tourism, Capitol Complex, Carson City, NV 89710; 800-NEVADA-8

New Hampshire Office of Travel & Tourism Development, P.O. Box 1856, Concord, NH 03302-1856; 603-271-2343 or 800-386-4664, extension 145

New Jersey Division of Travel & Tourism, 20 W. State St., CN 826, Trenton, NJ 08625-0826; 609-292-2470 or 800-JERSEY-7

New Mexico Department of Tourism, Room 751, Lamy Building, 491 Old Santa Fe Trail, Santa Fe, NM 87503; 505-827-7400 or 800-545-2040

New York Convention & Visitors Bureau, Two Columbus Circle, New York, NY 10019; New York City: 800-NYC-VISIT, New York State: 518-474-4116

North Carolina Division of Travel & Tourism, 430 N. Salisbury St., Raleigh, NC 27611; 919-733-4171 or 800-VISIT-NC

North Dakota Office of Tourism, 604 East Blvd., Bismarck, ND 58505-0825; 701-224-2525 or 800-HELLO-ND

Ohio Division of Travel & Tourism, P.O. Box 1001, Columbus, OH 43216-1001; 614-466-8844 or 800-BUCKEYE

Oklahoma Tourism & Recreation Department, 2401 N. Lincoln Blvd., 500 Will Rogers Bldg., Oklahoma City, OK 73105-4492; 405-521-2409 or 800-652-6552

Oregon Tourism Division, 775 Summer St. NE, Salem, OR 97310; 800-547-7842

Pennsylvania Department of Commerce, Fulfillment House, P.O. Box 61, Warrendale, PA 15086-9910; 717-787-5453 or 800-VISIT-PA; For Pocono-specific information, call 800-POCONOS.

Rhode Island Tourism Division, 7 Jackson Walkway, Providence, RI 02903; 401-277-2601 or 800-556-2484

South Carolina Division of Tourism, P.O. Box 71, Columbia, SC 29201; 803-734-0122 or 800-346-3634

South Dakota Department of Tourism, 711 E. Wells Ave., Room 513, Pierre, SD 57501-3369; 800-S-DAKOTA

Tennessee Department of Tourist Development, P.O. Box 23170, Nashville, TN 37202; 615-741-2159 or 800-836-6200

Texas Department of Commerce, Tourism Division, P.O. Box 12728, Austin, TX 78711-2728; 512-462-9191 or 800-888-8-TEX

Utah Travel Council, Council Hall, Capitol Hill, Salt Lake City, UT 84114; 801-538-1030

Vermont Department of Travel & Tourism, 134 State St., Montpelier, VT 05601-1471; 802-828-3236 or 800-VERMONT

Virginia Division of Tourism, 901 E. Byrd St., Richmond, VA 23219; 804-786-2051 or 800-VISIT-VA

Washington Division of Tourism, P.O. Box 42500, Olympia, WA 98504; 360-753-7288 or 800-544-1800

West Virginia, Travel West Virginia, State Capitol Complex, 2101 Washington St. E., Charleston, WV 25305; 304-558-2286 or 800-CALL-WVA

Wisconsin Division of Tourism, P.O. Box 7606, Madison, WI 53707; 608-266-2161 or 800-432-TRIP

Wyoming Division of Tourism, I-25 at College Dr., Cheyenne, WY 82002; 307-777-7777 or 800-225-5996

National Parks

National Park Service, Office of Public Inquiries, P.O. Box 37127, Washington, DC 20013-7127; 202-208-4747

Adventure Travel

America Outdoors, P.O. Box 1348, Knoxville, TN 37901; 615-524-4814

Specialty Travel Index, 305 San Anselmo Ave., Suite 313, San Anselmo, CA 94960; 414-459-4900 or 800-442-4922

EUROPE

Austria National Tourist Office, P.O. Box 1142, New York, NY 10108-1142; 212-944-6880

Belgium Tourist Office, 780 Third Ave., New York, NY 10151; 212-758-8130

Cyprus Tourism Organization, 13 East 40th St., New York, NY 10016; 212-683-5280

Denmark Tourist Board, 655 Third Ave., New York, NY 10017; 212-949-2333

Finland Tourist Board, 655 Third Ave., New York, NY 10017, 212-949-2333

France Government Tourist Office, 610 Fifth Ave., New York, NY 10020; 212-838-7800

Germany National Tourist Office, 122 East 42nd St., 52nd Floor, New York, NY 10168-0072; 212-661-7200

Great Britain British Information Services, 845 Third Ave., New York, NY 10022; 212-752-5747

Greece National Tourist Authority, 645 Fifth Ave., Olympic Tower, New York, NY 10022; 212-421-5777

Hungary Tourist Board, One Parker Plaza, Suite 1104, Fort Lee, NJ 07024; 201-592-8585

Iceland Tourist Board, 655 Third Ave., 18th Floor, New York, NY 10017; 212-949-2333

Ireland Tourist Board, 345 Park Ave., New York, NY 10154; 212-418-0800 or 800-223-6470

Italy Government Tourist Board, 630 Fifth Ave., New York, NY 10111; 212-245-4822

Luxembourg National Tourist Office, 17 Beekman Place, New York, NY 10017; 212-935-3589

Malta National Tourist Office, 249 East 35th St., New York, NY 10016; 212-213-6686

Monaco Government Tourist & Convention Bureau, 845 Third Ave., 19th Floor, New York, NY 10022; 212-759-5227

Netherlands Board of Tourism, 255 Lexington Ave., New York, NY 10017; 212-370-7360

Norway Tourist Board, 655 Third Ave., New York, NY 10017; 212-949-2333

Portugal National Tourist Office, 590 Fifth Ave., New York, NY 10036; 212-354-4403

Spain Tourist Office, 665 Fifth Ave., New York, NY 10022; 212-759-8822

Sweden Travel & Tourism Board, 655 Third Ave., New York, NY 10017; 212-949-2333

Switzerland National Tourist Office, 608 Fifth Ave., New York, NY 10020; 212-757-5944

Turkey Tourist Office, 821 United Nations Plaza, New York, NY 10017; 212-687-2194

For a free copy of *Planning Your Trip to Europe*, which offers helpful planning tips and travel information, write to

European Planner, P.O. Box 1754, New York, NY 10185.

CANADA

Alberta Tourism, Vacation Counselling, 3rd Floor, City Centre Building, 10155 102 St., Edmonton, Alberta, Canada, T5J 4L6; 403-427-4321 or 800-661-8888

British Columbia Tourism, Parliament Buildings, Victoria, British Columbia, Canada, V8V 1X4; 604-685-0032 or 800-663-6000

Manitoba Travel, Department 20, 7th Floor, 155 Carlton Street, Winnipeg, Manitoba, Canada R3C 3H8; 204-945-3777 or 800-665-0040

New Brunswick Tourism, P.O. Box 12345, Fredricton, New Brunswick, Canada E3B 5C3; 506-453-2444 or 800-561-0123

Newfoundland/Labrador Department of Tourism & Culture, P.O. Box 8730, St. John's, Newfoundland, Canada A1B 4K2; 709-729-2830 or 800-563-6353

Northwest Territories Tourism, P.O. Box 1320, Yellowknife, NWT, Canada, X1A 2L9; 403-873-7200 or 800-661-0788

Nova Scotia Department of Tourism and Culture, P.O. Box 456, Halifax, Nova Scotia, Canada, B3J 2R5; 902-424-5000 or from Canada: 800-565-0000, from the United States: 800-341-6096

Ontario Travel, Queen's Park, Toronto, Ontario, Canada, M7A 2R9; 416-314-0944 or 800-ONTARIO

Prince Edward Island Department of Tourism, Parks and Recreation, Visitors Services Division, P.O. Box 940, Charlottetown, P.E.I., Canada C1A 7M5; 902-368-4444 or 800-566-0267

Quebec Tourisme, C.P. 20 000, Quebec, Canada G1K 7X2; 514-873-2015 or 800-363-7777

Saskatchewan Tourism, 1919 Saskatchewan Drive, Regina, Saskatchewan, Canada S4P 3V7; 306-787-2300 or 800-667-7191

Yukon Tourism, P.O. Box 2703, Whitehorse, Yukon, Canada Y1A 2C6; 403-667-5340

SOUTH PACIFIC/ASIA

American Samoa Office of Tourism, P.O. Box 1147, Pago Pago, American Samoa 96799

Australian Tourist Commission, 2121 Avenue of the Stars, Suite 1200, Los Angeles, CA 90067; 310-552-1988

China National Tourist Office, 333 W. Broadway #201, Glendale, CA 91204; 818-545-7505

Cook Islands Tourist Authority, 6033 W. Century Blvd., Suite 690, Los Angeles, CA 90045; 800-624-6250

Fiji Visitors Bureau, 5777 W. Century Blvd., Suite 220, Los Angeles, CA 90045; 310-568-1616

Guam Visitors Bureau, 1150 Marina Village Pkwy., Alameda, CA 94501; 800-US3-GUAM

Hong Kong Tourist Association, 590 Fifth Ave., New York, NY 10036; 212-869-5008

India Government of India Tourist Office, 30 Rockefeller Plaza, North Mezzanine, New York, NY 10112; 212-586-4901

Indonesia Tourist Promotion Office, 3457 Wilshire Blvd., Los Angeles, CA 90010; 213-387-2078

Japan National Tourist Organization, Rockefeller Plaza, 630 Fifth Ave., New York, NY 10111; 212-757-5640

Korea National Tourism Corporation, 3435 Wilshire Blvd., Suite 350, Los Angeles, CA 90010; 213-382-3435

Macau Tourist Information Bureau, P.O. Box 1860, Los Angeles, CA 90078; 800-331-7150

Malaysia Tourism Promotion Board, 804 W. Seventh St., Los Angeles, CA 90017; 213-689-9702

Micronesia FSM National Government, Department of Resources & Development, Capitol Postal Station, P.O. Box 12, Palikir Pohnpei 96941 Federal States of Micronesia

New Caledonia Destination Nouvelle-Caledonia, 39–41 Rue de Verdun, Immeuble Manhattan, P.O. Box 688 Noumea, New Caledonia

New Zealand Tourism Board, 501 Santa Monica Blvd. #300, Los Angeles, CA 90401; 310-395-7480

Northern Marianas Visitors Bureau, P.O. Box 861, Saipan, MP 96950

Palau Visitors Authority, P.O. Box 256, Koror, Republic of Palau, 96940

Papua New Guinea Tourist Office, c/o Air Niugini, 5000 Birch St., Suite 3000, Newport Beach, CA 92660; 714-752-5440

Singapore Tourist Promotion Board, 8484 Wilshire Blvd., Suite 510, Beverly Hills, CA 90211; 213-852-1901

Solomon Islands Tourist Authority, P.O. Box 321, Honiara, Solomon Islands

Tahiti Tourism Board, 300 N. Continental Blvd., Suite 180, El Segundo, CA 90245; 310-414-8484

Thailand Tourism Authority of Thailand, 303 E. Wacker Dr., Suite 400, Chicago, IL 60601; 312-819-3990

Tonga Visitors Bureau, P.O. Box 37, Nuku'alofa Tongatapu, Tonga

Vanuatu National Tourism Office, 520 Monterey Dr., Rio del Mar, CA 95003; 408-685-8901

Vietnam National Department of Tourism, 80 Quan Su St., Hanoi, Vietnam

AFRICA AND THE MIDDLE EAST

Israel Ministry of Tourism, 350 Fifth Ave., New York, NY 10118; 800-596-1199 or 212-560-0600

Egypt Government Tourist Office, 630 5th Ave., Suite 1706, New York, NY 10111; 212-332-2570

Kenya Tourist Office, 424 Madison Ave., 14th Fl., New York, NY 10017; 212-486-1300

Morocco National Tourist Office, 20 E. 46th St., Suite 1201, New York, NY 10017; 212-557-2520

South Africa Tourism Board, 500 Fifth Ave., 20th Fl., New York, NY 10110; 800-822-5368 or 212-730-2929

LATIN AMERICA

Argentina Tourist Information, P.O. Box 1758, Madison Square Station, New York, NY 10159; 800-722-5737 or 212-582-7833

Belize Tourist Board, 421 Seventh Ave., Suite 201, New York, NY 10001; 800-624-0686 or 212-563-6011

Brazil Tourism Office, 55 East 59 St., New York, NY 10022; 212-759-7878

Chile National Tourist Board, 9500 South Dadeland Blvd., Suite 510, Miami, FL 33156; 800-825-2332 or 305-670-6705

Colombia Consulate General, New York, NY; 212-949-9898

Costa Rica ICT, APDO 777-1000, San José, Costa Rica; 800-343-6332

Guatemala Tourist Commission, 299 Alhambra Circle, Suite 510, Coral Gables, FL 33134; 800-742-4529

Honduras Tourist Office, 1136 Fremont Ave., Suite 102, South Pasadena, CA 91030; 213-682-3377

Venezuela Tourism Association, P.O. Box 3010, Sausalito, CA 94966; 800-331-0100 or 415-331-0100

INDEX

About the Author

Geri Bain has been Travel Editor of *Modern Bride* since 1988 and is a nationally recognized authority on travel, honeymoons, and weddings away. She answers honeymoon questions from brides-to-be in her column in *Modern Bride* and is frequently interviewed by newspapers and magazines and on television.

Ms. Bain began her travel-writing career on a break from college, when she worked and traveled around Europe and sold one of her first articles to the *New York Daily News*. Her first publishing job involved covering developments in banking and real estate. She then returned to travel writing, first as a freelancer and then as features editor for *Travel Agent,* a trade publication. She also has two children's books in print: *Bruce Springsteen,* a biography of Bruce Springsteen, and *New Jersey,* a history of New Jersey.